THE

TIMEKEEPER'S

SON

THE

TIMEKEEPER'S

SON

a novel

Sara Baker

Deeds Publishing | Athens

Published by Deeds Publishing in Athens, GA
www.deedspublishing.com

Printed in The United States of America

Cover design by Mark Babcock, text layout by Killian Wyatt

Library of Congress Cataloging-in-Publications data is available
upon request.

ISBN 978-1-944193-56-0
EISBN 978-1-944193-57-7

Books are available in quantity for promotional or premium use. For
information, email info@deedspublishing.com.

First Edition, 2016

10 9 8 7 6 5 4 3 2 1

To my husband, Todd, who is not half-bad.

'Father, father, where are you going?
O do not walk so fast!
Speak, father, speak to your little boy,
Or else I shall be lost.'

—William Blake, "The Little Boy Lost,"
from *Songs of Innocence*

"For what is time? Who can readily and briefly explain
this? Who can even in thought comprehend it, so as to utter
a word about it? But what in discourse do we mention more
familiarly and knowingly, than time? And, we understand,
when we speak of it; we understand also, when we hear it
spoken of by another. What then is time? If no one asks me, I
know: if I wish to explain it to one that asketh,
I know not…"

—St. Augustine

SECTION 1:
THE DAY BEFORE

ONE

"Josh, you're going to be late. Come on!" Helen called.

It was the third time she'd called him. Josh's door remained closed. Hal looked up for a minute from the *Horomundi* journal, reading glasses magnifying his blue eyes. She could see how bloodshot they were. He looked tired and, suddenly, old, Helen thought.

"You shouldn't have to dig him out of bed every day, Helen. He's seventeen. He ought to be getting himself up at this age, for Christ's sake." Behind his head, the ornate hands of the cuckoo clock ticked, inching closer to eight. Helen's stomach knotted. She turned the pancake over and mashed it with the spatula. She hated always feeling defensive, always having to explain herself.

"He wouldn't get up in time for breakfast, and he needs his breakfast. You know that."

It was the same old argument. They were like tired actors, each repeating their stale lines.

"Let him go hungry."

It didn't warrant a reply. At one time, she might have fought him, but now she just plunked the plate of pancakes in front of him.

Josh's door opened, the hinge squeaking loudly. The boy emerged from his room, yawning, his dark, shaggy hair flopping in his eyes, grazing his shoulders. He wore baggy jeans and a rumpled Drive-By Truckers T-shirt. He slumped wordlessly in a chair, his long body unable to fit comfortably. His mother caught a whiff of unwashed socks and stale tobacco as she leaned over and put his breakfast in front of him.

Helen hovered over the table, holding the skillet and spatula. "Want any more?" she asked her husband.

"Naw, I've had enough, thanks." Hal closed his journal, looked at her for a moment, and then he turned to his son. "Sit up for god's sake, Josh." He tried to say it evenly, Helen knew, but nothing disguised his irritation. *Here we go,* she thought. *Here we go.* She turned and put the skillet back on the stove, picked up her plate, and sat down at the table.

Hal looked intently at Josh. Helen could see Hal's jaw muscle clench and unclench. She thought it looked like a little mouse twitching under his skin.

"Haven't seen a lot of studying going on around here lately."

Josh sent Helen a covert look, a look of dread.

"It is only the beginning of school, Hal."

Hal shook his head. "All the more reason to get off to a good start. I don't want to see another D in English like last semester."

"No, it's just… well, it's really hard for me." For a moment, his eyes were naked and pleading.

His father regarded him impassively. "And are you going to give up any time something is hard?"

Josh sat up straight. "No, sir."

3

Helen had to look away from Josh, from the hurt that crossed his face even as he tried to mimic his father's stoniness. Hal knew why Josh wasn't doing well. It was the same reason Hal hadn't done well in English. But despite all the talks Helen had tried to have with Hal, Hal insisted on making it a test of moral character.

"Well, what are you going to do about it, young man? Because a D is not acceptable to me."

Josh shifted uncomfortably in his seat, then looked his father in the eyes. "I'm going to raise it—*sir*."

Helen hoped she was the only one to detect the marked sarcasm in Josh's voice.

"See that you do. You waste too much time on that stupid filmmaking, that's the problem."

"Hal! There's nothing wrong with his filmmaking. It's, actually, very…"

"Very what, Helen?"

"It's, it's good for him. He's good at it. He enjoys it." She heard her voice go up an octave, sounding too plaintive.

Hal gave her a look, equal parts warning and helplessness. She knew he thought these outbursts constituted corrective parenting to her "coddling." But she thought they had more to do with Hal than Josh. He ignored Josh for long periods and then attacked him like this, out of the blue.

He unfolded his own long body from the chair and drained his coffee, looking at his watch. "Better hurry, son. You're going to be late." She knew he was trying to soften things, to back off a bit. But it just sounded awkward. He bent down and placed a dry kiss on Helen's cheek. "Bye," he said, but he didn't look at her.

The front door slammed, and Helen let out her breath. She got up and poured another cup of coffee. She felt her body expand, relax. Yes, Josh would probably be late. But she wasn't going to rush him. She was going to sit and enjoy looking at him.

Josh looked up and smiled at her. "Good pancakes, Mom." He wiped the syrup from his mouth with his finger and licked it, then grabbed her coffee cup playfully, "Just a swig, baby cakes."

"Oh, you." She tried to sound angry, but she loved his playfulness. He seemed to weather his father better than she expected.

He took a swig from her cup, then yelped. "How can you drink it black? Tastes like diesel fuel, Mom. My word to you is sugar and cream." He pushed away from the table, bent down to kiss her, and she smoothed the hair off his forehead.

"You need a haircut."

"Yadda, yadda," he said, but he grinned.

"Josh—"

He stopped grinning, catching the serious note in her voice.

"Josh, your dad, he wants the best for you, you know that, don't you?"

Josh's face froze, darkened. "Mom, I don't want to talk about it, okay? Leave it." He slung his backpack on his back. "Bye," he mumbled, and then the front door slammed again.

***

Josh felt lighter with each step he took away from the house. His breathing became easier, deeper, and his stride more energetic.

He noticed the mist lifting and sunlight threatening to break through. A light breeze stirred the oak and pecan trees, and the patterns of light and dark made the suburban street seem mysterious and inviting. A cat slinked by, and Josh framed it in his imaginary camera, one of those throwaway shots he loved so much in Chaplin's films. His friend Andy loved Tarantino—the bloodier the better for Andy—but Josh loved early films, the dynamic use of shadows in Bergman or the poetry of Fellini's dream imagery. "Man, why you like those old movies?" Andy liked to tease him. "Those black-and-white movies. I don't get you—you're a weirdo, Josh." But Josh would retort, "You have no sense of history, Andy. You loser." Andy would watch Wes Anderson or David O. Russell films with him, grudgingly admitting they weren't too bad.

By the time he got to the shortcut through the field, he was almost happy, despite the still-wet grass slapping his jeans. He didn't know what he'd do without Andy, without his friends. His friends and movies, that's what he lived for. The rest just seemed tedious, going through the motions.

He could see the red brick school just over the rise, but he wasn't quite ready to be there. He set his book bag against the old crooked oak that stood at the top of the hill and pulled a cigarette out of the pack buried in the bag. Sitting on his bag, smoking, he felt like he was stopping time. Here were no adults telling him what to do. He was free, and the world was his. Once he got inside those doors, it was all about schedules. He was always late, always losing track of time. Why couldn't he just hang out in his own head, move at his own pace? He could make things, beautiful things, if they'd only give him time. He rubbed out the cigarette, hesitated, then lit another one, inhaling deeply.

He surveyed the field of long golden grass and brambles with proprietary satisfaction. He and his friends picked dewberries there in the summers, and a lot of kids made out and smoked dope there. But what Josh loved about it was its wildness. He tracked deer, not to hunt but to photograph. He spent hours watching beavers build their dam at the pond that glinted like a coin in the now-yellow grass. He knew where the blue heron had a nest, and where to avoid snakes. He had even seen a fox once. It had seemed a magical creature, like the foxes in Kurosawa's films. He had come across it in the field at dusk after staying late to work on a project at school. Suddenly in the path appeared a small dog. It turned toward him, its nose sniffing, then stopped. The animal's coat shone copper in the afternoon sun, its ears quivered, its tail curled magnificently over its body. Then it was gone. The encounter had seemed important to him, as if the fox had recognized Josh as a kindred spirit, another brother of the woods.

He rolled the cigarette butt between his fingers. He imagined trying to tell his father about the fox. Ha! It would just irritate him. Like this morning. What was it about him that made his dad so angry? He was trying, didn't he see that? It was like nothing he did was right. He didn't even see the good stuff. He didn't do drugs, he had pretty good grades, he worked. Man, what did it take? Josh felt defeated before he began; there was no chance of pleasing his dad.

A hawk took off from a dead pine tree, startling him. The morning sun had warmed the pines so that the air was sharp with resin. He picked up his heavy book bag and started slowly down the path. Maybe he should skip school—it was such a

7

glorious day. But he'd miss his friends. And besides, school was okay, except for English.

He used to like English, he liked stories, anyway, but the mechanics of reading and writing were just too laborious for him. When he was little and could listen to stories on tape, that was great. Now, he had to read so much and he was so slow that he never caught up. He didn't want to tell his mother that he'd stopped taking Adderall—that even though it helped him think, it made him feel weird and jumpy. He worried that it took his creativity away. She'd kill him if she found out, and then he'd have both of them against him.

He emerged from the field, crossed the busy road, and trudged up the hill to the school. He stood a moment in front of the heavy industrial gray doors, then reluctantly opened them.

***

The slammed door seemed to reverberate for a long time. Helen surveyed the kitchen—the dirty dishes left on the table, the orange juice container sweating into the newspaper, the half-eaten pancakes, the coffee getting cold in her cup. She had plenty to do, but her body seemed to have turned to cement. A familiar weariness settled over her. She recalled how she used to hustle Josh and Hal off in the mornings, eager to start her day, do the housework like a dervish and get out of the house, makeup on and everything, and work a full day. How had she done it? It wasn't just getting older, it seemed, it was something else.

Buster, her aging basset hound, nuzzled her hand in her lap and looked at her with the eyes of a disappointed lover. Lately, she had been slighting him in his walks.

"Okay, boy, you win today," she said, patting his old freckled fur. She'd leave the dishes and laundry and picking up for later and get out of the house. Maybe it would improve her mood.

She pulled on an old sweat suit and rooted around for her sneakers. Catching sight of herself in the mirror, she frowned at her burgeoning hips. She thought she should do something about her hair, which hung lank and dark against her face. But the thought of finding a style, never mind a hairdresser, was overwhelming. She bundled her hair back into a ponytail, wrapped an elastic band around it.

She whistled for Buster, rattling the leash, and he came lumbering toward her, his pink tongue hanging out in anticipation. She hadn't wanted a dog. Hal had gotten it for Josh, a hunting dog one of his friends was getting rid of because it couldn't hunt. Little did she think that in the end, Buster would be her most constant companion.

Stepping outside into the still-cool air and sunshine lifted her mood. She walked along the asphalt—no sidewalks in the subdivision—and didn't meet a soul. Most of the houses were brick ranch, and even though they had lived in Oakwood Estates for almost fifteen years, Helen knew few of her neighbors. It seemed everyone worked and kept to themselves for the most part. You only saw people when something happened, like the time that Mills boy wrapped his Corvette around a telephone pole and the Jaws of Life came or the time Tina Sanderson's husband beat her and she sought refuge in their next-door neighbor's house, a woman who had long since moved away. Helen didn't know the "new" people who had already been there five years.

Helen reached the bottom of the hill and had to decide whether to climb it or take the longer, flatter route home. She leaned over, gasping for breath. Sometimes she was shocked at her own lack of fitness. As a full-time nurse, she had been on her feet all day. Now, just working weekends, she took it too easy the rest of the time. She turned onto the flat route, telling herself that next time, she would climb the hill.

In the empty landscape, the scene in the kitchen replayed itself over and over in her mind. It filled her with sadness, a familiar pain like a stone bearing down on her chest. Helen had watched Hal's features, once soft and hopeful, grow sharper and grimmer every year. It wasn't that he didn't love her or Josh; no, he was an exemplary husband and father, doing always what he'd said he'd do, anxious to provide for them, responsible to a fault. He paid the bills, kept the cars in working order, fixed the plumbing when it leaked, spent his weekends on household repairs. He didn't gamble or drink, was faithful, demanded very little of her. She had known other women who complained about their husbands' over-controlling natures, the need they had to have their wives look a certain way, to entertain, to spend all their free time with them. Helen had secretly envied them. Hal hadn't seemed to notice how she looked, or that they had no friends together, or that she spent more time going to the movies alone than with him. As time went on, he retreated more and more into himself, becoming like his clocks, steadily ticking along, allowing nothing to disturb his routine.

Sometimes she felt like probing his flesh to see if he was real, imagining that underneath, she might find a robot, as in some sci-fi movie. It was only when he was angry that she was able to glimpse what he might be thinking or feeling. And that seemed to happen more and more over minor things, when something wasn't put back in the proper place or when Josh played his music too loud. Then it seemed as if his anger was out of all proportion, as if it was fed from another, deeper, source.

Panting now, Helen could see her house. Buster was dragging, too, and his ears perked up at the sight of it. "Boy, we are a sorry pair," Helen said, and Buster looked at her with sad hound eyes.

Helen knew that Josh needed his filmmaking, just like she needed her painting. She had given up painting after Josh was born, but recently had rooted around in the basement for her old arts supplies. She set her easel on the back porch when Josh and Hal were gone, attempting watercolor still-lifes or pastel landscapes. She'd work for a week or two, happy with the process, then decide her work was cramped and amateurish. Despite her frequent discouragement, she kept at it. Neither Josh nor Hal had any idea of her passionate agony; when they came home, dinner was always ready, and she was there, listening to the stories of their days, as if she happily had no other function. She kept her restlessness to herself.

Josh, unlike her, well, he would do something with his passion. He'd already won a small prize, and what she'd seen of his work seemed unusually good. Although, what did she know of the film world today? She had been a movie buff before she'd been married, priding herself on keeping up with experimental and international films. That girl she had been, though, seemed like another person altogether. But even if she didn't keep up anymore, she recognized Josh's passion when he breathlessly told her about a film. He had even invited her to watch "The Great Beauty," a surreal Italian film, with him--a rare event. She had been impressed with the way he talked about it, stopping frames and making her look carefully at the shots.

It hurt her that Hal couldn't understand this part of Josh. It was as if Hal couldn't step outside his own disappointment long enough to actually see his son. Josh had craved his father's approval and been disappointed for so long that now he simply hid himself from Hal. But Helen knew he still cared what Hal thought.

She thought of Josh as he left this morning, his impish, lop-sided grin, his dark hair with the sweeping cowlick falling over his eyes, his deep-blue eyes and high cheekbones, the rumpled too-large T-shirt, the baggy jeans on his tall, rangy figure, the way the boy still lived inside the man frame. It was all changing, she knew, so fast, and he was on his way away from her, and so she treasured each ordinary moment.

Helen let Buster into the backyard. The sun was bright now, and the hydrangea leaves glazed with last night's rain. A yellow garden spider had woven a web in the leaves, and Helen thought how she'd like to try to sketch it. Instead, she opened the door, determined to conquer, if nothing else, the chaos in the dark kitchen.

TWO

Meg usually got to school early. She liked the quiet of the classroom before the storm of kids hit, liked to putter and straighten, bringing in some new item to share with them—a feather or shell or cicada skin or perfect transparent casting of the insect with all its parts. She brought her thermos of coffee and sipped it, hot and bitter, contemplating the possibilities of the coming day. She anticipated her students in their essences, free of the green snotty noses, the red-rimmed eyes, their fidgeting inattention. She sat in stillness, the weak sun coming in the grimy window, the coffee warm in her hand, and she was filled with love.

By the end of the day, having spent two-thirds of it trying to bring some semblance of order to the classroom, Meg wondered how she could go on another day. Since when did second grade become a battlefield? Today at lunch she had sustained a bite on the arm when she had attempted to catch Andre as he danced around the table, grabbing food off lunch trays. He had learning problems, but there was something else there, something fierce and primitive, in his tarantella. Earlier, Keesha had come to school with welts across her back, which Meg had found when she saw blood seeping into her white T-shirt, and Nick had fallen asleep again before lunch. Her planning period had been spent reading a memo delineating new curriculum standards, mandating a reduction in PE, music, art, and recess. Another memo reminded her the school would lose its Title I funding if the students didn't perform well on the standardized test, and the implication was also they might lose their jobs. That might frighten the younger teachers, but Meg knew they'd have a hard time trying to replace them. No one wanted to work at McKnight Elementary. She didn't. In the middle of the day, she'd had the sudden urge to scream, "Let me out of here." She wasn't supposed to—it wasn't in the official curriculum—but after lunch she fit in ten minutes of quiet time. Everyone put their heads on their desks while she shut off the lights and put on some ambient music. She looked at her charges draped over their desks; they looked for those few moments like what they were—children.

It was a short reprieve. The lights went on, and she began force-feeding the sterile curriculum, always aware of her time constraints. They were not interested in spelling except when a word reminded them of a dirty word. Then they'd spell it out, complete with rap rhymes. She tried to make science hands-on as much as she could, letting them do experiments and walk freely around the room, but that had backfired one day when she found Danny in the resource closet with Allegra, both of them half undressed, bumping and grinding. It made her furious with the parents, but then she had to remember that half the kids there had been born to teenage girls. Still, when the kids came in reeking of tobacco, sour-breathed and exhausted, she wanted to send them all to foster homes or, better yet, just set up the school as an orphanage.

Janelle was one of the casualties of all the chaos. Ebony, with gorgeous green eyes and a sturdy little body, Janelle shrank from the more boisterous kids. She was shunned by them, too, partly because she was reading above grade level and was always eager to answer questions and partly because of her complete disregard of them. So they teased her, and she would spend most of recess glued to Meg's side, and sometimes Meg would look up from what she was doing in class and see Janelle's eyes silently beseeching her. Meg didn't know much about her home situation, except that her grandmother—primary residence?—sometimes called to have her sent home to her aunt's house. There was a light in Janelle's eyes, a hunger for order and intelligence, but Meg could see that other forces were dimming it. Meg panicked, wanting to pluck her out of the chaos, but what could she do? The kid soaked up attention like a parched plant soaks up rain. When the children lined up to go home, Janelle waved and waved to Meg until she disappeared out the door, and there was something anxious in the waving, something that made Meg want to call out, "Hold on till tomorrow."

Today, as always, there was the last-minute rush to make sure notes and papers got stuffed into the right book bags and lunch boxes got into the right hands, that car riders and bus riders got in the right lines, Meg leading the bus riders out. Returning to her room, she sat down, spent, to sort through the directives and admonishments that never ceased flowing from the administration. The statistics and quotas, the obscure educational jargon seemed more and more foreign to her, having little or nothing to do with the living, breathing children she was trying to teach. Tears of rage and helplessness started up in her eyes when she read that the board had decided to cut the number of aides per school because of funding issues. What the kids needed more than anything—more than computers, more than fancy building upgrades—were people. People to know them, to care about them.

She threw the weekly board update in the trash and looked at her disheveled room. It no longer held promise, but smelled of defeat—unwashed bodies, stale air, and the acrid chemical smell of whiteboard markers. There had been small triumphs in the day: Dariel's broad freckled face breaking wide open when she finally, finally made it through a chapter book by herself, Peter's grubby warm hand on hers during story time, Janelle's drawing of an African princess on the moon. She tried to keep these in mind, to not let a tide of bitterness overwhelm her. She entertained the idea of just walking away. But of course she wouldn't, because she'd wake up at 5:45 the next day, make her coffee, eager to get to this very same room, and by then Jamal, Keesha, Peter, Dariel, and all the others would be restored to their ideal, shining selves.

***

Meg slammed the door and threw her keys on the hall table. "Hi, honey," she called. She heard David's chair squeak and then a muffled "I'm on the phone." She shrugged to herself; so what else was new? She heaved the groceries onto the kitchen table and sorted through the mail. Pricey catalogs, bills, solicitations from every good and worthy cause. She threw the solicitations away and half the catalogs, although there were a few she couldn't resist. She poured herself a glass of wine and flopped on the couch. She felt as if she were reassembling her molecules into a coherent person.

She picked up the pretty catalogs and leafed through them aimlessly. Women posed in open fields, against wide blue skies, looking romantic and rested. Beautiful horses grazed in the background. They wore long, flowing skirts in earthy colors, their slender necks draped with turquoise and coral, shiny hair blowing in wisps across their faces. They seemed to be communing with nature, having deep, soulful thoughts, or sitting on a hay bale, waiting for the Marlboro Man to ride up. No elementary schools in sight.

She took another sip of wine, felt her body begin to loosen and warm. The newspaper sat in front of her where David had left it, and she thought about picking it up. She should, she thought, care about the larger world. But her brain was fried, and so she turned the page of the catalog and drank in its carefully staged fantasy.

David came in, leaned down, and kissed her. She patted his stubbly chin. Ever since he had started working from home, he'd been sporting the "rough and ready" look.

"You look beat." He sat down next to her, moving her legs onto his lap.

"Yeah. The usual. Everyone's cranky. It is too hot to be in school—I don't know why we have to start in August. Whatever happened to starting after Labor Day? Plus, the kids need more recess. What day is it, anyway? Wednesday? Well, maybe I can hold out till Friday. How was your day?" Their cat, Ginger, leaped onto David's lap and her legs, fitting himself into a nook.

"Can't complain. We're still having a hard time convincing the commissioners that we need to zone for more affordable housing. But we'll get there, just have to keep chipping away at them."

Meg sighed. That's what she loved about this man, his determined focus. He didn't oscillate like she did, up and down the scale of hope and despair. He just quietly and systematically kept burrowing away at his goal until he achieved it. The only thing was, ever since he started his consulting business, he worked much harder than when he'd been teaching. They had less time together. And she resented it. It was a case of the shoemaker's children going shoeless, only in this instance, they had no children, so she went shoeless.

She brushed the hair out of his eyes. "Why don't you take me out to dinner tonight? I know its decadent, but there's that little bistro that's opened up down on Newton Street. And leave your cell phone at home."

He hesitated, glancing almost longingly at his office, then turned to her and grinned. "Well, it is pretty decadent… but I think I can swing it. I guess I'll have to shower and shave?"

Meg looked up at him and grimaced. "Oh, *yeah*, as the kids say."

The evening had cooled by the time they went out. It wasn't far, so they walked. The leaves of the old oaks and pecans rustled in the evening breeze, casting shifting shadows on the brick sidewalk. They walked past Victorian homes in various stages of renovation, past new condos and old brick apartment buildings. They admired the Johnsons' garden, with its wisteria arbor and roses, and they gossiped about their neighbors—how the Walcotts' dog kept getting into everyone's garbage, but old Mr. Walcott denied it; how the Nortons' oldest daughter had just won a coveted scholarship to UNC; how the new couple down the street seemed overwhelmed with the demands of both a toddler and a new baby.

"I need to go down and visit them," Meg said. "On a weekend, when I can think straight. Maybe make some bread."

David grabbed Meg's hand in his and kissed it. "I love you," he said, and she knew he was all there now, with her.

They fell into a synchronized stride, despite their size difference. Middle-aged love was vastly underrated, she thought. They knew each other so well now. They didn't have to explain themselves to each other, or defend this or that habit or trait. Most of those battles had been fought. Still, even now, David would surprise her, and she'd get a glimpse of depths of him that she hadn't imagined. Sometimes it was an offhand observation about a person, or a response to a book or movie.

She hoped they wouldn't see anybody they knew tonight—she wanted him all to herself. She was glad David was loved and appreciated, but she would sometimes prefer he had a lower profile. She was relieved to see the outside tables at La Maison looked sparsely occupied.

"This is really nice," David said, taking in the enclosed garden, the lights strung in the trees, the candles flickering on white damask tablecloths. Baroque music floated serenely around them. Ah, this was what she wanted—David, relaxed, not striving, not fighting another good fight. They ordered a bottle of fumé blanc and took time perusing the menu. The breeze stirred the leaves overhead, sent whiffs of rosemary and sage from the kitchen garden their way.

"Well, honey, what are you going to have?" David asked her. She could tell by his voice that despite his earlier hesitation, he was beginning to enjoy himself. Meg knew that underneath David's genuine concern for social justice and his overwhelming work ethic, there lay a secret sybarite. She loved it when he peeked out.

"Chicken marsala. And you?"

"Lamb. And I think we should get appetizers. Maybe that mozzarella salad?"

Meg looked at him archly. "Caprese salad? Decadent. But if you insist."

"I do, oh, I do." He laughed expansively at himself.

David poured Meg another glass of wine, and she thought briefly that perhaps she shouldn't indulge, knowing tomorrow was another school day. But that spasm of conscience passed like a gentle ripple in a pond, and she lifted her glass.

David leaned toward her, his beautiful gray eyes focusing all their laser-like intensity on her. She still felt a thrill when he looked at her like that.

He hesitated, took a breath. "I have something to tell you."

Meg thought, *We're going to a beach in Mexico? A ski trip?* She laughed. "Okay. Don't look so serious."

He sat back in the chair, his eyes now looking away. "Well, it is rather serious."

Cancer? Heart disease? Meg's stomach lurched.

"You're all right, aren't you?"

He looked back at her, alarmed. "Oh, no, not serious like that. I'm fine. Actually, very fine. I've decided to run for Congress. We need a good representative in our district."

Meg stared at him, relieved he wasn't dying, but still unable to take in what he had said. *What drives you?* she wanted to say. *Law school, social work school, community organizing, teaching, your own consulting business, now this? Why do you never seem satisfied with what you accomplish? What about us?* she wanted to shout.

"Why?" was all she could get out.

He was looking at her carefully, gauging how to respond. "Honey, don't look so dismayed. Look how hard we've been working to effect change—I mean, you can see it yourself every day—but things move so slowly. We're not getting the funding we need, but it's more than that. It's this creeping abdication, this refusal of the government to govern. I always feel like I have my fingers in the dike—and I'm running out of fingers. I want to make a real difference, not just put out fires." He leaned toward her again. "Come on, give me a smile." He put a finger next to her lip, gently stroked her face.

She tried to smile. She wanted to be supportive. She knew he was right, and she knew he would do a good job. Still.

"David Masters, savior of the world." It slipped out, a venomous little snake.

Darkness had gathered around them, and in the soft candlelight, she couldn't read his face.

"I'm not trying to save the world. Just this world, this place. For the children. Meg, we've abandoned our children. *You* know. We've betrayed all the promises—"

"I know, I know, the Great Society. I was there, too. It's just—"
He took her hand. She withdrew it.

"It's just what?"

"It's just that we're only mortal. And we only have so much time. We've dedicated ourselves to this fight. But I'm tired. Sometimes I just want to run away." She thought of the models in the catalog, the horses in the background, the space, the peace.

"Ah." He sounded surprised. Why would that surprise him? Didn't he see how much she craved being with him? She loved her work, but it wasn't everything. She'd been experiencing a restlessness lately, a need for—what? Reward? Fun?

"You have so much energy. You're so unselfish. But I'm selfish. I want to be with you. I want to forget about pressing problems sometimes. But you can't seem to ever let it all go. Have you thought about what this means for us?"

"I've thought hard about it."

"It means we will be separated, that I'll see less of you than I already do." She could hear her voice, strained and high.

He leaned forward again. She watched the flickering light mold and remold his face. It was full of conflicting expressions—frowns, the long crease between his eyebrows, lips turned up in a determined smile.

"Look, I won't do it if you don't want me to. I understand your feelings." He said this woodenly, and she thought, *Right.* He couldn't understand her; he was just built too differently. It was up to her to understand him.

"If I prevented you from doing this, you'd resent me."

"No, Honey…"

She shook her head. "Yes, you would. I know you." She took another sip of wine. Maybe she'd call in sick tomorrow. "But if you do this, you have to promise me that we will have frequent trips, frequent vacations alone, together. Not just for official business. And we'll go out more. We're not grad students anymore, we don't have to be so prudent, so damn *good*."

He nodded eagerly, all his enthusiasm back. He looked like a child that had gotten away with something. "It really is for the children, Meg, for your children."

She knew what he meant, but shook her head and said softly, "I don't have any children."

He became stone. All the warmth between them, the ease, evaporated. Finally, he said, "Do you have to go there?"

She hadn't meant to bring it up. Apparently, it was closer to the surface than even she realized. She thought she had dealt with it, put it behind her. But it was always there, her ghost motherhood. The huge absence of a child of her own was as present as any real child could be.

"I'm sorry," she said. "That wasn't fair."

"No, it wasn't." He shifted his gaze to somewhere behind her head. They sat in silence. Meg could hear the muffled sounds of dishes being banged about in the restaurant's kitchen and the high-spirited bantering of the kitchen staff. Snatches of soft piano jazz drifted around them, mixed with the strident tuning of cicadas. She picked up her knife and studied it.

There was nothing to say; it had all been said and done. The endless rounds of painful, expensive, invasive treatments. Her pleading with him to adopt, his refusal. All that painful history was there in the air between them. *How come*, she couldn't help thinking resentfully, *you always get what you want? And I get to be the good wife, standing beside you.* Her love for him vied with her anger.

David had signaled for the bill, and busied himself checking it. Tentatively, she reached over and touched his hand. When he finally looked at her, it was with the rueful look of one old soldier to another.

THREE

Hal Lovejoy puttered in his shop, tidying and dusting, checking to make sure each clock was running on time before he left for the evening. Tonight he oiled the works of the French mantel clock, polished the case of the Babbitt grandfather, and carefully wound the pendulum wall clock. It was only when he was satisfied that each mechanism was in good order and the clocks were synchronized that he felt he could go.

He found himself increasingly reluctant to leave in the evenings. It was a pattern that had deepened in recent years. Helen scolded him, said he should make more time for family, that Josh would be gone in a year, and wouldn't he be sorry? Well, yes, he would be. He already was. But he didn't think that spending more time at home would help anything. It would only make things worse. The truth was, Hal adored Josh, but had no idea how to be with him. It had been easy when Josh was a kid; then Hal did lots of things with Josh—Cub Scouts, camping. But these days his son only endured him. He had even tried teaching the boy about clocks, only to be rebuffed by Josh's blithe dismissal. "Hey, Dad, it's a new day—ever hear of digital?" He worried about the kid incessantly, worried about his flighty ideas, but talk to him anymore? It just wasn't possible. Oil and water.

No, he thought, taking the day's earnings out of the till, *better to avoid conflict.* He shoved the drawer hard, put the money and credit card slips in the bank bag, and stepped out into the night. It was hot still, without a breeze, and after the air-conditioned shop, he found it suffocating. He noticed that Dragon Tattoo across the street was still open. He saw the leather-clad, pierced, and bearded proprietor moving back and forth, felt the deep bass beat of the music from the parlor throb through his body as he walked to his car. He'd been surprised to learn that Sam was only a few years younger than he was. *Having a kid, it ages you,* Hal thought, but he'd always felt old, even when he was young. He'd always been cautious, wary of adventure, never one to mix with people.

There weren't many people out tonight. Their part of town didn't get much foot traffic. People had to want to find them—the clock shop, the tattoo parlor. It might be better for business if he moved his shop to the mall, but he didn't want to go to the trouble. His was, as they say, a niche market. A shrinking niche market. Few people these days cared about antique clocks or appreciated them for the exquisite machines or works of art they were. At least no one in the hamlet of Milledge, Georgia, that is.

Not even Helen understood his fascination with clocks. He had tried to teach her, too, tried to convey the magic he felt each time he saw the intricate workings of a timepiece. No, not even Helen understood. In more civilized parts of the world, the ancient art of horology was respected. Since he was a kid, he'd been fascinated by the rich history of timekeeping. He had always wanted to be part of that almost occult horological brotherhood. He had dreamed of being the George Daniel of American horology—a dream that seemed vainglorious and shameful now. Yet he still nursed a hope, in some dark, small recess of himself, that he would still make his mark. Not that anyone knew—it was a secret he barely knew himself.

The air was heavy with the scent of honeysuckle. Hal stopped a moment to enjoy it, to enjoy the evening sky. The day's heat lingered. It made him think of the soft days when he'd courted Helen. He thought of the sweetness he'd felt then, and it made him wince. What young idiots they had been. Walking into marriage as if it were a lark.

He heard the whistle of the train, and then the familiar chug and rattle as it passed below him through the old cotton warehouses. He loved trains almost as much as he loved clocks. He understood how they worked, understood the world from which they emerged. Unlike this new world with its incessant communication, incessant "networking." Josh, with his head buried in his computer, even Helen—Hal couldn't understand it. It seemed disordered, all that chatting and pinging. When did anyone have time to think? He himself liked to close the door of his workshop, liked the uninterrupted quiet. It was where he felt most at ease.

He pulled out his key and unlocked the door of his battered old Chevy truck and got in. He sat there for a long while. Then he turned on the engine, put the car in gear, and headed home.

***

Helen checked her watch nervously. Hal had been staying later and later at the shop. For someone obsessed with time, he seemed to lose track of it often enough.

She covered the pork chops she'd fried with foil, and put them in the oven to keep warm. She could call him, she supposed, but he was usually testy when she did. He hated phones, hated to be rushed out of his routines. She considered taking out her sketchpad, but she didn't want him to find her engrossed in it when he came home, couldn't endure the thought of his cutting comments.

She got up and opened the fridge, took out a bottle of Sauvignon Blanc, poured herself a glass, and sat down at the table. It's come to this, she thought, drinking alone. She watched the rosy light fading behind the broad-leafed poplar tree, the east-facing kitchen growing dark. She didn't turn on any lights. The dark suited her.

How had they come to be the people they were now? Hal bitter, his anger always just under the surface. And how had she become so sad?

She sipped the wine, watching the shadows lengthen, listening to the ticking of the clock.

She honestly didn't know which was worse, Hal's absence or his anger.

Hard as it was to live with his anger, it was the dull ache she felt for him that was hardest. For hadn't she been with him as he struggled all those long years to get his mechanical engineering degree, only to fail in the end? Now, of course, she had learned that his peculiar problem was not unique to him, but a common diagnosis with treatments and allowances made for it.

Attention deficit disorder. But not then. Then, no one had ever heard of it. How they had both suffered, Hal with his shame and frustration, Helen looking on helplessly.

She had always known Hal was bright—he could take apart and put together any piece of machinery; he could patch electricity, plumb, build anything. His intelligence was spatial, mechanical, tactile, but not verbal. He knew intuitively how much weight a structure could bear even before he calculated it. He had a refined and economic aesthetic sense as well, and could redesign a lamp or radio to make it work or look better.

Still, he struggled. Reading was torture for him, and his writing indecipherable. She had retyped all his college papers, putting them in Standard English, but she could not take his tests for him. He had never finished one college exam on time, and so his grades deflated, finally dragging so low that all his efforts amounted to nothing. His parents had blamed him for being lazy, and none of his fine attributes had been recognized or mentored. It seemed for many years she alone had stood by him, and for that he resented her, resented her being privy to his pain.

And so he had retreated into his clocks, building around him a world he could navigate. He refused to talk about the failed degree, to acknowledge that part of his life, and it hurt Helen, for she had never felt so close to him as in those years when she had helped him. He might forget, but she couldn't forget—not the sight of his pale face and clammy palms, or the animal anguish in his blue eyes.

Josh had eased the silent pain that grown between them. Unperturbed by his father's reserve, baby Josh would light up at the sight of his father, burrowing into his side, clapping his hands on his face, or rolling on the floor with him. Later, they built towers and bridges and disappeared into their own imaginary worlds of *Star Wars* and *Lord of the Rings*, stories Helen knew little about. As Josh grew, they took fishing and camping trips, spending long weekends away from home. It seemed to Helen that it was easier for Hal to be a father than a husband, that his son gave him a solace that she could not. Still, she was happy for them.

That all changed when Josh began to have trouble in school. When the school counselor contacted her and suggested Josh might be gifted but had attention problems, everything in her wanted to cry *no!* and hang up on the woman. It was a nightmare repeating itself. But slowly, with the help of the school, she came to understand that Josh's fate didn't have to be his father's—that his story could be different. Her gratitude for that fact flooded her with hope and seemed to shake her out of a stupor she had been in.

But when she brought it up to Hal, that bitter underground stream found its way to the surface.

"There's nothing wrong with Josh, goddamn it, woman— why do you have to go looking for trouble!"

"But, Hal, listen, they have these tests…"

"Tests, smests—a bunch of goddamn interfering women over at that school with nothing better to do. Tell them to leave my son alone."

Helen took a deep breath. "I can't do that. I can't condemn him to a life, like…" And then she stopped, horrorstruck. She had brought up the unmentionable.

Hal's face was livid, but his eyes brimmed with pain.

Then, icily, he said, "You're going to do whatever the hell you want anyway. I can't stop you. Don't ever speak to me about it again!" And they hadn't.

Josh responded well to the medication, and his reading improved. He also started developing a wider set of friends, so that by the sixth-grade year, the camping trips had dwindled to nothing. Helen tried to get Hal to initiate some activities with Josh, but he just put her off. "He's got his own friends now. He doesn't want to hang with his old man." Helen wanted to say, *He'd jump at the chance.* But she learned to save her breath. Hal wouldn't listen.

She should be ecstatic that she had so much free time now that Josh was busy and Hal too. Isn't that what she always had dreamed of? Yet Josh still needed her, and while he did, she couldn't relax her vigilance. She had to be a firewall between him and his father. Or was that, she wondered, an excuse? An excuse not to face her own disappointed dreams?

She heard Hal's truck putter into the driveway. She got up, put away the wine, turned on the light, and lit the fire under the beans. Was it relief or dread she felt?

***

"I want to run through the halls of my high school," Josh sang lustily with John Mayer as he looked at the photos he had taken for the drama club's new production of *The Taming of the Shrew.*

The music echoed his feelings. He knew there was something better on the other side of his life in high school, and he could just about taste it.

He loved working alone in the journalism room, playing with the editing suite, manipulating the pictures. He plugged in his USB cable and downloaded the new photos and videos. Libby, the beautiful, the talented, played Kate. He had done a whole series of shots of her for the yearbook. He enlarged and cropped, filled in shadows, corrected colors. He had yet to say one word to her, and not even his closest friend, Andy, knew how he felt about her. It seemed enough to him to simply study her image, memorizing her pale oval face and soft brown curls. She was, he knew, shy, and only really came alive onstage. He liked it that she was a puzzle, liked it that she wore glasses and always looked a little disheveled and distracted. She sat next to him in English, and the class was sweetened by her presence. He was awed by what she saw in books that were to him dense and opaque. When she read her own poetry aloud, she lost her distracted air and became quietly authoritative.

He hadn't asked her out not because he was shy. He wasn't inexperienced with girls—he'd had one or two girlfriends, if you counted Cindy Reilly, but then that hadn't really counted, because she had been passed through just about every boy's hands in their class, in some form or another. *There* was a girl who held nothing back. But his brief infatuation with Cindy's black eyeliner and plunging necklines had given way to boredom, and his fumblings in the school parking lot were something he attributed to another, lesser Josh.

No, the reason he hadn't approached Libby was that he had

a plan, and he didn't want anything to jeopardize it. He'd made a few film shorts—one had won a small local prize--and now he wanted to make one for a national contest. A film professor at the local college had liked the last one he'd done, and had told him about the contest. He hadn't told anyone, not Andy, nor his mother and certainly not his father. He was going to film it at night, during and after work at the Video Library. He'd found a script on the Internet that he liked, a story with a perfect role for Libby. He knew some of her friends pretty well, and he felt sure they would be able to persuade her to at least give it a try, because he planned to give all of them either a role or a job.

Josh studied the images of Libby on the journalism computer. Wearing a wimple and a low-cut Elizabethan gown, she commanded the stage. Even in stills, it was clear that when she was onstage, everyone else paled. He pulled up the video of the performance, marveling at the mobility of her face, the perfect timing in delivering her lines. She was going somewhere. Everyone felt it. And he was, too. He was going to get out of here and be somebody. He allowed himself to imagine an opening at Sundance, heck, even at Cannes. He saw himself in ten years, walking up a red carpet, nodding and waving, the promising new director. And on his arm, Libby. He even imagined her in a gown not unlike the one in the photos.

Oh, he had plans for her. He gazed at her multiple images. He was surrounded by Libbys—smiling, frowning, laughing Libbys—and they were all his.

FOUR

David Masters thought how crazed—as in crazed porcelain—the road looked, with its patches snaking over the gray asphalt, all of it ghostly under the city lights. This road, one of the main thoroughfares in town, was really a disgrace. The city had plans to repave it, but he doubted it would be done any time soon—money was tight all the way around.

The night was blessedly cool. He liked jogging late at night, liked the quiet, the way the movement and the dark cleared his head. Besides, in August it was the only time cool enough to move. He needed the time alone, away from the ringing phone and faxes and email. He was, on the whole, pleased with his life, which had become fuller and more satisfying than he had ever dreamed possible. And yet the downside was he never had a moment to himself. Which was why at twelve thirty he'd found himself turning off the lights to his office, putting on his jogging shoes, and slipping silently into the night.

The streets were almost entirely deserted. He turned up Boulevard, passed old Victorian and Queen Anne–style frame houses that were in various states of renovation. Many of his friends now lived on this wide oak-lined street, a street that had once been the pride of the town, had passed into dereliction, and was now being brought back to life by artists and young families who had lots of vision and energy. He ran by gardens and yards—some littered with children's toys, some full of weeds, others with moonflowers gleaming in the dark. He ducked under the giant mimosa that hung in front of his friend Elspeth's home, its feathery fronds brushing his face.

David had helped Elspeth move into that house when that tree was a barely a sapling. Then, most of the houses on the street were student dives or belonged to old folks so frail that they looked no more substantial than the brooms they swept their porches with. He'd leaned over her rotting porch railing and told her she ought to cut that thing down, it was just a weed. The honeyed taste of the beer she'd given him seemed to mingle with her irreverent laugh. "No," she'd said, "I intend to paint that tree." And so she did, dozens of large voluptuous paintings of fuzzy pink mimosas; one of her mimosa paintings now hung over David and Meg's bed.

His footfalls echoed loudly in the empty street. Here and there a light flickered in the recesses of a house, or he caught the iridescent gleam of a cat's eyes peering at him. It seemed to him that he was the only moving thing in the landscape, as if everything around him was caught in the freeze-frame of a grainy black-and-white film. It was eerie, but also exciting, surreal, the way in dreams he flew above places both familiar and strange.

He turned onto the ironically named Easy Street. Here, the houses were smaller as they tumbled down to the railroad tracks and the old cotton warehouses. Still predominately black, there was little gentrification on Easy Street. Some of the poorest people in the county lived here, and had for generations. The poverty here was entrenched, as persistent as chickweed and just as hard to eradicate. David passed by unpainted wooden frame houses with weedy, indifferent yards, yet he also passed brightly painted houses or ones that boasted a profusion of sunflowers or cannas.

David ran on, at a nice, even pace now, angling down toward the river. He turned onto Odd Street, where his friend Anthony had grown up. It had been so long since he'd been here, and now in the dark he wasn't sure he could find Anthony's house. But there it was, distinguished as always by the overgrown hydrangeas almost obscuring the house. He slowed and stopped for a moment, catching his breath. Who lived in it now, he wondered. In the dim light it looked much smaller than he remembered it, shabbier, but seeing it again, he could almost smell the cornbread and vinegary collards that were always on the stove.

Anthony. They had been too young to realize how novel their easy friendship had been in those newly desegregated days. David hadn't even really thought about Anthony as "black" until high school—he'd just been Anthony. In elementary school they'd shared books on dragons, had played on the soccer team and ridden their bikes all over town. Anthony, quick-witted, on the track and chess teams, seemed to be the original whiz kid. David hadn't understood Anthony's growing bitterness, hadn't understood that even while Anthony seemed comfortable in his world, he was straddling two worlds. It was only now that David understood. Other black kids made life hard for him, turned on him, even as Anthony must have seen that he would never have the kinds of opportunities David took for granted. So in the last years of Vietnam, Anthony had lied about his age, and enlisted.

David started running again. At the time, Anthony's enlisting had seemed almost like a personal betrayal to David. Over the years he'd turned it over in his mind, why Anthony had done it. Was it just to get out of here? Just to get benefits? A VA loan so he could be the scientist he'd dreamed of being? Was it a calculated risk or a foolhardy adventure? Or was it some fatalistic streak that had always been there? Anthony had come back minus an arm but with a drug habit. David lost touch with him—he had surfaced every now and then, broke, strung out, then just disappeared, until he disappeared altogether.

David sighed, sped up as if he could outrun his memories. He had come under the train trestle and was running parallel to the river. The houses here were sparser, the trees lining the river—poplars, beeches, river oaks—were large and dense. River bottom land—for generations, the poorest of the poor had eked out a living on this mosquito-infested, flood-prone land. Now, ironically, the land had environmental value and was being bought up by the city for a greenway.

Star Richardson had lived down here, the woman who had helped raise him. He thought of her long-fingered broad hands with the pink palms and oval nails, those work-worn hands that had calmed him or gripped his shoulder in warning when he'd transgressed. She lived near here, if she still lived, rearing her children and grandchildren and probably, by now, her great-grandchildren. She'd been a proud card-holding member of the NAACP, but what had it changed for her? She had raised all those generations of children on her meager wages. He wondered if any of her brood were students in Meg's school.

Meg's school. What a mess. Well, better not to think about that now.

His feet pounded the street in a steady staccato. He tried to clear his mind, to empty it, but it wouldn't empty.

He had started drafting a history of the town, the unwritten history of the African-American community in Milledge, Georgia. It was crazy, with all the work he had to do, but this project had an urgency for him. Maybe it was because of Anthony, because of Star. As if he were trying to summon up ghosts, pieces of himself. Or maybe it was more practical than that, something that could be used to inspire Meg's kids, to show them their story was worthy of being told. There was so much to be proud of, from the thriving black middle class that had sprung up after the Civil War, to the nationally syndicated columnist who had gone through their very same school system. The kids needed models. But even as he thought that, he felt the overwhelming weight of what was against them—the economy, the drugs, the gangs.

He hadn't told Meg about it; he hadn't mentioned it to Meg; it was bad enough that he was entering this campaign. She worried about him needlessly. He liked hard work, was easily bored.

The shadows of the trees in the streetlights grew larger and more ominous, his breathing more labored, the echo of his footsteps louder. A large pale owl swooped down into the pool of light cast by a flickering streetlight. *Probably hunting rats,* David thought. He didn't like the idea of coming across a wharf rat, or

38

whatever else might be lurking in the shadows. Like someone from the homeless camp down by the river. A homeless man had died there recently, killed by two women from the camp. Another man had set a fire that had gotten out of hand, burning most of the tents in the camp. The police had closed down the camp for a while, but he knew that it was slowly filling up again. He veered to the right, up a gentle hill, headed back toward the lights of downtown. No, he didn't want to end up on the police blotter.

He turned onto Prince, pounded past the board of education building, and the whole school dilemma intruded on his thoughts again. What could they do at the local level? The state had no money for school construction, despite the local extra sales tax. Schools were using trailers for overflow classes, enduring leaking roofs, broken heating systems, decrepit bathrooms. There was no money for badly needed ESOL classes. Next year there would be a state-mandated increase in class size, and the state was taking away all the unfilled teacher positions. The state was even threatening to take away preschool and after-school programs.

Every day there was new chaos to contend with. David remembered coming home from New York after his brief law career there, ready to make a difference. He'd gotten involved in every kind of social activism, and it seemed for a while that progress was inevitable. Now, those days felt like an anomaly. The NAACP had waned, and all the old problems of fatherless households, high school dropouts, and pregnant teens continued. Health care was less available and more expensive than ever. The environment no longer seemed to top anyone's agenda: The city would clean up one creek, only to discover another one just as polluted. There was something in the well water of a rural community causing high cancer rates. But people were working too hard now to make ends meet to pay attention to all those things. It was every man for himself.

David slowed down and then stopped at the top of the hill, breathing hard. All around him was the sleeping town: from this vantage point he could see the railroad tracks faintly gleaming in the glow from the lights of the chicken-processing plant, where hundreds of Hispanics toiled. The hills gently rolled away from him to the north, tiny pinpricks of house lights barely distinguishable from the stars overhead. He breathed in the air, thick with the sweet smell of honeysuckle, of grass wet with dew. He stood in front of an abandoned row of apartments, some with boarded windows, others with doors hanging cockeyed from hinges, all of it overgrown and buggy. The sight filled him with exasperation and tenderness. All of it, he felt—the chicken plant, the train whistles in the night, the lights arraying the black hills, the broken and the poisoned, all of it belonged to him and he to it.

David turned south, back toward home, picking up speed on the downhill. He hit level ground, and now it was only minutes until he would be at his front door. He loved this stretch, when he felt exhilarated, at ease. He passed the trendy new renovated warehouse district, the old New Way cleaners, the illuminated Huddle House where a few insomniac souls bent over the counter like supplicants, passed the quiet gray Episcopal church, and contemplated again the disrepair of the road when he heard a screech behind him and that crazed pattern rose up to meet him.

FIVE

"Oh, man, you ain't gonna make me pay that, are you?"

Josh looked the guy in the eyes. Sometimes he cut his customers a little slack, but he didn't like the look of this guy. Tall, muscular, tattooed, gold chains around his neck, he looked like the kind of guy who could make trouble.

"You can't take out new movies till the fine's paid. Sorry, that's the deal."

The man glared at him.

"You can talk to the manager if you want." Josh thought this came out well, cool and firm, but he was a little nervous because Carl was a nerdy little wuss and this guy was big. Josh glanced at the videos stacked at eye level on the counter—*Raunchy Nights*, *Two Girls and a Big Cock*, *You'll Get Yours*. Josh wanted to commend him for his *excellent taste!* But then again, the dude didn't look like he had a sense of humor.

The man seemed to be weighing his options. His heavy aftershave and a sweaty, musky smell wafted across the counter. Josh forced himself to look nonplussed, but he was beginning to sweat. This guy was really big. He glared at Josh, but Josh just looked back, smiling, he hoped, blandly. Finally, muttering obscenities, Big Guy dug into his pocket, pulled out a fistful of greasy bills, and threw them down on the counter. Josh was counting out his change, the guy giving him dirty looks, when Libby walked in.

He almost didn't recognize her at first. She wasn't dressed for an Elizabethan play. Not that he hadn't seen her in school clothes, but in his mind she seemed most herself wearing a long dress and wimple. But there was something else different, besides her jeans and peasant blouse. It took Josh a moment to recognize it—she wasn't wearing her glasses. She must have been wearing contacts, because she had a dreamy, unfocused cast to her eyes. She looked nervous, and kept tucking her hair behind her ear. The big, angry guy almost knocked her over on the way out.

Josh quickly scooted out from behind counter. He was astounded she was here, although she had agreed readily to come when he'd finally called her and told her about the project. Suddenly, the *Video Library* seemed entirely too nasty, with its stained carpet and pockmarked sheetrock, the nerdy goths slinking down the aisles, heavy metal music hammering off the walls. It wasn't worthy of Libby. But she didn't seem to notice.

"Hi," she said. "So this is where you work, huh?"

"Yeah. It's not the greatest place… it's a little sleazy, but there is a big storeroom in the back we can use." Josh hadn't wanted to work on the film at home, hadn't wanted to explain the thick quiet of his house to his friends. Nor had he wanted to face his father's sardonic comments. No, definitely not at home.

"Here, come sit with me behind the counter. I have a few more minutes before my shift is over." He led her to a high stool behind a stack of videos. She shifted onto the stool, dropped her purse at her feet.

"So, what's this film about?" She turned her large eyes on him in that way she had of suddenly focusing all her attention. It was almost too much for him.

"It's about this Muslim girl—she comes here from the Middle East—and she's in high school. Her parents are real strict, suspicious of everything. They won't let her go out with her friends. So she starts sneaking out, saying she's spending the night with a friend. On the night of the prom, she borrows a dress and goes. She gets drunk and ends up in the back of a car with some boy. She's not sure what happened, is terrified she has lost her virginity, and doesn't know what to do."

Libby nodded. "Could be good. You have a script?" Josh took a deep breath. "Yeah, but I really want you all to improvise. That's the way Altman directed, you know, put the situation out there and then see what the actors do with it."

"I've never worked without a script before." She blinked myopically.

"It'll be good, you'll see. You'll have a lot of freedom."

"Who'm I playing?"

"Amber—the Muslim girl."

"That's not a very Muslim name."

"No, that's her American name. She made it up so she wouldn't stand out. Her parents call her by her Muslim name, but not her friends… a thread we could develop."

"I see." Libby sounded slightly dubious.

"It'll come together, you'll see."

The bell on the door jangled, and in walked Andy and Susie. Andy's elfin face, dwarfed by his mop of brown curls, made him look like a Muppet. He bobbed up and down to the hip-hop music that was now playing, came up to Josh, high-fived him, and pirouetted on one foot. Behind him trailed Susie, short and rounded and blond—a perfect 1930s heroine. Josh wanted to do a noir-style short just to feature her. She had the right mix of vulnerability and toughness. He hadn't told her yet.

"Susie, you know Libby, right?"

Susie nodded, smiled shyly at Libby. "Hi."

Libby seemed suddenly aloof, perched on her stool. "Hi," she said, voice flat and uninflected. He could see Susie flinch. Susie always acted tough, but she wasn't, really. Libby was the best actress at school and had a reputation as an intellectual. Susie was probably a little afraid of her. Josh wanted them to get along, hoped Susie wouldn't get into her defensive mode.

"Okay, man, tell us w'as up," Andy crowed. Wherever he went, Andy bounced with enthusiasm.

Josh was flooded with affection for his friends. Here they were in this trashy place, ready and willing to play with him, nobody questioning whether his idea was any good or not. They just assumed it was good. They assumed he knew what he was doing. They were his real family.

"I'll close up in a few minutes, close out the cash register, and straighten up here, and then we can get started. I've got copies of the script for everyone here"—he pointed to the stack of papers on the back counter—"so why don't you all read through it while I finish up. Then we'll improv some scenes and, you know, try 'em out in the back. I'll tape 'em, and we can see what works."

"But what about clothes and scenery and all that?" Susie looked petulant.

"Oh, this won't be the final thing… just, y'know, the process. Like, get it into our heads, see how the dynamics between people are."

"Okay."

Josh turned the Open sign over, pulled the blinds down, went through the aisles, straightening up video jackets, picking up trash from the floor. He closed out the register and watched his friends reading. Libby had a look of total absorption on her face, Susie looked skeptical, her jaw furiously working a wad of gum. Andy bounced on his toes, a look of puzzlement on his face.

"So, okay, let's get started." Josh ushered them into the back room.

At first, they wanted to stay tethered to the script, but Josh weaned them off. He focused on the scene between Amber and her parents: he wanted to show how hard it was for Amber to understand her parents' traditionalism and how hard it was for them to understand her desire to be like her peers.

"But I want you to also try and show her inner turmoil, Libby, because she also wants to please her parents. She's caught between her own conflicting desires."

Libby nodded thoughtfully.

"Okay, here's the setup. Amber's parents have discovered she wasn't at her friends' house. The mother is distraught, expecting the worst, the father is trying to calm her down and get the story from Amber. Amber is trying to cover for herself, but she's on the verge of breaking down—doesn't know what she did when she was drunk. Okay, got it? I'll shoot this, and then we can review it."

Susie and Andy arranged themselves on the couch, Andy with his arm around Susie, who wept into a paper-towel hanky.

Libby sat stiffly in front of them. Josh went for a wide shot, getting them all in.

Susie: "How could you do this to us, your family? What will people say? I feel like I don't know you anymore."

Andy: "Answer your mother."

Libby: "I don't know what you're making such a big deal about. It was just a dance, okay? It wasn't an orgy."

Susie: "But you lied. You lied to us. How could you?" Here Susie looked hard at Libby and Libby returned the stare.

Libby: "You force me to lie. You bring me to this country and expect me to act like I'm still in Pakistan. Everyone thinks I'm strange. I just want to have some fun, be like normal kids."

Andy: "But these kids—they are godless. The girls dress like whores, and the boys are lazy and ignorant. This is not who we brought you up to be."

Libby: "You're just looking at the outside… you never give anyone a chance." Here Libby looked petulant. "I might as well be dead, the way you want me to be."

Josh focused the camera on her face, which alternated between fear and a false bravado. *Good, good,* he thought.

Susie: "Better dead than a whore."

Libby stood up, then crumbled, turning away from her parents. Josh zoomed in to her face, catching the fear and confusion and rage.

"*Cut,*" Josh called out. "Hey, that was great. Really. Let's play it and see what you think."

They rewound the video and sat down on the couch to watch. Josh sat next to Susie, whose eyes were bright and eager. He watched his friends watching the video. Libby's look of concentration was almost spooky. As the scene came to an end, Josh flicked it off and said, "What do you think? I liked the way there is some overlapping of the dialogue—sort of Altmanesque."

There was a pause as the others all stared at Josh.

"Josh, I never know what you are talking about, dude." Andy threw a waded-up piece of paper at Josh's head.

"I thought it was pretty good," Susie said. "Libby was real good."

"Yeah, man, girl, how do you do that with your face and all?" Andy turned to Libby admiringly.

Libby just shrugged. "Actually," she said, "I thought the dialogue was a little hackneyed. Maybe we should stick to the script."

Josh saw Susie freeze and Andy look puzzled. Susie's face was getting harder and harder.

"Bitch," she murmured.

Libby blinked. "What?"

"You heard me. How dare you come in here all high and mighty and start with, 'Actually, I thought the dialogue was hackneyed'—whatever the hell that means. What do you think this is, the Actors Studio? We're just trying to make a little film here, not do Shakespeare, for god's sake."

Libby looked genuinely baffled. "But, but I thought we were going to critique it—to try and make it better. That's all."

Josh began to feel a panicked, airless feeling. He wanted to stop them, ease off the conflict, but he didn't know how.

"How about a break, girls?" Andy said affably. "I just happen to have some fine Mexican weed here—might give us all a different perspective." He took a pouch out of his jeans.

"Good idea, Andy," Susie said.

Libby looked panicked. "Uh, no, thanks. I don't smoke."

Susie smirked. "Why doesn't that surprise me?"

Libby turned to Josh. "I've really got to go. Tell me when the next rehearsal is, okay? I think we made a good start…" Her voice trailed off.

"Yeah, sure," Josh said and got up to let her out. He felt sick to his stomach.

"Good-bye," she said awkwardly to the others, halfway to the door.

"Bye-bye," Susie sang out in a falsely bright soprano.

"See ya," said Andy.

Standing outside the door, Josh tried to make excuses for his friends, even while he made excuses to himself for Libby's coldness. Apart from his crush on her, she was the real thing, and she could make or break his video. He didn't want to lose her. He realized that she really hadn't meant to alienate anyone, that she was just that much of a craftsman about her work. He found himself at a loss for words, and then found himself leaning down and kissing her. Startled, she drew back and then returned his kiss. He was surprised at how yielding she was.

"Okay, we'll get the kinks worked out, don't worry," he murmured.

She pulled back as if to get him in focus, then smiled at him. "I'm not worried." She hitched her shoulder bag on her shoulder and dug out her keys. "I think it's going to be good." Then she strode off toward her car.

Josh stood in the dark lot, watching as she backed the

old Impala out and left. The smell of asphalt and exhaust and stale cigarette butts rose up around him. Yes, maybe it would be good.

When Josh came back, Andy's and Susie's faces in the cloud of smoke were impassive. Josh felt so many things—elation at the kiss, unfamiliar anger at his friends, confusion about how to smooth things out—that he wasn't sure how to act.

Andy held the joint out to him. Josh hesitated—he didn't usually smoke, didn't like to mess with his head.

"Aw, come on now, don't be a Goody Two-Shoes like snooty," Susie said. "Tooty-snooty, hooty-mooty..." Susie started laughing, fell over on her back on the couch.

Josh wanted to explain that Libby really didn't mean to be a jerk, that she was just a perfectionist, but he could see they were in no mood to indulge him. And he couldn't alienate them. If he did, who would he have? His mother's sad, drawn face and sloped shoulders appeared before him. He took the joint and inhaled and passed it back to Susie.

Expelling the fragrant smoke, he waited his turn for another hit. He didn't feel anything at first, then he noticed that he felt lighter, happier. A tight place in his chest seemed to loosen, open. *How could anyone be opposed to this stuff,* he thought, anger and confusion withdrawing their sharp tentacles. Andy passed the roach to him. "Yeah, man, good stuff," he said, taking another long drag. Maybe he was too serious, too over-controlled. Maybe... but he forgot. The thought floated pleasantly away.

"Hey, man, don't hog it," Andy said playfully, taking the burning roach from his hand. "God, I'd love to see old Libby on this stuff. See what she's really like."

Susie snorted. "Yeah, that'll be the day. Uptight bitch. Snotty-rotty."

Josh felt an urgent need to try and make his friends understand about Libby. "She's all right, y'know. Just very... serious."

Susie's eyes fixed on him. "Oh, my god, are you, like, in love with her? Why didn't I get that? That is so, so, like, wrong, Josh." Susie started crying.

Josh put his arm around her. "Don't cry, Susie."

"She'll so eat you up and spit you out, Josh. She doesn't care about you like we do."

Andy sighed. "Here we go. Susie, come on, I got to get you home or your mother won't let me near the house again." He took her firmly by the arm. "See ya, man," he said to Josh.

Josh held up his hand. "Yeah, man, see ya."

***

Josh sat alone in the dark room. He suddenly felt very lonely. He didn't want this project to fall apart. He punched the play button. Yeah, Libby was good. He began to see more possibilities, ways they could elaborate the scene. He paused on the last frame, on Libby's face. It hovered there in the dark, her eyes wide and vulnerable. Man, she was something.

He felt a sharp pain behind his eyes. He couldn't lose his friends. He'd have to try to get Susie to understand. He shivered in the dark. He picked up the tattered end of the roach, lit it, and inhaled. He didn't feel anything but burning in his throat. *Stuff's overrated,* he thought. *Better get home. It's past midnight.* There wasn't anything more he could do about his friends tonight.

He got in the car, strapped himself in, turned on the radio, and eased the car into traffic. That's when it hit him, the last toke. "Whew," he said out loud, shaking his head, his eyes straining to see the road wavering between his headlights. Whew, how weirdly still everything was at night, like a ghost town.

Josh noticed something out of the corner of his eye, something moving, and then, before he could notice anything else, he realized he'd hit something, he'd braked, that something had happened, that he better get out of the car, better do something. But all he could do was sit there. He didn't want to get out of the car. He didn't want to know it, whatever it was.

SECTION 2:

THE DAY AFTER

SIX

There was nothing that Helen could grab on to, no experience or idea or person. Nothing had prepared her for the dark empty street, for the wailing siren, for the red light strobing across their faces. Nothing had prepared her for the sight of a man limp as a rag doll being strapped onto a gurney, nor for the knowledge that her son, her Josh, had put him there. And nothing had prepared her for the force of Hal's fury, or Josh's stunned, pale face as his father stood over him, screaming. She didn't know how long she had stood there, shrinking back from them. Time seemed to stretch out, so that the scene in front of her sucked up all the past, all the future, in an endless black hole.

"Stop it, Hal," she said finally, forcing herself out of her stupor. As she drew closer, she smelled the vomit, felt herself beginning to get sick. She flung her arms out to Josh, but he shook her off. She backed off, feeling useless, embarrassed.

Josh hugged himself, his body convulsed in shudders. He was pale, his eyes empty, alien. A policeman came over to him and began asking him questions and writing things in a notepad. Helen started to say something, but Josh shot her a warning look. He looked so dutiful, so earnest. She strained to hear what they were saying, but then she saw Josh nod docilely and the policeman take him by the elbow and put him in the police car and drive off.

Panic came over her as the lights of the police car grew smaller and smaller, then disappeared into the dark. Ever since they had gotten Josh's frantic call just a short twenty minutes ago, she had rushed single-mindedly to him, only to have him seem to be just out of reach.

Hal had stopped screaming, at least. He seemed suddenly drained of energy, his shoulders sloped, his arms hanging limply at his sides, his eyes wide and blank.

Hal turned to her, his usually impassive face wrenched out of all recognition. "You!" He jabbed a finger in her face. "You! This is what happens when you let him do any goddamn thing he wants!" His face was so red, the veins standing out in his forehead and neck, that she was afraid he'd have a heart attack. She reached out to touch his sleeve, to try to calm him, but he hit her hand away, then sat down on the curb and sobbed into his hands.

Helen couldn't breathe. He had only cried once in their life together, and that had been when she'd broken their engagement.

Another cop came over to them, startling Helen. He suggested to her that they needed to get to the station—bail would be set, and then they could take their boy home. The cop was young and tall and kind, soft-spoken. "I don't think they'll keep him there, ma'am," he said reassuringly.

"They ought to just keep him there," Hal muttered. He had turned away from her and the cop, and she could tell by his ragged breath he was fighting for control.

The cop touched her shoulder lightly, encouragingly, and she blurted out, "He's a good boy, really."

"I know, ma'am. Lots of kids hit some bumps along the way—I did myself."

She nodded, wanting to take his hand and kiss it.

Hal got up, shook himself, then grasped her arm, hard. "Come on, let's get it over with." He pushed her toward the car and into it. "You know who that man was, don't you? David Masters?" He didn't look at her, looked straight ahead.

She shook her head.

"He's that liberal activist, that's who. The guy who organized the poultry workers, who works with refugees. The one everyone likes so much... That's who your son just ran over." He turned away from her. Her stomach churned, her heart raced. Who? Poultry workers? She had no idea what he was talking about. Everybody else knew what was going on and she didn't know anything. But it didn't matter, didn't Hal get it? Josh mattered, he was the only one she cared about. She didn't give a damn who that man was, just as long as he didn't die and make her son a murderer.

When they got to the station, Helen rushed over to Josh, but still he wouldn't look at her. She gulped back the words she'd wanted to say. Hal sat down on a bench, staring straight ahead. They took Josh away for a drug test, and as he passed her, she thought his eyes looked dilated. Josh had been open with her about his drug experiments in the past, but he had told her that he didn't like pot very much and that anything else was out of the question. Well, maybe he was lying. Another shudder passed over her. Something else she didn't know that she thought she knew. Her idea of who she was, who they were, was whirling away, coming apart so fast she felt dizzy.

Helen sat down next to Hal. The fluorescent lights of the police station drilled into her head. Angry prostitutes were brought in, men drunk and swearing. A black woman came in raging that she'd kill him this time, and Helen saw her gentle cop push the woman forcibly against the wall while a female cop patted her down. She was stunned. All of this existed, she knew in an abstract way. But what did any of it have to do with Josh, with her?

Hal ignored her. When the sergeant brought Josh back, Hal went over to them. Helen strained to hear what they said. She saw Hal hang his head and pass his hand over his eyes, saw Josh stare past his father. Then the sergeant turned and led Josh away. Only then did Helen see the handcuffs behind his back. She thought he might look back at her, but he just walked through the gray double doors. The doors swung listlessly behind him. Josh was in jail.

Helen went over to Hal. "How long?" she asked.

"They don't think it will be more than overnight. They'll set bail tomorrow."

"Bail?"

"Yes, Helen, bail."

"But, how much?"

"Between five and fifteen grand."

Helen sank down in the seat. It was so much.

"But we'll get him out tomorrow? He'll come home tomorrow? I mean, Hal, it was an accident!"

"He was driving under the influence, Helen. He'd been smoking pot with his so-called friends."

Helen looked away. Why did Hal always make her feel like it was her fault?

"He told me he didn't like pot," she offered timorously. "I just can't believe—"

"I don't want to talk about this anymore. Let's go home."

They drove home in silence. Helen could see Hal's jaw popping in and out, but other than that he made no movement or sound. A tight, cold knot coiled in her stomach and began to creep up her diaphragm. She cast small furtive glances at Hal, hoping he would turn to her, maybe put his arm around her, anything. But he didn't, he just pulled into the driveway, put the car into gear and got out, slamming the car door hard behind him.

She sat in the dark car, the cold seeping into her bones, unable to move. She looked out at the basketball hoop in the driveway, at the bedraggled boxwood hedge, at the stars suddenly bright in the sky. It was all familiar, and yet unfamiliar. It was as if she were seeing these things for the first time. Slowly, she opened the door and willed her body to move.

Inside, Hal was already in his pajamas, brushing his teeth. He didn't turn when she came in. She stood in the bathroom doorway, staring at his flannel-clad back. She waited, willing him to meet her eyes in the mirror. He kept his eyes down, then turned and brushed past her.

A blow to the stomach could not have been more effective. Was Hal going to ignore the way he treated her tonight? Were they simply not going to talk about what was happening? Was it going to be business as usual, like his goddamn clocks? Wind them up and off they go, ticking without variation, in a long monotonous routine? Slowly, the heavy cement in her began to move. Something hot and liquid began to take its place.

"I think you'd better sleep in the living room." That's what came out of her mouth, although she hadn't planned to say anything.

He turned to her in surprise. His eyes widened at first with what looked like bewilderment, but swiftly narrowed. He contemplated her, an icy look on his face. She knew this look, the look of white fury, when he fixed her in his sights as if he recognized her as his true enemy.

Circling around her deliberately, he went over to his side of the bed. "I can do you one better. You want to handle this all by yourself? Well, have at it. I wash my hands of the two of you." And he took his suitcase from under the bed, and methodically began to pack underwear, socks, shirts, and pants.

Helen didn't do anything to stop him. She went into the living room. Ordinarily, she would have been all over Hal, gentling him, apologizing, anything to keep him from some threatened action. But a strange numbness took over. She didn't seem to care what he did. She was only aware that she was very, very tired. So she sat on the couch in the dark and waited for the next thing to happen.

He walked through the living room. At first he didn't see her. Then, startled, he stepped back. "I'll stay at the shop. I'll pay the bills as usual. I'll make arrangements for bail. Other than that, you two don't really need me around, anyway." And he was out the door. She heard the familiar rough cough of their Chevy truck starting up and then heard the engine whine and the whine grow fainter. He was gone.

She was still clutching her purse under her arm. She put it on the coffee table and took off her jacket and put it over her.

In some ways, it occurred to her in her altered state, she had been waiting for this to happen all Josh's life. The shoe to drop, the ax to fall, however the saying went. She'd been holding her breath since he was small, waiting for the rages, the tantrums, the frustrations she couldn't seem to help him contain. All those years, fearing that his impulsiveness would finally do him in.

There had been the early years when, even as a toddler, he had been so easily upset. When he was five, they'd gotten separated at the zoo for just a moment, but even after she found him, he couldn't stop crying, and they had to leave. All those years in grammar school, waiting for him to come home and face the homework battle, the broken pencils and hitting his head and saying, "I'm stupid," or worse, "I wish I were dead." And then, thankfully, finding some help for him, finding out it wasn't all her fault, but still her radar was always up, worrying that some stress or other would set him back. She was, she realized now, exhausted with the vigil she had kept.

And she had been waiting for it all to be too much for Hal, holding her breath, trying to defend herself, defend Josh, trying, trying so hard to make it all right. Fighting the fear that the worst would happen, that he would leave her.

And now it had happened. The worst thing. And all she felt was numb. And relieved? Was that the feeling? No more finger in the dike; the dike had broken, and all she could do was watch the water rise.

The silence now was more companionable. She let her breath out. She lay on the couch for a long time, her eyes open, listening to the sounds of the empty house. The cuckoo clock struck, then struck again, and she didn't bother to count how many times. Finally, she got up and shuffled to the medicine cabinet and dug through the dusty collection of pill bottles, finding at last a bottle of Klonopin that wasn't out of date. She shook a pill into her hand. It was as if everything that had happened would be dissolved by the little white sphere. She found her way in the dark to her bed and waited for oblivion to take her.

***

Hal had once rented out the room over the shop, but that had been years ago, before the business became self-sustaining. He still used the kitchen and bathroom—the kitchen to make coffee and lunch during the work day. But he hadn't really taken it in for years, and when he'd made his angry declaration to Helen, in his mind's eye he'd framed it as both more comfortable and cleaner than it turned out to be.

He stood in the middle of the room, blinking. The weak overhead light cast a dim pall over the old futon bed, the bare linoleum floor, the shabby orange tweed chair. It was cold, and Hal wondered if the space heater still worked. The room smelled like cats, and he vaguely remembered he'd thrown out the last tenant because he'd secretly kept cats in there. Hal hated cats.

He flung himself on the futon. He felt miserable and stupid. Why had he stormed out? He longed for his own bed, for the clean familiar odors of his home. And yes, for Helen, for the warmth of her, and for Josh.

But then his anger and resentment came back fourfold. It rose in him, a bitter, sickening tide. No, it was just as well. They'd shut him out long ago, the two of them. It was as if they willfully misunderstood him, refused to see that he was hard on Josh only to help him, prevent him from wasting so much of his life. He, Hal, had made enough sacrifices for two lifetimes, and if there was any redemption to be had in his own suffering, wouldn't it be in saving his bright boy from more of the same?

He and Helen should have been a team. But Helen always felt she had to protect Josh from him, and this stung him more than anything, her not trusting him. She'd always supported him before. Her belief in him had been the one thing he'd held on to in all the bleak years. He was stunned how that had eroded away, how he had been made the enemy.

Well, to hell with them.

The anger burned off any lingering regret. To hell with them. Let them see how they do without him. Neither of them will be anywhere on time, Josh's grades will tank, nothing in the house will be maintained. He'd be surprised if they managed to empty the garbage or get the recycling bins out on the curb on the right day.

He pulled the thin comforter on the futon over himself and shivered. He needed to sleep, clear his head for dealing with all the crap in the morning. But when he closed his eyes, the scene of the accident came back to him: the man's body awkwardly splayed out on the road, the police lights turning everyone blue,

Josh running up to him, as if he, Hal, could somehow fix this, this worst of all possible things. But it was too late, it was all too late. They'd made a wrong turn somewhere, and the worst had happened. It was broken, and nothing Hal could do would fix it.

***

"Dad got me out. I'm going to school." Helen stared up at Josh's face swimming above her, trying to place where they were, what time it was, why he looked so odd and grim. She realized she was still in bed, and was ashamed of it. She looked at the clock with panic—it was nine thirty. Slowly the events of the night came back to her. Josh looked awful. His skin had a bluish tint. His breath smelled stale. His hair stood up in webby black clusters. His blue eyes had gone flat and hard, all the warmth and merriness extinguished. She wanted to tell him to stay home, but as if anticipating her, he said, "I have to. The probation officer will meet me there."

She struggled against the fog in her head, against the bed covers strangling her. "Let me make you something to eat," she said hoarsely.

"Mom! I can't eat, okay? Let me go."

She wanted to take his hands and ask him what happened last night, why he'd been smoking. She wanted to tell him she didn't care who David Masters was, she didn't care what Josh had done, she would fight for him. Instead she lay back against the pillows. "Is there anything I'm supposed to do?" she asked. "Your father didn't tell me…"

He shook his head, picked up his book bag. He walked out of the room woodenly, as if he couldn't quite control his body and was being very careful to look as if he could. He slung the too-heavy book bag on his left shoulder and leaned to the right like an old soldier, and left the room. The front door slammed shut, and the silence, which had retreated to the corners of the room, crept back to her. This time she didn't struggle against it, but turned into it gratefully.

***

It was all mixed up for Josh—the fight between Susie and Libby, the joint, the kiss, braking as the guy appeared out of nowhere, the sickening thud of the car hitting something, the delay between the sound and what it meant, the guy lying there twitching, his shorts twisted weirdly on his legs, his head at a strange angle, and then the dark sticky blood seeping underneath, the retching sound that was coming from him, and then the lights and sirens, and then Hal. When he looked up, his father's face was the only thing in focus, and Josh was flooded with relief at the sight of it. He wanted to jump into his arms and cry, "Daddy!" like he used to when Hal would come in to soothe him out of a nightmare. He could almost feel Hal's hand smoothing his hair, telling him it would be all right. But then Hal's face distorted into something else, like some Stephen King horror movie, something dangerous and rageful. And that's when Josh knew he was wrong. He, Josh, was guilty. And there was no help for him.

Now, walking to school, his mouth cottony and dry, his legs like the sacks of sand he'd hauled last spring to make a dam for the flooding river, it came over him again. There was no way out of this. He didn't know who he was today, but it bore no relation to who he was yesterday.

His father had gotten him out of jail and explained about the trial date, about the probation officer, about who they'd get as a lawyer, about how he'd have to go into treatment for substance abuse, everything, but he never looked Josh in the eye. His voice was cool, mechanical; he almost seemed to enjoy it. Josh was used to his father's disapproval, but this was something else—something icy, something hard. His father had dropped him at the house, telling Josh that he would be staying at the shop for a while—if Josh needed him, just call him there. Then he pulled away from the curb and drove down the street, and Josh felt a longing, a homesickness come over him as the car disappeared.

He had seen the headlines at the newspaper stand on their way home. Everyone would know, even if they didn't print his name because he was a minor. But Josh found with surprise that he really didn't care. He tried to blame Andy, but he couldn't. It was just the luck of the draw—Andy smoked all the time and never got caught; Josh hardly ever smoked. A curious detachment settled over him. What will be will be. Except. Except for Libby. Suddenly he remembered Libby, and suddenly he knew he cared. She wouldn't have anything to do with him now.

The backpack was heavy, and he shifted it on his back. He

was almost through the field, and the sun beat down on him. Sweat trickled down the back of his neck, behind his knees. He squinted in the bright light, saw the sunlight flash off the cars parked in the school parking lot. For a minute, he thought about not going in and facing them at all, of just staying in the field, or even of escaping, somehow. He stood and smoked, relinquishing the heavy backpack for a while. He tried to think of this as a film and how he would direct the protagonist. Yes, in the film version of his life, he would decide to split, hotwire a car, and head for Mexico. He would also be taller, have six-pack abs, and be a babe magnet. But that wasn't really his style. In the film, he would be as he was, thin, disheveled, confused. That was more like it. Not an action film—no, a quiet film. A quiet, stupid film where he didn't have a chance.

He reached down to pick up his backpack, and suddenly he saw David Masters lying there with the blood seeping out. Josh got sick all over again. He vomited in the tall scratchy weeds. It was real, it wasn't a movie. And the man might die. And then he would be a murderer.

He got up, wiped his mouth on his sleeve, combed his hands through his hair, then plodded slowly toward the redbrick building.

SECTION 3:
DOG DAYS

SEVEN

News of David's accident rippled throughout the town, slowly at first, then with increasing speed and disbelief. The accident made the front page of the local paper, and the front page of the bilingual paper. It was the subject of conversation at the courthouse, the YMCA, at the Waffle House, in the poultry plant. For many who had worked with David, or for whose causes he had worked, it was unimaginable that such a giant could be felled. For those who had seen a new future through his leadership, who had shaken off their apathy and worked and hoped for change, that hope began to seem like a mirage. Their grief and shock were both intensely private and yet communal. People walked around dazed, their hearts yearning toward David. Hardcore agnostics found themselves staring into space, formulating fractured prayers. Even his political opponents sent Meg notes of sympathy and encouragement. Petty concerns seemed just that, petty, and life suddenly seemed more capricious, mysterious, and also more significant than before David Masters' accident.

Meg at first was inured to the mood that gripped the town. Sequestered in the ICU with David, she was aware only of him lying under the white blanket, unmoving. She felt not quite real, as if she were in a TV show, as if she were acting the role of the shaken and aggrieved wife. She was sure this was an odd crimping of time, some alternate reality she had stepped into by accident, and which she would step out of soon and resume her normal life.

She didn't know what to do. She felt awkward, and strangely resentful that no one had taught her how to handle something like this. All the useless things you grow up learning, she thought, all the effort put into learning chemistry tables and algebra equations, but no one ever talks about what to do when your husband lands in the ICU. She brushed his hair off his forehead, held his hand, talked to him, and waited for him to respond. When he didn't, she felt an unseemly desire to yell at him, to shake him out of it, and, at other times, to run away, to go home and find him, the real him, there.

Time folded in on itself, so that it became not a forward line, but an endless cycle. There was only this: a thick now of half sleep, of machines whirring like cicadas, of blinking lights and bells going off, punctuated by doctors' rounds and nurses briskly taking vital signs, adjusting machines. There was no day or night, no weather or seasons. Because there was no time, she experienced neither hope nor fear.

She sensed she was in shock, and that later, the solid reality of it would hit her, but for now she was content to be in this cocoon with him. She focused intensely on each small practical matter—answering phone calls, writing notes, making plans for the substitute. She did these things automatically, as if another self were doing them, while her real self was simply matching her breath to David's, letting him know she was there.

It was only when they moved David out of the ICU that Meg understood that this had not just happened to David and her.

So many he had worked for or with over the years came

to the hospital, filling the fourth floor waiting room, giving it the air of a party or an activist group meeting, so that Meg was embarrassed by the noise, hoping they wouldn't bother the other meager visitors. Meg began taking flowers to the nurses' station, and when they protested, down to the maternity ward. Although it was a Catholic hospital, Meg noticed some of the nurses pursing their lips disapprovingly at the unlit votives and Our Lady of Guadalupe holy cards piling up on the windowsill. She had thought about discouraging the Latino contingent from bringing rosaries and holy medals and the African American contingent from bringing food, but in the end realized not only that she couldn't stem the tide, but that she shouldn't.

She had complained of all the excess to one of David's old friends, Raleigh Williams, a black minister who had come to visit David. Raleigh had always been a comforting presence to Meg, one of the few people she felt able to open up to. "Of course you don't need all this, Meg, but they need to give it." And then he had turned to David, putting his hand over David's, and had sung "Amazing Grace" in a low, rich baritone. When Meg emerged from the room to give them time alone together, she caught in the up-tilted faces of the nurses and patients in the hall the lingering resonance of the song.

And so she accepted the gifts, became reconciled to the strange and motley parade through the waiting room. Meg brought some of the votives and medals home and took to going by the homeless shelter with bags of tamales and tortillas, fried chicken and yams, more food than she could ever eat. Despite the exhaustion that set in having to talk with so many people, in telling the same story over and over about how the doctors didn't know when or if he would come out of the coma, Meg felt each encounter nourished her. She felt upheld by love, and when, in the dark hours of the morning, she was alone with David and the green light of the monitor, the knowledge of all those people loving David consoled her.

***

David always knew when Meg was with him. Her voice came to him as if down a long corridor, but he felt what she was feeling as if there were no skin separating them. Today she was burdened, and he wasn't sure if he heard or felt her sighs. What is it, what is it? he wanted to ask, and his heart contracted. He felt her sit on the bed and take his hand. There was a heaviness in her, more than usual. He had always worried about her, her tendency to over give—whether at school or in friendships, even to him. He could feel it now, her emotional weariness. She felt everything deeply, couldn't leave things behind, so that when she came, it felt to him as if a whole roomful of people were there—the children she taught, her friends, the cashier she knew from Bell's.

Then he drifted off, and when he came back, he knew she was gone.

Peggy Lee came to him then, perched on his bedside.

At first he had been surprised by the singer's presence. He remembered listening to her albums, lying on the floor of the living room when he was a kid, staring at her doe-eyed blond visage, her velvet voice wrapping around him, hinting at an adult world full of irony and remorse, of men who left women, and women who toughed it out. It was as if he had conjured her somehow. At first he'd been shy—as if he still were that boy—but now he was getting used to her visits, looked forward to them even. He could talk to her. She understood everything.

"She was here again?" Peggy's tight-fitting aqua dress shimmered as she kicked off her shoes and lit a cigarette.

"Yes, and she seems so sad." They had fallen into an intimate easy way that was new to him.

She gave him a long, slow look. "What do you expect?" Her voice seemed particularly husky today, particularly world-weary.

"I know. Still, I wish I could comfort her, talk to her."

"There's nothing you can do about it, babe."

"But I'm a doer. That's what I am."

"Guess you're going to have to be something else. It's not all bad, y'know. Just seems like it at first."

"What's good about it?" He wanted to believe her, but he didn't know who he was if he wasn't fixing things, changing things.

"Buck up, chum." She gave his arm a comradely shake. "Come on, I'll fix us a drink."

David could hear her humming under her breath, her hips swaying, her platinum hair just brushing her bare shoulders. He smelled the juniper-scented gin and olives and caught a whiff of her cigarettes. He wanted to protest that he never drank hard liquor, but when she handed the glass to him and winked at him with her catlike eyes, he felt all resistance melt away. He didn't know where he was heading, but if Peggy was there to guide him, it would be okay.

***

Into the second week, the doctor gently suggested that Meg return home, resume her schedule. "There isn't much you can do here," he said. "It is going to be a process, and I don't know how long. It will be better for you to try to get back to normal."

But this is normal, Meg thought. *And how will he breathe without me here?*

He was telling her something about time, something she was supposed to grasp: ". . . it could last two to five weeks. After that..."

Leaving the hospital felt like a betrayal. How could she leave him there alone? She blinked her eyes at the blue sky, the bright sun, the flowers and traffic. It all seemed too much, and she felt unfit for it. The worst was the house, with its stale air and piled-up mail. Her neighbor had let the cat out and brought in the mail, but several plants had died. The message machine flashed F for full. She opened the door to David's room, saw his many notes and opened books, just as he'd left them. She hesitated in the doorway, began to shake. The pen on the pad was uncapped, and she should cap it, but she wasn't sure she could bear to see his handwriting. She felt a passing irritation—why couldn't he ever cap his pens? And then thought, *He's not dead. He'll be back. And he'll need his pen.* She walked over slowly, capped the pen, and laid it gingerly on the yellow pad, her hand lingering on his spidery, indecipherable handwriting. She jiggled the mouse, revealing the monitor's wallpaper, her own face, pink from exertion from their hike in Banff, happy. The email icon flashed on and off—there were hundreds of new emails. What should she do? Should she cull them? Keep up with them? She was back in it now, back in time with its incessant demands. How was she going to take care of her work and his, too?

Meg ran a bath, poured a glass of wine. Slipping into the warm water, she let it enclose her. Something was coming at her, the way a storm approaches quickly or a large wave knocks the wind out of you, so that you come up gagging. It was coming now, and she would have to face it. Despite the warm water, she shuddered.

She was again at the scene of the accident. She had wakened at half past two that night, alone in an empty bed. She was used to David's late-night runs, but he had never been this late, and she had been seized by dread. Without changing out of her pajamas, she'd thrown on her jacket and gotten into the car, rehearsing the scolding she would give him when she found him. She hadn't expected to find him on a hospital gurney, surrounded by EMTs, blue emergency lights garishly strobing his inert form.

It wasn't only the eerie unreality of David so passive, so broken. It was also the boy's pale face, his eyes staring out of his head, his mouth slack, seeming to hover above David as he was hustled into the ambulance. And it wasn't just him; it was his father screaming at him, his mother backing away in horror. The whole tableau kept repeating itself over and over in her mind, the boy pinned there, unmoving, his face stricken, the car door open, the blood on the pavement, David's still body on the gurney, the father's face red with fury, his voice the only human sound.

What sorry people. Did they have any idea what their son's carelessness had taken from her? After all the hard years, she and David had finally landed in a relatively calm and happy place. The cup of their marriage began to seem half full, not half empty, sometimes brimful. She finally had understood that all the people Dave helped were not in competition with her, that he needed them in his life to be who he was. Dave had finally—oh, how long she had wanted it!—begun to initiate time spent with her alone, sometimes suggesting a shopping trip, a drive in the country, a game of chess. She had wanted more of him, more of that.

Last fall, on impulse one long, empty Sunday, they'd gone for a drive in the country. They passed fields of goldenrod and pastures dotted with hayricks, the late-afternoon sun gilding everything with its warm light. It seemed to her that the gentle hills and white farmhouses and horses and cows were unusually beautiful, and she wondered why they didn't drive out there more often. They drove to a small park with a covered bridge and a river with rocky shoals, where they'd waded, sitting finally on warm granite rocks, watching the silvery water rush by. On the way home, they'd stopped at the rundown Fish Shack for fried catfish and hushpuppies, dipping the hushpuppies in honey—the honey golden, the fried hushpuppies golden—and popped them in their mouths, joking about the thousands of calories they were consuming. They'd gone home tired and satisfied, like two kids spent after a day on the playground.

Meg sipped the wine and tasted salt. She was unmoored. Why should she feel sorry for that boy? At least he had his parents and they had him. She had no one.

EIGHT

Meg's hands on the steering wheel shook. She was there for the trial, but she wasn't sure she could handle it. Wasn't sure she really wanted to hear all the details again, but even more, she wasn't sure she could bear to see those people again. Meg had asked around about the family, but no one seemed to know much about them. They seemed to have lived quietly, under the small town's gossip radar. It was almost as if they didn't really live in Milledge. In her mind she imagined a slovenly, neglectful mother, someone who smoked and racked up debt buying shoddy goods on the shopping channel. The father watched NASCAR and drank beer and didn't bother to vote. The boy had been brought up on video games and fast food, was a troublemaker, a druggie, a punk.

Meg was glad no one knew much about them. Meg wanted to be vindicated in her judgments of them. She didn't want to have to revise her opinions, or lose the focus of her wrath. She did learn, finally, from school gossip, that the mother was a nurse at the hospital, the very hospital that was now keeping David alive, a fact that made her blood run cold. And the father had a small shop that repaired antique clocks and watches. And the boy, well, the boy was considered a good kid. Meg sniffed. What kind of good kid would be DUI, would almost kill her husband?

The boy had been charged with driving under the influence

and reckless driving. But all that would change if David died. The state wanted to make an example of him because of David's high profile, and have him tried as an adult. At first Meg had thought this unfair, but now she didn't want to waste energy on what was fair or not. It wasn't fair for David to be lying in the hospital.

Meg was tired of caring. David had cautioned her for years that she internalized too much, that she brought all those children home with her. And she knew he was right. She just didn't know any other way to do it. Yesterday, she had learned that Janelle had not been in school because an older cousin had molested her, and the children had been taken by DFCS. Janelle, her Janelle. The news had left her feeling enervated. There was so little she could do for her students, really. The whole enterprise seemed doomed.

Meg looked at the granite courthouse. It was a rainy, overcast day. She wondered vaguely if her umbrella was in the trunk. She watched the rain slide down the windows, watched as an oil slick formed on a puddle. She wasn't sure she had the energy to cross the parking lot.

She blew her nose, then checked the mirror. Her mascara was smeared, her nose red; she looked like hell. She spit on a tissue, wiped away the black mess, patted powder on her red nose, and reapplied her lipstick. She wasn't one for makeup usually, but she couldn't show up for this with her raw face. Despite the makeup, her face in the mirror looked startled and brittle, her hair severe in its bun, gray strands falling around her thin face. She pulled out the pins, brushing her hair loose. She wasn't sure she looked any better, but at least she looked less severe. She steadied herself and got out of the car, locked it, and straightened her shoulders. It had been years since she had experienced such a feeling of dread.

Inside the courthouse, people stood in the corridor, chatting in soft voices. The corridor was well lit, the carpet deep, the woodwork polished to a high shine. The halls of justice, Meg thought. So civilized. It all seemed pleasantly normal, a place where wrongs were righted, a place far removed from the messiness of the accident, the monotony of the hospital. She found the room she was supposed to be in and slunk into the red plush seat at the back. She watched a few people drift in, but no one she could identify. She began to wonder if she was indeed in the right place when a knot of people emerged through the door, whispering tensely.

"What you don't seem to understand, Helen, is that it doesn't matter that he isn't a regular drug user. They don't care. He just has to go through with it to show good faith."

"But it was just once, they need to know that." The woman's voice was thin, imploring.

"That's not the way it works, Helen. Get a hold of yourself. Just let him do it." The man put his hand on the small of the woman's back and propelled her forward.

It was them. Meg sank down in her seat, tried to look at them from the corner of her eye. *Why,* she thought, *am I afraid they'll see me? I didn't do anything wrong.* Meg recognized the father from the night of the accident. She remembered his contorted red face as he screamed at the cowering boy. She half expected his face to be frozen still into a mask of rage. But it wasn't. He looked perfectly normal, tall, lanky, his face tense, put but pleasant enough. He almost didn't seem to be the same man.

Meg caught a glimpse of the mother, who, in turning toward her husband, looked in Meg's direction. Her shoulders drooped forward, as if she were perpetually protecting herself. She was overweight, dressed sloppily in pants and a sweater, her dark hair hanging indifferently from her wide, pale face. She had the dull, amazed look of someone drugged. The boy followed behind her, looking, it seemed to Meg, strained and uncomfortable in what was clearly a new suit. He walked stiffly, his face flushed. Behind him was the lawyer, tanned and jovial, nodding and greeting people.

Her lawyer had pressed a civil suit, but Meg had waffled. The family's insurance was good, was covering all the medical expenses. Meg simply didn't feel up to a fight. She had the impression of swarming sharks sniffing blood.

A few more people drifted in. Some had notepads, most of them looked official. There was a girl with a camera. The door at the side opened, and the judge came out. A woman, Judge Carmichael. *When did all the judges become women?* Meg wondered. Meg had heard that this judge was tough but compassionate. The charges were read—he was charged with DUI marijuana, reckless driving, endangerment, and speeding. The boy, Josh, stood up. Meg could see the red tips of his ears, the pale exposed neck of a new haircut.

"How do you plead?"

"Guilty, Your Honor." The boy trembled visibly. His mother put a hand on his arm.

"You can sit down."

Josh sat down, glancing anxiously at his mother, who gave him a slight nod, a ghost of a smile. Meg could imagine the nods and smiles she might have given him all along—his first drawings, his first ride on a two-wheeler, his first crush. An ingrained habit. Even here, now.

Meg saw the boy relax a degree, held in his mother's look. The father sat, stony faced, staring ahead.

Meg exhaled. The beloved voodoo dolls she had created had to give way to these people. They were just ordinary people. A mother and son. The old pang came back to her, the persistent haunting emptiness, no matter how many children she had mothered along. It wasn't the same. David had thought it would be, but it wasn't. No, she wasn't going to sue this boy, put his mother through any more.

Because of his age, his clean record, the drug program he'd enrolled in, the fact that David wasn't dead—all of these—he was given a fairly light sentence. His license was revoked for a year, he was given two years of community service at the Good Shepherd, a school for disabled children, and he would have to meet his probation requirements. Meg was stunned and relieved. It was fair, and fairness was what David had spent his life fighting for.

Suddenly, Meg felt as if she should do something, make some connection, she wasn't sure what. They were in this together, in some strange way, weren't they? Maybe it was the boy's stricken face. Maybe it was the thought of having lost Janelle, of not wanting another child lost. Maybe it was her early conditioning as a Quaker. She didn't know. But something impelled her toward them. Meg scooted out of her seat. They were ahead of her, in single file, the father first, then Josh, then the mother. Meg hung back, not sure how to approach them. Then the mother stopped at the water fountain. The father and son rounded a corner and disappeared. Meg took a deep breath and went over to her. The woman looked up at her as she unbent from the fountain, a puzzled expression on her face.

"Excuse me," Meg stammered.

"I'm sorry. Go ahead," the woman stepped away from the fountain, dipping her head obsequiously.

"No, I mean, I don't want—I, uh, I want to talk to you."

The woman frowned. "To me?" She looked around, with a panicked expression, for her family.

"I just wanted to say—I know it was an accident. You have a good boy there—I'm glad the sentence wasn't any harsher."

The woman's faced blanched. "You're, you're... ?" She stammered, her eyes narrowing as she began to understand.

Meg nodded. The woman stared at her.

Meg went on. "I'm sorry..."

The woman stepped back. *"You're sorry?"* She steadied herself against the wall, shaking her head. Then, in a choked voice, "What do you want from us?"

"Nothing. Really."

"Look, I'm sorry about your husband, but leave us alone!" She gave Meg a hurt, hard look, then turned and walked quickly away.

Now Meg slumped against the wall, her heart was pounding. How stupid she was! Was she insane? The woman, the mother had looked at her as if she were. It must be getting to her, the lonely nights, the long visits in the hospital. How pathetic that she thought she could reach out to those people.

She waited a few minutes to make sure they had cleared out, trying to calm her breath, trying not to cry. It was raining harder now, and she had never gotten her umbrella. In her rush to leave the scene of her humiliation, she slipped on the bottom granite step, twisting her ankle slightly. She limped to her car, wrestled with the lock, her reflection in the wet window that of a bedraggled ghost. She slammed the door shut and gripped the wheel, feeling as if she were escaping something.

***

Now that Hal was gone, all the clocks in the house had either stopped or told the wrong time. At first it was disconcerting to Helen. Their life together had always followed a punctual, orderly progression. Now the oven clock said 5:20 and the wall clock said 3:05 and then the digital bedroom clock—always a bone of contention—just blinked 12:00 because there had been a power outage somewhere along the line. Her cell phone ran out of power, and she didn't bother to find the charger. Ditto the computer. Helen managed to keep appointments by her wristwatch, but if that battery went, there was no telling what might happen—she might just spin off into timelessness. She was getting used to time without clocks. It had first felt like chaos, but now it felt like freedom.

For the first two weeks, she had wandered around her house in shock. The house seemed strangely hers and not hers. The lampshade in the living room—had it always been so dingy? Who had chosen the color of the couch—an insipid mauve? The passion she had poured into making curtains, choosing rugs, fighting over what height to position picture frames—all that seemed to belong to someone else.

She had gazed dispassionately at the family portraits, the school pictures. Who were these people? She seemed suddenly not to know, their lives as opaque to her as strangers'. Their family, that cozy bastion she'd sought to make, had crumbled like a gingerbread house left out too long. They had all been playing house, but then an unscripted actor from another play had wandered onstage and the whole thing fell apart. Now Josh went to school, to his community service, and to his room without a word to her. She only knew he was there by the dirty dishes in the sink, the piles of unwashed laundry, the slammed doors, and the throbbing music seeping through the closed door.

Her days had been spent in a kind of fugue state, walking through the house, examining it like an anthropologist. But gradually, over the last several weeks, she had gotten used to the absence and the screaming emptiness in the bed and kitchen, in the den and living room, and had grown calmer. Now, the emptiness seemed like spaciousness. It was companionable to sit in the mornings, watching a green anole climb on the holly bush, to sit with her coffee and watch the patterns of leaves on the table change as the day made its slow, deliberate rounds.

Since she had taken a leave of absence from work, she gave up trying to have a schedule. She slept until she felt like getting up, she ate watching TV, she let her clothes fall where they fell and didn't pick them up. When she ran out of underwear, she went to Walmart for more. Before, she would never have gone to Walmart, but now she went because it was close and cheap and anonymous.

Cruising the brightly lit aisles there, she often felt like an alien who had just landed on the planet. When had everything changed so much? She had no idea how to check herself out in the automated checkout and was exasperated by her own ineptitude. She found herself staring openly at people—the young tattooed mothers; the teenagers with their pierced belly buttons, most of them spilling out over their jeans; the Hispanics speaking rapidly, moving in large clusters that seemed so comforting somehow. She was seized with strong feelings for these people, feelings she couldn't account for, feelings of love or revulsion she didn't particularly like or approve of. There was the server at the meat counter, a soft-spoken black woman with unfortunate scarring over her face, as if she'd been plucked out of a fire. Her expression was unchanging, one of seeming meekness, her eyelids permanently cast down. But then, Helen thought, how would one know what she was really thinking, with that face? Maybe she was seething inside, maybe she was filled with hostilities that sprang up unbidden, so that inside she was really muttering "stupid bitch" or "spic" or "flaming asshole" as she handed the meat over the counter. Maybe she was like Helen.

Inevitably, when she got home from these excursions, she was met at the door by Buster. She was thankful for the dog, that there was someone in the house to greet her, some movement and noise to fill the place up. She loved Buster, but she didn't always like him. Buster smelled. Buster drooled. Buster farted. He was needy, and invariably nosed her elbow, just when she sat down with a cup of tea, spilling it all over her. She could only pet him so much. Still, he made her feel less alone.

She and Josh were awkward with each other when their

paths did cross. She used to know everything he did. She used to know his friends, and enjoyed the way the house filled up with their laughter. Now she knew nothing. The silence between them had grown and calcified like a coral reef. She hated the silence more than anything. She wanted to talk with him, but she didn't know what to say. She hardly knew this new Josh—abrupt, closed, impatient. When he was home, in his room or watching TV, she found herself on edge, both anticipating and dreading some kind of communication.

She knew she had behaved badly that night. It had been a betrayal to shrink from him, at first. He must have seen the horror on her face. And while she wanted to hug him, to soothe and reassure him now, she was also aware of another feeling she didn't want to own, a white-hot anger. She was angry with him for the shame he'd brought them, for the scrutiny that made her hide, for, most of all, not telling her what was going on. For closing her out. She struggled not to blame him for driving Hal away, but it was hard.

She felt Josh had been ripped from her by a torrential current, and she was on the bank, looking on helplessly. There was nothing she could do but watch, and there was no way to know if he would grab a floating log or go under. The current was taking him around the corner, out of sight.

Now she struggled with the key in the lock, Buster barking ferociously on the other side of the door. She got the door open and called, "Josh?" She couldn't remember if today was his day for community service or not. Her voice echoed hollowly in the dark front hall. She threw her keys on the table. "Josh," she called again, more loudly. There was no answer, only the sound of Buster's tail thumping the carpet. The sight of Buster gazing back at her adoringly made her groan.

She threw herself on the couch. "I need to talk to someone," she said into the emptiness. Buster thought she was talking with him, and thumped more loudly. "Jesus, Buster, I need to talk to someone human," she cried. She thought of calling her mother. Her hand crept over to the phone; she picked it up and cradled it in her lap. But she dialed no number, just curled around the phone, weighing what to do next.

Helen's mother had always been a shadow woman. That was the term Helen had come up with. When she thought of her mother, it was a memory of trying to hold on to someone who wasn't really there, someone who didn't want to be there. She remembered clasping Ruth around the neck so hard at night when Ruth tucked her in that Ruth had to pry Helen's fingers off her. "Go to sleep now, honey," she'd say in her raspy voice, the sweetish odor of cigarettes wafting over Helen. "Go on now," she'd say, an edge of irritation in her voice. "I'm going downstairs, and I don't want to hear a peep from you—got it?" And Helen would shrink down under her covers, flooded suddenly with shame, at what she wasn't sure, at herself for being not what her mother wanted.

Nevertheless, she longed for her mother now, the old, primitive longing. She sat alone in her dark, stale-smelling house and longed for her mother's touch on her brow. Her mother had always been attentive when she was sick, as if her daughter were suddenly in focus, and she would lose her impatient edge. Ruth would sit on the edge of the bed, talking soothingly to Helen. She wanted her mother's voice now to reassure her that there was some way out of this mess her family was in; that Josh at least would be all right.

She rehearsed what she might say—that Josh had been involved in an accident, that Hal had left her, and how she was going to be breezy and matter-of-fact and act as if it all were just information. Maybe she would go down there for a visit, sit on the sand and try to get her bearings. Maybe she would bring her watercolors and work under the pine trees and forget that she ever had a husband or a child. Maybe she would lose twenty pounds and her mother would take her shopping and would admire her new figure and they would gossip together about the people her mother was always talking about.

Helen slowly hung up the phone, and her bright, sun-washed vision faded. It began to dawn on her that there was no one for her, no one to go to. She was on her own. She sat there, trying to let the realization penetrate. It felt both cold and bracing, somehow liberating. She had lived for Hal, for Josh, and now they were inaccessible to her. There was nothing she could do about them. She would have to live for herself.

Helen was vaguely aware of a car door slamming, of Josh coming in. The door opened, and Josh swooped in, turning on lights as he went.

"Mom, why are you sitting here in the dark without any lights on?" He peered into her face.

"I didn't notice it getting late, I guess."

"What time did you get up today? What did you do?" There was a demanding, irritated quality to his voice.

Helen started to give an account of herself, and then stopped, laughing. "Boy, this is role reversal."

Josh sat down, scowling. "I don't see what's so funny." He inspected her carefully, a hurt look on his face. "Are you—okay?"

She started laughing then, tears pouring down her cheeks. When she finally caught her breath, she gasped, "Do you mean am I cracking up?"

Josh shifted uncomfortably in the chair opposite her. He looked like he wanted to leave more than anything, but couldn't.

"Well, are you?"

She tried to calm down. She reached over to touch his hand, but he flinched away. She rummaged in her purse for a tissue, blew her nose. His eyes stayed riveted on her.

"No. I promise. I'm not cracking up. It was just funny to me, there for a minute. You know, I used to be the one trying to get you going in the mornings…ahh, well, I haven't had a good laugh in a while." She wiped her eyes with the back of her hand.

"Mom, this can't go on. You can't go on like this." Something in his voice thinned, wavered.

Helen regarded her son as if she had just met him, as if he weren't hers. *What a fine boy he is,* she thought. *How caring.* She took his face between her hands and kissed his forehead. "You are right, son. I can't go on like this. I'm going to shower and clean up this house. Are you going to be here for dinner?"

Josh squirmed uncomfortably. "I, uh, well, I made plans, you know, but, uh, maybe tomorrow…"

Helen smiled. "That's fine, just let me know."

Josh looked at her, wide-eyed, not sure what to make of her. She laughed again.

"It's okay, Josh, I'm a big girl. I can take care of myself. You don't have to worry about me." And for the moment, she meant it.

SECTION 4:
THE NEW NORMAL

NINE

Josh wiped the soup off Chondra's chin. Chondra looked up expectantly at him, eager for the next mouthful of beef and barley. Josh managed to get it in this time without causing Chondra to gag. She smiled at him, and he smiled back, his mouth stiff from lack of practice. "You've had a good lunch, Chondra." Josh tried to sound enthusiastic, but he was forcing it. Chondra made a crowing sound. Josh looked at his watch. Getting a cup of soup into Chondra had taken over half an hour. It was his first day at Good Shepherd Home for Special Needs Children, and he thought it would never end.

He hadn't really thought much about doing this community service. He guessed he was a little numb or in denial. He had thought, if he thought at all, he'd do some menial labor like cleaning or clerical work. So when he pushed open the steel doors and entered the noisy, crowded lunchroom, his first instinct had been to run. He couldn't help it. The sheer concentration of disabilities—what he later learned included cerebral palsy, Down syndrome, spinal injuries, autism—was too much for him. And the ugliness! The drooping eyelids, the drooling mouths, the little twisted bodies. Not to mention the smell—overcooked broccoli, musty clothes, sweaty bodies. Josh hated that part of him that was so sensitive to things like smells and blood, but he couldn't help it. He was clearly the wrong man for the job.

Yet he hadn't run, and somehow he ended up with Chondra, who seemed to find him a fascinating object of contemplation.

He felt a hand on his shoulder. It was Ms. Jones, the formidable director of Good Shepherd. "Good job, Josh. Ms. Marbry will take Chondra back to the activity room now." She nodded to Ms. Marbry, then turned her attention back to Josh. Her gaze was like a lighthouse beam searching him out. A large, black, middle-aged woman, Ms. Jones moved steadily and serenely among the children and staff. Josh could imagine her attired in native West African headdress and clothes, reigning over a village with absolute authority. Josh found her a little frightening. She was bossy and abrupt from what he could already see, and had little patience with incompetence. It was his first day, but he had already seen her scold one of the aides for taking too long a smoking break. He was a little afraid of her.

Now she said to him, "Let's take a walk. I want to show you around," as if he were a casual acquaintance to whom she was showing off her estate.

Josh wanted to mention that he hadn't had a chance to eat, but he didn't dare, scooting back his chair quickly and scrambling to follow her through the metal double doors down a long corridor.

Ms. Jones gestured to the left, through an open door. "This here's the quiet room. We put kids here when they can't control themselves."

Josh was shocked to see the walls were padded, that there

were mats on the floor. Ms. Jones's rich, honeyed voice was unperturbed. She traveled steadily on ahead. "And here is the activities room, where you will be spending most of your time."

Josh peeked through this door and was relieved to see a room with a bank of windows, bright posters on the walls, soft music playing. He saw Chondra pecking at a keyboard with what looked like a stick in her mouth.

"What is she doing?" Josh asked, nodding to Chondra.

"She's learning to write."

At that moment, Chondra caught sight of him and stared, the pointer in her mouth now pointing at him.

Ms. Jones moved on. She opened a door to another hallway off of which were bedrooms and bathrooms arranged in suites. "…Used to be a nursing home, so there was very little retrofitting necessary…" Josh wasn't listening. He was looking at the room they were in, with its family pictures and stuffed animals on the bed. It was like any kid's room, he guessed, only neater. But there was something depressing about it, if only the slightly medicinal smell wafting from the bathroom.

"Josh?"

Josh glanced up at Ms. Jones. She was looking at him, her arms folded across her ample breast, her flat brown eyes fastened on him. A knot of dread gathered in his stomach. He hated it when adults got that earnest tone in their voices—it always meant a lecture. He looked away.

"Ma'am?"

"I want you to know that I don't care what you've done."

He started to say something, to protest that he hadn't done anything, but remembering, stopped himself.

"Because here, you have a clean slate. All I care about is that you show up, do the job, and are nice to the kids. Do you understand?"

Josh could feel himself go red. He wished his skin was dusky like hers, that it didn't register his feelings faster than a mood ring.

He looked right at her. "Yes, Ms. Jones."

"Good, then. You go on back to the cafeteria, and Ms. Marbry will tell you what to do."

He turned to go, then turned back.

"Thank you, Ms. Jones."

She smiled briefly, a gleaming white crescent. "You're welcome, Josh."

He turned back and walked down the hall to the cafeteria, the crowing cacophony already giving him a headache. How could this be his life? How could this have happened to him? This was so not who he was. He couldn't cope. He knew himself. He was very good at a few things, and anything to do with children or medicine or anything physical, he was useless. What had he thought he would do here? Maybe push a broom? He'd talk to Ms. Jones later, ask if he could just wash dishes or something like that.

He spotted Ms. Marbry leaning against a door frame.

"Ms. Marbry? Ms. Jones told me to find you and you'd tell me what to do next."

A tough little woman with the arms of a professional wrestler and the raspy voice of a lifelong smoker, she gave him a tight smile.

"Well, we've got some diapers to change."

Josh tried to control a need to gag, but as always, he betrayed himself.

"Hey, kid, it ain't no big deal. Just think of them as your kid brothers. Didn't you ever change a diaper before?"

"I, I don't have any siblings."

She shrugged, pushed off the doorframe.

"You'll get used to it."

The first kid he had to change was Marius, a black boy about six who had been injured, Marbry said, in an accident. She talked about him as if he weren't there, but Josh could see that the kid was taking it all in. She showed him how to spread the towel on the bed, then lift Marius—who was not light—onto the towel, peeling away his pants, then the sodden, dirty diaper. It wasn't as bad as Josh had expected, although he held his breath the whole time. Marbry criticized his wiping job, but he thought she was too rough. He glanced up at Marius, who looked resigned, absent.

By the time he got home that night, he was exhausted from lifting kids out of wheelchairs onto toilets, from the hands that always seemed to be reaching for him, but even more so from the assault of so many feelings—pity, revulsion, fear. He fell gratefully on his bed, but when he closed his eyes he saw the picture of Marius one short year before, a healthy five-year-old on his tricycle. Some jerk like him had changed all that in a short second. It was too much, too much to bear.

He opened his eyes again, glad at least that his room remained unchanged. As soon as he closed the door, he felt himself reassemble into his real self. His eyes traveled around the room, to the familiar posters for R.E.M., the Drive-By Truckers, and Lil Wayne; the swimming trophies; the model airplanes hanging over the bed; his childhood books from Tolkien to Harry Potter. They fell on the award for first place in the youth division at the annual Houston CineFest. The poster for his film, *Edge of Shadow*, was tacked below it, a black-and-white photo of Andy in a fedora, slouching against a door. Josh took it all in and allowed himself a brief moment of satisfaction. He still couldn't believe he'd won that award.

He'd thought at that moment that everything between his father and him would change then, that his dad would see that he wasn't a loser. But Hal had just glanced at the award, mumbled congratulations, and gone right back to what he'd been doing, fiddling with some clock gears. Helen had taken him out, bought him an expensive meal, beamed at him. At the time, he really hadn't cared that much. His mom always did things like that, and he knew she was trying to take the sting out of Hal's indifference. Now, he wished he'd been more appreciative. What he wouldn't do to have his old mom back, instead of the distracted ghost who shared the house with him.

There was another contest coming up, the Chicago International Film Fest. He had planned on sending another short there, the one he'd started on the night of the accident. He hadn't really thought of it until now, but suddenly it seemed possible again. There was still time, although just barely. He should look at the preliminary work they'd done, see if there was anything salvageable from that night. Suddenly, he wasn't tired. He was alert, focused.

He crawled across the bed to his computer and clicked on the file. He took a deep breath. He was a little scared about bringing that night back, but curious, too, to reconnect with it. Maybe it wasn't any good, maybe he would just have to give it up, but he had to at least find out.

He watched intently. It wasn't bad, no, not bad at all. He liked how everyone stayed in character, how the scene began to coalesce. This, this is who he is, he thought, not some orderly cleaning up shit for retarded people.

He replayed it. Libby's face filled the screen. Josh sat back in his chair. God, she was so good. Subtle. The way her face changed just slightly as defiance and fear fought for the upper hand. The others were clearly not in her league. She took his breath away.

If he wanted to do this film, he'd have to talk with her. And he'd have to find time, and he didn't know how that would happen with the damn Good Shepherd Home. And it would mean getting Susie and Libby together, and they would fight, and everyone would be doing what he was doing now, which was trying not to remember what happened afterward.

A headache began pounding in his right temple. Two months to go before the deadline. It was impossible; what had he been thinking? His small peak of elation began to fall. Why was everything against him? Exhausted again, he lay back on his bed, and soon was asleep, dreaming a surreal dream where he was trapped in a circus, a freak among freaks.

TEN

Meg listlessly straightened the papers on her desk. She'd found herself yelling today, something she'd sworn she'd try never to do. She hated it when teachers yelled. She usually lowered her voice or used hand signals to get her class back in control. She also hated worksheets and making kids stay at their desks without moving around. Yet lately she'd fallen back on worksheets, happy if she could make it through the day with minimum effort. Most of the kids didn't notice, but she'd caught Janelle and Dariel gazing at her quizzically. Janelle in particular had become sullen and withdrawn, which only made Meg feel worse. *It's the best I can do!* she wanted to yell at them.

She stooped to pick up the broken pencils, gum wrappers, erasers, and bits of construction paper that littered the floor, then pushed the chairs flush with the desks. Alante's desk was stuffed—she bent down to see papers and a shirt and broken crayons all crammed into the small space. She made a mental note to help him organize in the morning during announcements. No wonder he could never find anything.

She paused before turning off the lights, noticing that she hadn't changed the display on the bulletin board—it still said "Welcome Students" and featured pictures of summer activities—swimming, biking, et cetera. She needed to put up a new display, one appropriate for fall, but the chore, one that she usually liked, now held no interest for her. She'd been back two weeks, and yet she hadn't returned to anything like her old ease in the classroom. Every task overwhelmed her, and she couldn't seem to focus. She was just putting one foot in front of the other. She didn't know how she would make it to the holiday break.

She turned off the lights and picked up her purse, closing the door behind her. She nodded to Jolene at the office and stepped outside into the cool afternoon. And then it began: the ruminations about Josh, the memory of his young voice pleading guilty, his mother's voice saying, "But it was only this once." And Meg remembering her own youth, all the times she'd smoked pot and how it had seemed so innocent then, the times had seemed more innocent. She had never envisioned consequences like the one that had caught up with Josh. If Josh had been her child, would she have been more understanding than his parents? Surely, she would have been better than his stony-faced father.

Even now, as she headed to the hospital, the boy's white face at the accident, his expression of disbelief and need, struck her with renewed force. That stunned expression, and then that man, yelling, yelling at him. The violence of it all, not just David, already felled, but the boy and the father. Coming upon the whole thing, like stepping into a war zone, or being caught in a natural disaster.

She needed to talk with someone, someone who wouldn't judge her, who would listen and help her understand why she couldn't stop thinking about this boy. She didn't understand her own feelings—her anger, her pity, her despair, and, particularly, her *interest*. Especially after it had been made so clear to her that her interest was unwanted. But she couldn't not think about him, because every time she stepped into David's hospital room, she was reminded of how he got there.

She found a space on the ground floor of the hospital parking deck and was grateful not to have to circle endlessly. Her world had constricted so much that the issue of finding a parking space had become a major preoccupation. She put the car into park, turned off the ignition, and sat, gathering herself together. She felt, suddenly, how tired she was. She knew she was stalling, bracing herself to see David. Between visits she convinced herself that she'd gotten used to seeing him in that bed, but each time she walked through that door, it always felt like a new shock. It was always too real.

She got out of the car. She would tell David about Josh. He may not be able to understand her, but then again, he might. She chose to believe he would.

***

David felt Meg come, felt her take his hand. He strained to understand what she was saying, but he couldn't. I'm sorry, Meg. It is just too hard today. As if she heard him, he felt the bed jostle, felt the air around him empty.

Peggy Lee walked languidly over to the bar and shook up two martinis, looking at him with that all-knowing smile. The sound of a clarinet tuning up came from the back room. She began to hum, then sing throatily, "'I didn't know what time it was. Then I met you. Oh, what a lovely time it was. How sublime it was, too! Grand to be alive, to be yours...'" She poured the drinks into glasses, brought them over.

"We'll make this a quick one, darling. I have to go onstage in a few minutes." She gave him the martini. It was icy cold, the olive salty as he rolled it around in his mouth. She sat next to him, slouched down on his pillow. He could smell her Givenchy. She smiled down at him and kissed him on the forehead.

"Don't leave me," he whispered.

"Don't worry. I'll be back, darling. I'll always come back." And then she was gone.

David was alone then. *Meg, Meg.* There was something he needed to tell her. Something, just out of reach. He strained to remember.

He sipped his martini. He longed for a cigarette, although he hadn't smoked since he met Meg.

Then he was back at that Common Cause meeting, picking his way around all the people sitting cross-legged on the floor, people dressed in jeans and tie-dyed shirts, anxious to get back to the kitchen where they told him he'd find food, the potlucks being half the reason he'd joined the group in the first place. That and the fact that, newly divorced, he'd gotten sick to death of his own company. He smelled curry and brown rice, saw the piles of salads, and his heart sank. No meat anywhere. It was just then that he felt himself being looked at. He glanced up and saw a slight girl with an elfin face and dark hair, perched on a stool. She looked as if she were about to burst into laughter.

"Uh, hi. Didn't see you sitting there."

"Well, I saw you." She grinned.

"What's so funny?" David wasn't used to being laughed at. Did she know who he was?

"Guess you don't really like what you see, huh? Tofu curry not really your thing?"

"How did you know?" Was the girl a mind reader?

"You should see the look on your face. Pure disgust." Then she laughed, a deep belly laugh that didn't seem to go with her small frame.

He stood there, indignantly ready to prove her wrong, when he realized how stupid that would be.

"You've got me," he said ruefully.

"Yeah, well, don't worry about it. I could go for a nice juicy hamburger myself."

"And miss the program?" he said, slightly askance.

"Well, I just meant, theoretically—" Now she looked embarrassed.

He took her in. She sat there, her head tilted to the side, her hair brushing her shoulder, her eyes shining. Common Cause seemed suddenly less compelling.

"Forget theory," he said, emboldened. "Come on, let's sneak out of here and get some real food."

She hesitated a minute. But just a minute. Then she hopped off her stool. "Okay, let's go," she said. And they were out the door, never looking back.

Oh, Meg, Meg, he thought, aching for her now even as the memory of their first kiss began to wane, even as he dissolved with it.

***

By the time Meg got home, it was late. She'd stopped at the drugstore to buy a few unnecessary items, just an excuse not to face the silent house. The house was dark, not a light on. She fumbled with the key, opened the door, flipped on every light and the radio as she made her way to the kitchen. She poured herself a glass of wine and nibbled on some crackers and cheese. She didn't cook anymore, just grazed. She often didn't realize she'd forgotten to eat until she woke at two in the morning, hungry, but there was rarely anything in the fridge, now that people had stopped bringing food by.

She didn't read anymore, or go out, either. Jane, her closest friend at school, had urged her to go for Friday drinks, but she had demurred. All she could manage was school, hospital, then a quick retreat home. If you could call it that.

What she did do was stare at the TV. She clicked it on now, flipping through the channels. She stared incredulously at a hysterically opinionated woman with bleached hair and a wide red mouth, spouting off about how Obama was going to "take away our guns" on the supposed news hour. Is this what was considered news? She flipped the channel. There were reruns of *When a Man Loves a Woman*, of *I Love Lucy*, and some Fred Astaire movie that seemed to always be on. She just wanted something to take her away, something beautiful or mysterious or engaging.

She clicked frenetically. She landed on National Geographic Channel, paused. On the screen was a tall, spare man wearing skins and holding a spear. There was something about the way he held himself, a quiet assurance as he walked slowly with a young boy at his side. They seemed to be herding cattle, the animals silhouetted in the blazing sun hanging on the horizon. The camera lingered on the pair, the sunset shimmering orange behind them. The narrator's soft, cultivated voice intoned the salient facts about the Masai, a seminomadic people who resisted Westernization.

She let the narrator's British lilt wash over her as she watched the women weave baskets and bead bracelets, their faces bright, laughing at what she imagined were jokes and gossip. The sunlight warmed the mud hut they sat against. It made her feel deeply alone, as if she had misplaced friends, sisters, mothers, as if some ancestral village memory of sitting and weaving and talking was stirred. Meg watched in fascination as their hands moved like quicksilver. The decorated walls picked up the ochers and browns and blacks and patterns of the skins they wore; it was all of a piece. The narrator calmly explained the division of labor in the culture—the women built the huts, cooked, sewed, and beaded. The men hunted and cared for the cattle. The young children played around the women, the older boys hunted with the men. Meg stared at the screen, entranced.

Then the screen flashed on the handsome, toothless face of a woman proudly wearing her red-and-black headdress. "Women become elders after bearing four healthy children," the narrator said. Meg sighed, poured another glass of wine. Well, that would leave her out. She picked up the remote to switch the channel, irritated. But suddenly there was singing, the narrator's voice again: "The Masai sing to bring in the day, to close the day.

They greet each other with song." The children's faces were so—alive. Meg couldn't help but think of the children she taught every day, how dull some of their eyes had already become. She thought of Jamal, of Keesha, of Aliya greeting each other with songs rather than taunts.

The picture changed to warriors stalking a gazelle, their bodies lithe and muscular, their aim sure. Then a picture of a herd of zebras. Now the closing credits: the same picture that had arrested her before, an older man walking with a young boy, herding cattle, the two of them unhurried, the cattle ambling alongside them. Behind them the huge sun set over a slow-moving river. It looked so peaceful. It looked so real. It looked like paradise.

Meg was seized with a longing to be Masai. She could write a grant to take her students to Kenya and learn the Masai ways. How crazy this life was! No, her children did not greet the day singing, they didn't laugh and play—not with recess being only fifteen minutes long. They were caged, and she was the zookeeper.

The hospital, too, another cage. Today in the waiting room, waiting for the nurses to finish some procedure, Meg had been overtaken with claustrophobia. Gone were the lively groups that had supported her during the beginning of David's ordeal. Maybe it was her foul mood spilling over, but the other inmates of the waiting room reminded her of *Twilight Zone* clones, lumpy and dull. They reeked of cigarettes, a smell that always made Meg slightly nauseated. But they didn't seem to notice her. The older couple's and young man's attention were riveted on the wall TV, where the wheel of fortune turned. There, a fat woman with long, unkempt hair, a straw hat, a T-shirt, and sweatpants jumped around the set, her hips and breasts jig-gling. She had just won a thousand dollars. Meg stared herself. A thousand dollars was a small consolation for complete loss of dignity. But evidently not for that woman.

Now Meg began to cry, out of frustration, at the memory of the revolting woman, and her own secret, shameful misan-thropy. She cried for the vast unfairness of life, for the stupidity of the world around her, for the cruel separation from her hus-band. She clicked off the TV and sat in the quiet room. In the next room, she could see David's computer monitor's sleeping light glowing faintly. Something that had buoyed her up, her conviction that she could make a difference, that people were basically good, now seemed a convenient delusion. It seemed to her the ugly, the crass, and the mean were the forces that were winning. Maybe her faith in mankind, her belief in change for the better, had really been David's all along.

She pushed herself off the couch and wandered into David's office. She turned on the light and sat down at his desk. "David, David," she murmured, as if she could conjure him, as if she could, by osmosis, soak up the faith she'd lost. She stared at the papers on his desk: the yellow legal pad with his almost illegible writing, the piles of folders, the pens scattered over the surface. She felt almost guilty for being there, for transgressing. Then, out of her own compulsive nature to order things, she began to file and sort, amazed as always at how David could get anything done with his lack of organization. At the bottom of a stack of files, she came across a folder called the Lost History. Puzzled, she opened it.

Inside were copied newspaper clippings, old photos of what

looked to Meg like shantytowns in the thirties, an article about some black neighborhood called The Bottom, scribbled notes, articles on post–Civil War era black progressive groups, articles about prominent black leaders of the town, about the lynchings, about the sixties voter registration drives. All with scribbled Post-it notes, with yellow legal pages and David's chicken scratching. Meg sat, dumbfounded. She hadn't known he was doing this. It was so like him, the scholar in him, the need he had to illuminate dark places. But still, it felt like a small betrayal. She shook her head at her own pettiness. What else, she wondered, did she not know about him? What else would she never know?

SECTION 5:
THINGS TAKE
A TURN

ELEVEN

Meg passed the clock shop on foot four times before she found the courage to go in. It was an incongruous place, part of what remained of the old downtown—a place slowly emptying of mainstream businesses, leaving behind stout brick buildings with empty black windows. Here and there, trendy ventures had sprouted up, so that the poky little shop was not alone on its gentle hill, but was accompanied now by an elegant Thai restaurant on its left, a tattoo parlor and a futon store several doors down and across the street. Still, there was something forlornly brave and defiant about it, as if, being neither trendy nor mainstream, it stood for some forgotten middle way.

On the day she decided she would go through that heavy old wood door—no matter what—the air was beginning to crisp. Maybe it was the change in the weather that had given her the energy to finally go on this errand. Her grandfather's skeleton clock was something she had always intended to get fixed. Her idea had been to bring it into class and show her students not only how time used to be measured, but how gears worked. The fact that the repair shop belonged to Hal Lovejoy was only incidental, she told herself.

She had spent several hours searching for it earlier in the

week until, almost despairing, she had found it tucked igno-miniously in a dark corner of the attic. When she found it, its dome covered in greasy dust, she was surprised at how small and delicate it was. In her memories, it had seemed enormous and radiant, something golden, out of a fairy tale. She remem-bered her grandfather's freckled, gnarled hand pointing out the delicate gears, patiently explaining to her that dust must never get in the workings. Looking at the gray layer of dust, she had wondered, horrified, if it was irredeemably damaged.

Carrying it downstairs, she'd been surprised at how some-thing so light had figured so heavily in her memories. As a child, she'd wait impatiently for her grandmother to open her elegant front door, not to see her, but to run past her and make sure the clock was still there. She'd stand on her tiptoes, so that she was on eye level with it, and watch with satisfaction as the minute hand ticked around the ornate face. "Is it time to wind it, Grandpa?" she would call, hoping that it would be. And of-ten it was, because he waited to set it until she was there. He let her help him, too, if she promised to be careful. He would gen-tly push aside the pendulum and push the key into the winding square. Then, very carefully, she would turn the key three and a half times. Then her grandfather would replace the glass cover, and they would watch the gears magically click into place. Meg wouldn't leave the clock until it struck the quarter hour gong. "Oh, Margaret loves that clock more than me," joked her grand-mother, and Meg had to give her grandmother an extra kiss. But her grandfather would wink at her, and she'd wink back. They understood the clock was magic.

She'd carefully cleaned the dust off the glass, then gingerly lifted the dome. The once-shiny brass gears were darkened with age, but the clock itself seemed dust-free. It was sad to see it dulled, but the Roman numerals painted in white were as she remembered, as was the elegant curving facing. She wanted to start it, but was afraid she might damage it. The whole structure was delicate and marvelous, a device to measure the hours that gave those hours a weight and gravity that somehow the easy flicking of digitalized phosphorous didn't. Besides, it was her ticket in, the next task on the mysterious errand she felt compelled to run.

Why was it that she couldn't just leave Josh and his family alone? What was this itch she needed to scratch? Was it some misplaced maternal instinct? Some social worker inclination? What did she think she could accomplish?

The truth of it was, she wasn't thinking. It was more like feeling her way in the dark. In her solitary bed, she woke many nights, drenched in sweat, with the same dream: David lying broken and bloody, the father raging at the boy, his veins standing out on his forehead, the boy's face slack and pale and frozen, the three of them a ghastly tableau. It was the immobility of the figures that terrorized her. Some nights she was aware of the mother in the background, of her trying to call to the other woman. Some nights she was trying to get to David, but couldn't move past the boy and the father. Some nights there were rivers of blood lapping at her feet, or the flashing of ambulance lights that blinded her. It was as if she had to confront the actual people themselves to break the spell they held over her.

She felt like a character in one of the fairy tales she read to her classes: chosen to go on a mission she didn't understand.

The clock was like the gift to open the fairy hill, the one you tossed to the troll so you could slip inside.

Feeling the slight weight of the clock in her hand, Meg took a deep breath and pushed the heavy wooden door of the shop. In the dim light, the first thing she noticed was the old, scuffed pine floor. It made her think of the old five and dime of her childhood, the one with the penny candy and a musty proprietor. Here, it smelled of grease, like a bicycle shop, and it was filled with the ticking of myriad clocks. As her eyes adjusted to the light, she saw grandfather clocks and Empire clocks and ornate German cuckoo clocks and smooth, sleek modern clocks in blond cases. The ticking and humming of the moving parts were like the beating of a heart and the rush of blood through veins, and for a moment she felt light-headed.

She stood awkwardly in the middle of the floor, then trundled over to the counter and laid the clock on it. The counter was plain and workmanlike, and the man behind it, busy with gears, didn't look up from his work. No pretentious trendiness here. Another man came out of the glassed-in office. He was tall and lanky with blond hair going gray. He placed his hands on the counter on either side of the clock, and she noticed the grease under his fingernails, the long tapered fingers. He looked up wearily at her over his glasses.

"What can I do for you?" he said abruptly. She took a breath, looked at the lean, drawn face, the dark circles under his eyes. Yes, it was the father. The same face that haunted her dreams, and yet not the same. Not enraged. Her heart beat fast, and she was terrified that he would recognize her. She searched his face for any signs, but all she saw was a tick of impatience.

Meg cleared her throat. "Um, I retrieved this old clock from my attic. I don't know if it works or what shape it is in. I thought you could tell me." Her voice sounded too plaintive, unsure.

He sighed, looking down at the bundle with faint interest. "Attic, huh. Not good." He shook his head. "Well, let's take a look at it."

Carefully, Meg unwrapped the small delicate glass dome from its towel swaddling. The man pushed his glasses up on his nose and expelled a long breath. He carefully turned it around, like a jeweler examining a diamond, looking at it from several angles.

He squinted up at her. "Where'd you get this?"

Meg blushed. "It was my grandfather's."

"And where did he get it?" It was the terse, dry interrogation of a doctor with a neglectful patient, Meg thought.

"I have no idea. I mean, it was always there. I want to take it into my class, you see, to teach them about analog time. I thought they could see how the gears worked, maybe learn about Roman numerals, you know, things like that."

He didn't seem to hear her. "Hmm. Looks like an old skeleton clock. Probably a reproduction. Haven't seen one like it in a long time. Looks to be intact. Let's open it and look at the workings."

He carefully lifted the dome off its dark wooden pedestal and inspected the tiny brass gears, pushing on them gently. He scratched behind his ear, his face puckered in disapproval, and he tsked.

She felt herself blush again, and her courage failed her. This whole idea had been crazy. Now she just wanted to make a swift exit.

"That's all right," she said, grabbing the clock. "If you think it's too far gone—" She was angry now.

He put his hand on the clock. "I didn't say that." He looked at her as if seeing her for the first time, and his tone was gentler. "No, I think I can get it going again. I'll try, at any rate." As if realizing his first off-putting brusqueness, he attempted a smile. From under the counter, he drew a form and picked up a pen. "Now, what's the name?"

She hesitated. She had thought she should be honest, but she saw now that it would be too strange and disconcerting. "Valerie... Tate," she stuttered, and gulped, sure that she had been unconvincing.

But he didn't seem to notice and took the rest of her information, saying, "I don't know if there is a time constraint, but we're really backed up. It'll be two to three weeks, minimum."

"No hurry," Meg said, hooking her purse on her shoulder and making her escape past all the clocks that now seemed to be frowning and pointing at her, whispering, "Liar, liar." As the door closed shut behind her, she blinked in the strong sunlight, her breathing slowed. She was safe.

***

Hal took the clock to his office and closed the door. People were so careless of things these days. Just stuck it in the attic, a piece like this. It looked to be a reproduction, a good one, at that, of an eighteenth- or nineteenth-century skeleton. He wiped the cloth over the gray film on the dome. That woman clearly had no sense of beauty, of worth. She probably just threw things away and replaced them without any thought. Well, at least she wanted to teach about analog time, that was something in her favor, he supposed.

He sat down in front of the clock. With the dust wiped off, he could see that the mechanism itself, though tarnished, looked clean. He carefully lifted the dome off and put it to one side. He whistled through his teeth. The brass pillars were delicately turned, the whole mechanism pierced so that the fretwork appeared almost filigreed. The frames created lozenge shapes and sweeping arches so that it looked like a miniature cathedral. The face was burnished steel with engraved Roman numerals, the hands slender, the pointed end sporting another lozenge shape. Inside the face was a smaller face for the minute hand.

Of all the clocks he had repaired or collected, he had never seen one quite like this. Skeletons had always seemed a little gimmicky to him, their exposed works a sort of superfluity. The clocks were initially made to display the internal mechanism, and grew to be popular in Victorian England. Like all things Victorian, they seemed fussy to him. Still he had to admit, the engineering on this clock was amazing. He gently pushed on the escapement, felt the tension, which seemed neither too tight nor too loose. Hal whistled. The work was nice, very nice. The movement appeared to be fully jeweled. The wheels and arbors and plates were all in good condition. Someone had taken good care of it. The gears weren't worn, the winding shaft seemed to be intact. He knew that American reproductions like this were popular in the 1950s, or earlier, in the thirties. He was a little fuzzy on these clocks, he knew. He specialized in American clocks because those were the kind he came across most frequently. He got up and shuffled through a stack of magazines, flipping through *TimePiece* and *Reproductions Today* and *Clocks*, looking for references. He came across an article about cheap reproductions from China, but it was a new industry there, and the woman had said her grandfather had had it. As soon as Mike could fix the damn computer, he'd be able to do a search on it.

He picked up a new chamois cloth and began to gently clean the workings. He would have to take it apart, but he wasn't sure, now, without more to go on, if he should. No clock had ever made him feel this way, as if he might not be up to the task. He'd always been confident in his craft. But the clock before him seemed such an unreal, delicate confection that it gave him pause.

He oiled the works just enough, then began the winding. When he felt the key tighten just enough, he let it go. The clock began to turn, a little slowly at first, but then it regulated. He'd have to research the wheel period to find out what it was, but by his watch, it was just under eight minutes. Amazing! Up in an attic for years, and yet look at it! No flimsy digital clock would withstand time like that. The gears clicked, and there was a soft whirr, and around it turned, a marvel. He imagined it shining on its mahogany base and revised all his earlier opinions of skeletons. He'd been wrong. It was a thing of beauty.

Then his heart sank. That woman—what was her name?— wanted to bring this clock into her classroom. He would strongly caution her against it. Strongly. He felt protective of it, the way a lover feels about a person only he can see the true beauty of. It would be physically painful to let the clock out of his sight. But for now, it was his.

***

David heard a distant voice, felt the bed sink, jostling his legs. Meg. He listened intently, but her voice was muffled and far away. "Father," he heard, and "clock." He tried to place whom she was talking about, but then his thoughts were tugged as if by a stronger current in another direction. It was as if time were a river with currents and shallows, places to linger and others where he had no choice but to be carried along.

David followed his friend Anthony down and over dizzying hills until finally he had to yell at him to *stop*! He was so out of breath. Anthony slowed at the top of the hill and turned to look at him with languid triumph. "Ooh, you white boys are soft."

David pumped up the hill, wheezing, and when he finally got to him, "Who you calling white?" and punched Anthony in the arm.

"Let's go to my house and make Coke floats." David's mother always stocked the fixings for Coke floats.

Anthony grinned. "Okay, man."

He pushed off ahead of David and almost swerved into an oncoming blue Mustang. The driver leaned on the horn and gestured rudely at Anthony. David saw Anthony jerk back, his eye's wide, and he could feel Anthony's fear and anger lift off him in waves.

"You okay?"

Anthony nodded. "Bastard."

"You better watch where you're going."

"Hey, man, don't tell me what to do." Anthony gave him one of his warning looks.

David knew not to push it.

"Okay, let's go."

The street was empty again. They rode side by side on the wide street, the shadows from the fully fledged trees—oaks and magnolias and mulberries—cast moving patterns on the gray asphalt. The heat rose up from the street, and David could smell the sulfurous tar. They made wide, swooping figures, the breeze cooling the sweat on their temples.

They stopped as always at old Mrs. Moss's property. It was a city block, overgrown with kudzu and honeysuckle vines. The house, barely visible from the street, stood a shabby, weathered three stories tall. There was great speculation among the kids in the neighborhood about Mrs. Moss that she was a witch, per- haps, or a ghost. David had heard his parents talking about her drinking. He didn't know what that had to do with anything. All he knew was that whenever they sneaked onto her property to glimpse the giant goldfish in her pond or play in the stand of tall, dry grass that made great nests and hiding places, he would often glimpse a moving curtain, a hand and once even a shad- owy old face at the uppermost window.

Today, though, they had stopped for honeysuckle, which was at its early summer peak. Anthony got there first and threw his bike down on the pavement. It was always a race to see who could get the largest drop of nectar, and there was great skill required in pulling the stamen out properly without breaking it. The sweet smell of the flowers almost overpowered David. Anthony dangled the nectar above his tongue, and there was golden pollen dusting his brown chin. "Hmm," he said, shutting his eyes as the clear drop of liquid dripped into his mouth.

They lingered at the honeysuckle patch until David realized he was hot and still hungry. They hopped back on their bikes and rode over to his house. Anthony teased David about living in a mansion, but really the house was a modest clapboard cottage.

Anthony had been shy at first about coming to David's house. They'd walk home from school together, but Anthony would never come in. David had been to Anthony's house any number of times. Down by the river, the house was small and weather-beaten and dark. Anthony lived with his grandmother and mother and three other siblings in a four-room house that always smelled of vinegary collards and yams. But David liked it there. He liked that it was crowded and people were always jiving with each other; he liked the flowers Anthony's grandmother grew—cannas and hydrangeas and marigolds—and he liked it that Anthony seemed most himself at home, funnier, stronger, more sure of himself than he was at school.

And Anthony liked David's house. He liked the room, the light, the way David's mom was calm. He liked the quiet. He liked Coke floats, and the way David's little brother didn't bother them so much. He liked it that David could shut the door and keep everyone out, and they could play chess undisturbed, or listen to the radio.

They skimmed up to David's house, threw their bikes on the lawn, and went into the cool foyer.

"Mom?" David called. His mom was always there when he got home, even though she worked in the synagogue office in the mornings. Usually, she was in the kitchen, making something for dinner. David's kitchen smelled like garlic and paprika, and yeasty on Fridays when there was freshly baked challah.

"Mom?" David called again. The light was off in the kitchen, and there was nothing on the stove. They wandered through the house. It was more quiet than usual. At the back of the house, they found David's mom. She was in a small screened-in porch, curled up on the couch, a washcloth held up to her face. She looked like she'd been crying.

David could feel Anthony shrink back. David had never seen his mother this way.

"Are you sick, Mom?"

She shook her head slightly. Her eyes looked very far away. She was holding something in the hand that lay on her lap, and she lifted it to David. He took it gingerly.

It was a large stone. Wrapped around the stone, torn and bloody, was a note. "Get out of our town, nigger loving Jews."

The words our town hit him like a jab to the middle. It was his town, wasn't it? His and Anthony's?

"They threw it through the dining room window. I don't think they meant to hit me. I don't know." Her eyes darted nervously to Anthony; David could see his mother not wanting to upset Anthony.

Stupidly, because he couldn't think of anything else to say, because he wanted things back to normal, he said, as if nothing had happened, "Can we make Coke floats?" And his mother laughed, and looked relieved.

They didn't talk about it, but David could tell that Anthony was angry and maybe a little afraid, because he left after they had their floats on the porch. David watched him pedal away, and stood watching long after Anthony's figure had dwindled to a speck.

TWELVE

"Josh." Ms. Jones accosted him as soon as he was inside the door. Immediately guilty, he checked his watch to make sure he wasn't late.

But she smiled at him and took him by the elbow, as if she had a delightful secret to tell him. "Josh, I've been thinking of how best to use you."

Good, Josh thought. *Now maybe I can file papers or clean out the fridge.*

"You know, Marius is supposed to be mainstreamed next year. He is very bright, and he's at a point with his physical therapy that allows him more time to prepare. He needs much, much more stimulation than he's getting. So I thought I'd have you work with him doing some reading and exercises and games."

Josh's heart sank. Marius at the best of times was withdrawn. He made Josh uncomfortable because, unlike most of the other kids, until a year ago, he'd been a normal child. The others, most of whom where both mentally and physically disabled, affected him less, because he figured they didn't know the difference. But when Josh looked at Marius surveying the other kids, Josh imagined him running and playing and laughing. He imagined

Marius was thinking about that, about being whole, about not having to wear diapers.

Marbry had filled him in on the details of the accident one day in the break room. She seemed to revel in anything tragic or gruesome. The boy's twenty-year-old mother had been walking with him on the shoulder of the highway late one night. "They were going to the BP, y'know, right there on Highway 13. Going to get his favorite candy, red licorice whips." She exhaled through her nose and looked above his head, as if relishing the telling. "The paper said she must have realized what was about to happen, because she pushed him out of the way. The driver never stopped. They never found him. Anyway, she was killed and he ended up like that." She nodded toward the door behind which the kids were eating snacks and ground out her cigarette in the ashtray. "Stupid thing to do, walk out on the highway on a dark night like that."

The story had left Josh feeling ill, whether because of the image of the woman and child run over like stray cats or because of Marbry's smug expression or because of his own identification with the driver, he didn't know. So he avoided the boy. It wasn't fair, he knew, to blame Marius for his own unease. Yet he couldn't help it.

They were in the activities room now, where Ms. Jones had pulled out materials she wanted Josh to use with Marius. She showed him a beginning reader, a pile of books, games, and art supplies. "Take it slow at first," she said. "Make it fun. Don't be too ambitious. If this goes well, we'll make it a regular thing."

She was looking at him intently, waiting for a response.

Josh cleared his throat. "I'm, uh, I don't have much expe-

rience with this kind of thing." He hoped she'd hear his am-
bivalence, decide to get someone else. "Maybe you should find
someone more experienced."

"Well, this is how you get experience. Just do your best. I've
got faith in you."

Josh nodded, and Ms. Jones, seemingly not to be swayed,
left the room. Marbry appeared, wheeling in Marius, who didn't
look at Josh. Marbry gave Josh what looked like a smirk. "Good
luck," she said, and Josh winced. Marbry always acted as if these
kids were stones.

"Hi, Marius," Josh said, wheeling Marius over to the side of
the room where the light was still coming in.

"Hi," Marius said in a thin, high voice. Josh parked Marius
in front of an activity table and brought over the materials Ms.
Jones had given him. Marius turned his small head on his thin
neck and gazed out the window.

"Something interesting out there, Marius?"

"Uh-huh."

"What?"

There was a pause. "Nothin'."

Josh cleared his throat. "Well, there's lot's going on in here,"
he said, trying to sound avuncular. Trying to sound like on
Sesame Street.

The boy swiveled his head back. "What?"

He was a slight boy, with a finely molded head, dark skin, and
even features. His big hazel eyes looked at Josh with suspicion.

"Well, we've got games—Chutes and Ladders, Connect
Four, Uno, Dora the Explorer…" Marius just looked at him.
Josh imagined the boy was like a reptile that slid opaque lenses

over his eyes to protect them. To protect himself. "And we've got art supplies, we've got books." Josh gestured at the pile. His enthusiasm sounded pallid even to himself.

The ticking clock was the only sound in the room. Josh noticed that the light was moving away from them. It would be dark soon. Marius stared glumly at the pile of books. "Read," Marius said, then turned to look out the window again.

Josh sifted through the books. There were Berenstain Bears books, but he thought that the intact family might make Marius more upset. There was *Blueberries for Sal*, but how on earth would a black disabled boy in Georgia have an interest in a sweet-cheeked white girl in New England? He sorted through the books until he came to Ezra Jack Keats's *The Snowy Day*. Good—the boy was black and the mother was barely mentioned.

"Look, Marius," said Josh, gently touching Marius's shoulder. The boy flinched. Josh went on. "Look, here's a little boy like you. His name is Peter." Marius glanced at the book, and Josh read the first page:

"'One morning Peter woke up and looked out the window.' See Marius, I told you he was like you. He looks out windows, too."

Marius looked with a little more interest at the page. Josh went on. "'Snow had fallen through the night. It covered everything as far as he could see...'" Josh stopped again. "Have you ever seen snow, Marius?"

Marius shrugged, made a noise. Josh didn't know whether to take it as a yes or a no, but he went on. He read about how the city was covered in snow, about how Peter wanted to play with the big boys but was knocked down by a snowball. Marius appeared to be listening, but he didn't react, even when Josh tried to talk to him about the illustrations, the colors and shapes. Josh read about Peter making angels in the snow, about going home and taking a bath and finding that his snowball had melted.

Marius made some small sound like humph.

Josh shut the book dispiritedly. He had known he wouldn't be any good at this. Ms. Jones had the wrong idea. Marius's face was impassive. He sighed heavily and looked around the activity room.

It seemed to Josh that the ticking of the clock in the quiet room grew steadily louder and louder. He started to sort through the other books when he felt a hand on his arm. He turned to find Marius looking at him.

"My mama's an angel now," he said, and Josh flushed, didn't know how to respond.

"Yes," he stammered.

And that was all Marius said. But it was something, Josh thought, maybe it was something.

Marbry bustled in. "You kids have fun? I got to take him to get changed before dinner. Ms. Jones wants you." She nodded officiously at Josh, as if Josh had committed some transgression and she was in on it. Marius had turned back to his window, now a dark rectangle in the wall. Marbry took command of Marius's wheelchair and spun him around and out. But Josh thought that he caught the boy's eye just before he disappeared into the hall.

Ms. Jones simply wanted to know how it went. Josh relayed

it as best he could, sure that she would give up the plan. But she seemed to think it went well, and told him that and dismissed him with a wave of her hand. He thought as he left he was more tired than when he had to do a lot of heavy lifting.

That night Josh volunteered to stay and clean the activity room and wash up all the lunch trays. Marbry looked at him skeptically. "Don't you have homework to do, kid?" she said, lighting up a cigarette.

"Not much," he muttered, waving away the smoke. He wanted, more than anything, to be left alone. He wanted not to have to go home.

"Well, all right, then," Marbry had muttered, stubbing out her cigarette in a dish he had just washed. She gave him a long, considering look, seemed about to say something, then shrugged.

He did his homework, if he did it at all, in the early mornings. He wasn't doing very well in school, barely hanging on to a C in most classes, except for English, which he was failing. When his counselor called him in to try to motivate him about his "future," Josh felt like telling him to save his breath. What future? He didn't care. There was only the past, the time before, that seemed to matter, and that was gone.

He wanted everyone to leave him alone, but suddenly he was on all their radars. His dad was riding him like never before. Moved out, wasn't there, but was keeping tabs on him. Sending him odd emails, asking about how school was going. Sometimes he took a stab at being supportive, with platitudes about moving on with his life, not letting a thing like this define him. Like he'd been reading a book called *How to Motivate Your*

Criminal Son or some such thing. Questions about what kind of career path he was thinking of. Career path! *Oh, I don't know, Dad, how about diaper changer? How about interpreter of kids who drool and gag or see people as shapes? 'Cause now my film ambitions, you'll be glad to know, Dad, are dead in the water.* Hal had no idea, *no idea*, of what Josh's life was like. It was like he was talking to some imaginary, ideal son. It was so nuts.

And what about his mom? How could Hal leave them like that? Now that it was just him and Helen, Josh felt guilty half the time for neglecting her, but also irritated by her. She was either staring into space or reading art books. She'd let the house go to hell, and he had to remind her to do the shopping just so they'd have eggs and bread and milk in the house.

The whole thing gave him a headache. He scrubbed the glue and glitter and marker off the tables, swept the floor, emptied the trash, washed the trays, and looked around for something else to do. He saw that some of the Halloween decorations—the orange crepe paper and hanging witches—had fallen down. He picked them up and tacked them securely in place. It had gotten dark outside, and cold—he could feel it coming in the windows. Reluctantly, he shrugged into his jacket and picked up his book bag.

Outside, the parking lot was almost deserted except for the overnight staff's cars. Small rectangles of lights painted the darkened lawn, and Josh could see the shadows of the kids moving behind the blinds. He paused a moment, watching them, and felt a sudden pang of loneliness.

He had a long walk to the end of the property, and then a short walk to the main road, then the long bus ride home. The bus was dingy and stank of cigarettes and too many tired, sweaty bodies. The springs on the seats had long since worn out, and every bump jolted through him. He slung his book bag on his back, then took it off again, adjusted the strap, then hoisted it back. Head down, trudging along the dark drive, he realized that he was hungry and wondered if he had enough money to get a burger at Wendy's before the next bus. He had bus fare, but beyond that was anybody's guess. He stopped again to check his pockets, and when he looked up, one of the cars in the parking lot turned on its lights and pulled over to him. Startled out of his habitual solitude, he stepped back, worried it might be someone selling drugs or, worse yet, his probation officer.

"Thought you might want a ride. It's gotten kinda cold."

He peered into the recesses of the car, could make out a faintly recognizable figure. "Libby?"

"Yeah, it's me."

Josh felt disoriented, and then exposed. They'd passed each other in the halls at school, but he wouldn't meet her eyes. Not that he hadn't wanted to see her—no, that wasn't it. It was more that in his present state, he didn't want to be seen. He wanted her to see him as the director of an award-winning indie film, not a loser doing community service. This was the last place he wanted her to see him.

"What are you doing here?" he said, almost irritably.

"Well, I never get a chance to see you at school. You seem to be avoiding me. I heard you were working here, and I figured it was the only way I'd get to see you. Come on, get in, it's cold."

Josh did what he was told. He was stunned, but grateful, once he was in the warm car. It was a long, cold hike to the bus stop.

He turned to Libby. She wore large black glasses he hadn't seen before. She always surprised him, always seemed a little different each time he saw her, so that each time they met, he had to update his idea of her. Now, behind the glasses, she looked intellectual, and a little formidable. She met his eyes, but there was a tremble in her voice. "Do you want to get something to eat?"

"Yeah, but I'm not sure how much money I have."

Libby waved a gloved hand. "I've got enough." She swung the Impala out of the parking lot, into the busy street. Josh felt oddly relieved, now that the thing he'd dreaded most had happened. He *had* been avoiding her, avoiding talking about that night, the abandoned project, the kiss, the accident. When he was working, he never thought about the passed deadline for the festival, but here, faced with Libby, it all came back to him. Seeing her, he felt rubbed raw.

They didn't talk for a while, then Libby said, "Let's go someplace where we won't see a lot of people."

Josh nodded. "Okay." At first he wanted to protest, to take some control of the situation, but he didn't seem able to. He sat back in the capacious seat. It was strangely pleasant to just be carried along.

She drove out of town. He watched the strip malls recede, the traffic diminish, until they were out on the highway. They passed dark stands of pine and open fields dotted with hay ricks. Neither of them spoke, and Josh was grateful for both the silence and the darkness surrounding them. Finally, on the horizon, a neon sign blinked on and off, Pig Pit BBQ, and Libby turned in to the parking lot.

"Is this all right? I don't think we'll see anyone we know here." She turned to him, her face questioning and pale.

"Yeah, sure, great."

He followed her into the small brick building. Inside, the place was filled with mostly old people, and nobody from Milledge High. A thick haze of cigarette smoke rose up from the tables, and for a panicked moment, Josh worried they might see Marbry. He didn't want his worlds to collide any more than they had. One surprise at a time.

They were seated, and Libby took off her knitted hat, shook out her thick brown curls, and peeled off her coat. Her tight red sweater clung to her breasts; he couldn't help but notice, then panicked that she noticed him noticing. But her whole attention seemed focused on the menu.

"The barbeque sandwiches are good, if you like them." She looked up at him. A look of horror crossed her face. "Oh, my god, you're not vegetarian, are you? I forgot to ask."

Josh laughed. "At this point, I'd eat anything."

She looked at him earnestly. "Really?"

"No, yeah, I mean, I've never been a vegetarian. It's just, my mom used to cook, and now, well, she doesn't, and I'm pretty much reduced to school lunches." His laugh sounded forced, and he regretted his lame joke.

Libby wrinkled her nose and stuck out her tongue. "Yuck. Oh, well, my mom never cooked, anyway."

They ordered, and there was a lull.

Josh fingered the sugar packets, tried to think of something to say. Finally, looking up, he began, "Why—"

"It's just, y'know, the last time. It was like something started, then—" She looked away, then leaned toward him, her brow wrinkled. She was so serious. He didn't know anyone as serious as she was. She made him a little nervous.

Josh blinked. "It isn't you." He hesitated. Her eyes behind the glasses fastened on him unnervingly. "I've been avoiding everyone." He rearranged the packets into a square, waiting for her to say something. When she didn't, he said, "I don't understand why you'd want to spend time with me. I mean now."

"Why do you think, Josh?" Her voice was low and calm.

"Oh, I guess I'm interesting now that I'm a freak, a potential murderer, someone with a record…" He was trying to be funny, but it sounded like an accusation.

Libby shook her head. "No, I liked you before, before all that happened." She reached over to touch his hand, and he pulled it away.

"Besides, if you want to talk about freaks, I'm the number-one freak of the school."

"You're nuts. Are you kidding? The star of the drama department? Ms. Talent?"

"Yeah, but how many friends do I have? Have you ever seen me with anyone?"

Josh thought about it. "Well, now that you mention it, I guess not."

"And why do you think that is? Huh?"

Josh shrugged.

"Do you know where I live?"

"No."

"I live in a trailer."

"I don't believe it. You're making it up."

Libby shook her head. "I couldn't make this up." She shook her head, and looked, suddenly, very tired, and older. Behind her glasses he noticed dark circles under her eyes.

"But you are so, uh, cultured and stuff. And I mean, you wear nice clothes and all… you've lived up north. You don't sound like a hick or anything."

"Oh, yeah, we're cultured all right. Cultured up the wazoo. Just chronically broke, that's all. Hey, have you ever seen that street musician downtown, Scary Harry? Hm? The one that does all those impersonations and plays the accordion, guitar, and harmonica?"

Josh laughed. "Yeah, he's great."

"Great," she snorted. "Yeah, well… he's my father."

"No way."

"Way. Yeah, he's the reason I'm Ms. Talent, as you call me. I've been groomed for the stage. Do you know that as a child, I won singing contests all over the country? That I grew up doing commercials? Ever see the little girl on the Downy commercial? The one that helps the mom pour the stuff in the washer? With the curls? And the two of them singing, 'So soft, so soft, so Dowwwny soft'?"

Josh nodded his head, the jingle calling up the little girl in her overalls. "Wow. That is amazing. The Downy girl."

"That's nothing. I was in *Annie.*"

"Really?" Josh felt off balance, overwhelmed. Was she on the level? Was she a pathological liar?

"Really." She sighed, shrugged, and took a bite of the sandwich that appeared on the table.

"You're, you're lucky your parents support your creative interests."

Libby laughed, a short dry, laugh, and shook her head. "Support me? Are you kidding? I support them. My dad is the original stage dad, and if you think a stage mom is bad, you don't know the half of it. Oh, no. Daddy dearest is always working the angles. Children are capital to invest."

Josh stared at Libby, startled by the weary cynicism in her voice.

"Well, why did you move down here? I mean, there's not much happening here. Not anything."

"Well, Daddy got into a little trouble with the law, so we came home to Mama's side of the family. We're kind of lying low for a while." There was a pinched look around her mouth. "Not for the first time, either."

Josh forgot his food, stared at her. His own persistent cloud of pain lifted. Libby's story was far more interesting than his.

"What about your mom?" Josh asked.

Libby sighed. "Mama's a mess. I used to hate her 'cause she was such a drudge. He always takes things out on her, screaming and yelling at her. I didn't want to be like her. I was going to be a star." She puckered her lips as if tasting something bitter.

"Do you still hate her?"

Libby shook her head, her hair falling over one eye. "No, I feel sorry for her. I used to dream she'd take us away. Now I see she can't leave him. She's too frail. But I'm gonna leave." She looked straight at him, her eyes intense and fierce.

Josh said quietly, "Why are you telling me all this?"

She pulled her hair away from her face, flipped it over her

shoulders. "You're the only guy I've liked for a long time. I've always been afraid for anyone to know me, to find out about me. We moved a lot. You learn how not to let people in. I mean, why? You just have to leave and start over." She shrugged, her face hard.

"Yeah, well, I guess I wouldn't know. I've always lived here." Josh couldn't imagine her life, but it seemed so much more adventurous than his, even if it was hard. He thought of his house where nothing ever changed. The same furniture, the same pictures, the same smells. All the same, all his life.

"I mean you are so tight with your friends and all," she went on, pausing to butter a biscuit. "I guess I was a little jealous." She took a sip of tea.

Ah, Josh thought, *so maybe it wasn't all in Susie's head.* He wanted to bring up that night, but didn't know how.

Libby went on. "It looked, I dunno, so cozy. So when you asked me to come to audition…"

Josh choked on his sandwich. "It was hardly an audition…"

"I thought, well, maybe I could get in that group."

There was a pause. Josh winced, thinking of how awkward they all were that night.

"Guess I pretty much blew that, huh?"

She looked suddenly vulnerable. She really wanted him to answer that?

Josh looked away. She went on.

"I know. I get all icy when I'm unsure of myself. I know Susie hates me. She probably blames me for—"

Josh said gruffly, "Forget it. Don't worry about that. But now, why?"

Libby nibbled on a dill pickle, considering. "When you started avoiding me, I thought maybe you felt different, too, now. I thought, maybe I could tell him, maybe he'd understand."

"I still, I mean, wow...you always seemed so perfect, so untouchable."

"Naw," Libby said finally. "I'm a freak. Now you know."

Josh was aware of the George Jones song playing, aware of the waitresses circling with iced tea, aware of the smell of fried chicken. She looked at him expectantly. A part of him that felt forsaken, frozen, broke open. He was not alone. He reached over and touched her hand.

SECTION 6:

BABY STEPS

THIRTEEN

Helen stepped into the gallery timidly. Her heart beat fast, and she felt hot and sweaty and not a little nauseous. It had been years since she'd gone to an art opening, but the poster announcing it had mesmerized her with its bold and free use of color, the looseness of line. The painter's name was Olaffson, a local artist. She had stood transfixed in front of the plate glass window at the hobby store for a long time, pulled into the scene of the old cotton warehouse, its tin roof rich with purples and rusts, green shoots sprouting from its dim interior. It was clearly a picture of decay, but also of wildness and mystery. She felt her heart beat faster, her breath catch. Everything about the featured painting had been different from her crabbed, careful attempts. It made her want to enter the painting, to live in it.

She wanted to see his other paintings, to see how he managed to convey such freedom. *Wanted* was the wrong word. She *yearned* to see them. It had been so long since she had felt a desire for anything she almost felt sickened by the feeling, mistaking it for the beginning of a cold.

She hadn't made a firm decision to go, but had clipped the newspaper notice and put it on the refrigerator. Then this afternoon, she'd decided it would be too much effort. But as the time drew nearer, she found herself pinning up her hair and rooting around for a pair of black pants and the black sweater she knew was somewhere in the back of her closet. Her hands shook as she jabbed the pins in her hair. She wouldn't know anyone. Maybe she should stay home. Lethargy had come over her, and she felt the pull of her bed, but shook it off. At the last minute, she put on her old denim jacket and a beaded necklace and hoped she looked sufficiently arty to not be noticed. She left the house quickly before she could change her mind.

She'd found a place to park and made her way down the unfamiliar street jammed with secondhand stores and coffee shops. It reminded her of her student days, of the thrill of the slightly seedy. She remembered for a brief moment how it felt to be young and open, an adventure around every corner. Was she mad to have come here, she thought, stepping over some trash spilling out of the alleyway. She felt old and out of place and slightly panicked.

Still she'd pushed on, until the street number matched the number in the clipping. It was a storefront gallery, and through the window she saw a small group of people clustered around the cheese and wine, several more groups moving from painting to painting. She took a deep breath and pushed the door open. No one seemed to notice her. Nothing happened. Several people smiled distractedly in her direction. She poured herself half a glass of white wine, praying to remain invisible.

She chose a starting place. She didn't read the artist's notes, just took in the paintings or was taken in by them. They were large, luminous oils that made her feel she was stepping into a wider, more spacious world—this world, only sun washed, with a clarity of light that cherished every surface it touched. The pictures, abstract but recognizable, were of coastlines, wood-lands, dilapidated barns, but there was also a series of decaying urban buildings, equally as beautiful. The light lifted everyday objects out of the ordinary—streets that were clearly poor tenements were made lively with color and light. These paintings seemed to acknowledge the brokenness of the world, but they didn't end in pain. They seemed to say, "Yes, but look here." They made her feel, in some strange way, filled with hope. She forgot all about technique, about analysis.

Her curse was that she knew good painting. It was like having a good ear, but being unable to sing. Her own work lacked freedom of expression, was careful, tentative. Her lines were pedestrian, her colors muddy. It tortured her. Maybe if she had gone on with studio classes, she might have progressed. But she hadn't. Instead she'd gotten her nursing degree and fit in art courses whenever she could. She'd spent many hours on the fifth floor of the library, poring over luscious art volumes. She especially loved the moderns: Lucien Freud, Kandinsky, Rothko, and Arshile Gorky. But she had also loved Rembrandt, Vermeer, and the Dutch Masters. Her appetite had been promiscuous, voracious. She remembered her heart racing, her palms sweating, as she turned the pages of the folios. She couldn't believe that such a wealth of beauty was there, free for the asking. She had felt an intense, almost clandestine pleasure in these forays.

If she hadn't known what real painting was, she wouldn't have been so tormented. She would have been like the woman she used to chat with in the parking lot of Josh's day school—the woman said she "painted too—china," and "it was so much fun."

She stopped in front of a painting of a pecan grove and a dilapidated barn. The mellow light suggested a long, lazy summer afternoon. She recognized the regular arching of the pecan limbs over each other, the way the shadows patterned the canvas. Although loosely applied, the paint accurately evoked the precise curve of limbs, the feel of heat coming off the tin roof.

Helen became aware of someone at her left elbow. She turned and saw a short, wiry man gazing not at the painting but at her. She flushed, remembered herself again. He had white curly hair and intense ice-blue eyes.

"Sorry to startle you," he said, "but so few people know how to look at a painting. You seem to." He smiled, and the laugh lines around his eyes deepened.

"I, uh, used to study painting. I mean, you know, art appreciation courses and such. Nothing much, really." She felt the blush rising again, staining her chest and neck and face.

"And this painting, what do you see in it?"

"Oh, I don't know. I like the way the barn is so broken-down, but still beautiful. Like you could feel the sunshine on the wood, the way it would radiate onto your hand."

"Ah," he said, one eyebrow cocked. "You understand wabi-sabi."

Helen laughed nervously. "I don't know what that is."

"It is the beauty in the impermanent, in the weathered… it would take a long time to explain it." His friendly, penetrating eyes stayed on hers. "And you paint as well?"

"Well, I, uh, yeah, I fool around with it sometimes. I don't really know what I'm doing."

"Maybe you underestimate yourself. Look." He scouted around in his pockets, pulled out a somewhat creased card, and handed it to her. She noticed there was ink under his fingernails. "Here is my card. I'm teaching a painting class at the community art center. Maybe you would like to come? I think I would like to have someone like you in the class."

"But has it started?"

"Yes, but just barely. You would have no problem, I'm sure."

She looked down at the card in her hand. Andrew Olaffson. She looked at the paintings. Andrew Olaffson. She looked for him again, but he had moved away from her and was laughing and talking with some people near the refreshments.

She tucked the card away in her wallet. Flustered, she turned back to the paintings, but her reverie was broken. As she left, she picked up the artist's statement and some postcards of his work. She needed fresh air, needed to process what had just happened. She walked along the sidewalk, noticing only the cracks in the cement. Conflicting currents of fear and excitement flowed through her.

Her carefully constructed cover had been blown. She had hoped to be able to see the paintings without anyone noticing her, and instead she had been singled out for scrutiny by the artist himself. And he seemed like such an odd little man. But friendly. She loved his paintings. And he had invited her to his class. But why? Maybe he was desperate to fill it. But still—she didn't know what to do. It had been years since she had gone to an art class. Any group activity, for that matter. If she went, she might find out for good and certain that she had no talent. On the other hand, it might help her break through the im-

passe she felt so deeply. She might learn from him. She might—
what? For a moment she had that giddy feeling of being young
again, of daring to hope.

He had seen something in her. He had seen her. Who had
he seen? The door she had shut a long time ago cracked open
and let in a filament of light. Something like an idea of her own
possibilities began to stir in her, and she let herself feel that old,
now unfamiliar feeling. It felt like stretching an unused muscle.
It felt like something deep in her that was hers alone, a deep,
pleasurable secret. Her heart pounded, and she could feel the
rush of blood in her ears.

But. Her steps slowed, and she looked around at the shop
she stood in front of, a trendy clothing store, the headless mannequins sporting crocheted ponchos and worn jeans. If she
joined a class, there would be other people. It wouldn't just be
her and Olaffson. Her habitual unease around people would
have to be overcome. She imagined young women in jeans and
crocheted ponchos. They would talk about things she had no
idea of—art, movies, music. They would be bright and their
laughter silvery. They would do group critiques, no doubt. She
would be inarticulate. She felt her heart sink. She would be so
exposed. She thought about her paintings and drawings, about
how she'd never let people see them.

Then it hit her. People would know who she was—the
mother of the boy who ran over David Masters. She would be a
freak, something people talked about when they were standing
in line at Kroger. "Oh, ya know what? I'm taking an art class
with the mother of the boy that put David Masters in the hospital." "Oh, I thought he died." Helen imagined reactions, pity

or perverse curiosity. She steadied herself against the wall, trying hard to breathe.

It would be safer not to go.

She came to a stoplight and waited for the walk signal. There, that was the right decision. She felt a peace and relief at the thought of not having to go. The light turned green, and she stepped out into the street. A close call avoided. Time to close that door. What had she been thinking? She let go of the secret thrill, the momentary hope. Some things were better savored as pleasant might-have-beens. She needed to get a grip on herself.

Helen squinted now, trying to get her bearings. Where had she parked? Over by the bank on Hancock. She turned north. The sun was low in the west, the sky glowing pink. The orange-and-purple clouds cast a warm glow over the old redbrick buildings. Helen noticed how the roofs angled down the slope like old, slightly drunk companions, all jumbled together and holding each other up. She imagined how Olaffson would paint them, how he would convey the—what did he call it?—wabi something of this shabby, beautiful place.

She thought, with a start, *How would I paint them?* She pulled out some crumpled list paper and a pen and began sketching quickly. She stood concentrating, trying to breathe in the colors, to remember what they felt like. She felt alive, every fiber of her being concentrated on this moment, this sketch.

When she finished, she held the sketch up. *Not too bad,* she thought, squinting. She took out Olaffson's card again and studied it. What, anyway, did she have to lose? What else was there for her? An empty house filled with stopped clocks? A farty dog? Relying more and more on her chemical friends?

She shuddered. She had been waiting for Hal and Josh to come home, for life to become normal again. Standing there on the street, the light fading, she knew it would never be normal again. It was as if they all had been hit that night, and now they were bloody and broken, unable to see or hear or help each other.

She looked down at the card. She thought of Olaffson's face. He was kind, she thought. She was terrified to go. She was more terrified of what would happen to her if she didn't go.

Let people talk. Andrew Olaffson had singled her out.

FOURTEEN

Josh saw the white slip of paper sticking out of the row of gray lockers, and his heart sank. Even from the far end of the crowded hall, he knew it was his locker and he knew who the note was from. His steps slowed, and someone behind him rammed into him. "Hey, dude, slow traffic to the right." Josh shrugged, got moving in the stream of bodies, his nose assaulted by sweet perfumes, sweaty gym socks, disinfectant; his ears full of the murmured voices, shrieks, and banging of lockers. He reached wearily for the note. He stood there with it unfolded, holding it gingerly, as if it were a spider that might bite him. Did he really want to read it? He knew what it would say. But he couldn't help himself.

"Josh, I hope you know that you have traded your two only truly LOYAL BEST OLD FRIENDS for the Ice Queen. I hope you know that we haven't dropped you, YOU DROPPED US. LET'S GET THIS CLEAR. We are loyal, and we would stand by you IF YOU LET US. NONE of this would have happened if it wasn't for her. I WILL NEVER FORGIVE HER. Your TRUE FRIEND, Suzbug." And incongruously, there was a smiley face at the bottom of the signature.

Josh crumbled up the note and stuck it in his pocket. How

could he explain to Susie of all people that he and Libby were freaks, marked out in some way? That it was too exhausting to pretend to be normal? That it was a relief to be with your own kind? Susie's accusing, hard look, the face she turned to him these days whenever they saw each other, floated in front of his face. He couldn't get past that look, even if he wanted to.

Andy had cornered him in the field on the way home a week after the accident. Pale and strangely sluggish in his movements, he had asked Josh to forgive him. Josh had looked into his big brown puppy-dog eyes and hated him, his best friend, for the first time in his life. Then he got control of himself. "Look, you didn't put a gun to my head. I'm responsible for my actions." He wanted to believe that. But if Andy hadn't been there with his stash… "Look, man, drop it. What's done is done. I really don't want to go there."

"But," Andy started to walk next to him.

"I just want to be alone, okay? Is that too much to ask?" And he'd hurried off through the weeds, leaving Andy stranded.

He knew his friends still cared about him, that Andy would be Sir Galahad to his King Arthur. There was just no going back. It was as if he'd stepped through a membrane that separated before from after. In some weird way, it was as if he were floating above ordinary life, so that the whispers and exchanged glances when he walked down the halls, Susie's angry pointed looks, Andy's misery, didn't really touch him.

Now he pushed through the crowds, the last shrill dismissal bell ringing, all around him kids laughing, like inmates giddy at getting out of prison. They fell through the doors and out into the gray afternoon. His eyes scanned the parking lot for Libby's car. She always took him to Good Shepherd now. There she was, leaning against her mustard Impala, surely the ugliest car ever created. She didn't see him; she was talking on the phone and staring off at the baseball field. He liked looking at her without her knowing, drinking in her cascades of brown hair, her small heart-shaped face. She was gesturing with her hands, and he liked that, too, how she could become suddenly so animated. He liked the way she never looked like anyone else, the funky knitted sweaters she got at the thrift store, how they almost swallowed her small body, the vintage beads she wore with her T-shirts.

She caught sight of him and waved, turning her back for a minute to finish her call.

"Okay, Mom, look, I've got to go. Yeah, yeah, I know, I'll pick them up at six thirty. Bye."

She turned and looked up at him, her mouth tight.

"Got to pick up the twins? TKD?"

"Yeah, Dad's gone off with the other car. Parts unknown. Sounds like he's hatching a plan or something."

Josh felt helpless whenever Libby talked about her feck-less father. It seemed he was always creating chaos and Libby was always having to pick up the pieces. Now she jammed her phone into her purse and tried to smile.

"Let's get out of here. Want to go downtown, get a coffee?"

Josh nodded. He'd go anywhere with her.

As they nosed their way out of the crowded parking lot, Josh took her hand. She smiled a sideways smile at him, keeping her eyes on the road. She was so small and the car so big that she looked like a diminutive sea captain manning a giant wheel. Neither of them said anything.

Josh looked out the window at his schoolmates trudging home with their backpacks, at the people walking dogs, raking leaves, all the ordinary people in their ordinary lives. It was as if he and Libby were sailing by all the landlocked, buoyed on waves that were taking them farther and farther away from that mundane lot. They had plans, big plans. She believed in him, believed he would be a director, and he believed in her, man, he knew she had that spark, that something special. When they were together, the air vibrated with possibility.

They pulled up to Hot Corner. The car docked slowly in the small space. Josh could smell the coffee, and he was suddenly hungry. He was always hungry these days, it seemed, and now his mouth watered, imaging the cranberry scones and coffee awaiting them.

Libby grabbed his hand and turned away from the coffee house, pointing across the street. "Look, Josh, Archipelago is having a sale." She pushed her cat-eye glasses up on her nose. "Let's go check it out. Maybe you could find some old movie posters or some of those Coltrane vinyls, hmm?"

Josh hesitated, reluctant to give up his anticipated goodies. "Yeah, but we don't have much time—"

"Oh, please, Josh, I've always wanted to take you here. It'll be fun."

Josh nodded reluctantly, turning toward the store.

They stepped into the musty, dimly lit store. Victorian couches pushed up against sixties modern peg-legged coffee tables. A lava lamp glowed purple. A mannequin sported a wide-brimmed man's hat, and a red slip festooned its limbless body. Shelves were crowded with books, pottery, garish amateur paintings, and piles of old photographs. Josh picked up a photo of a family in stiff collars and long skirts. They looked so serious, so formal, and yet here they were, thrown carelessly into a dusty pile. It seemed wrong, somehow, that no one had claimed them.

Josh followed Libby through the cluttered aisles. A rusty bicycle dangled from one wall. From the ceiling hung chandeliers, paper lanterns, strings of chili-pepper lights. They wandered past racks stuffed with dusty vintage clothes.

"Wow, this is incredible. I can't believe I've never been in here."

"Look, Josh." Libby snatched up a leopard-skin toque, put it on her head, dug her lipstick out of her purse, turned away from Josh and then back again, posing like a sixties pin-up girl. "James, darling," she purred. "Stirred, not shaken, if I remember correctly?"

Josh blinked. She had transformed herself into a bombshell.

She laughed at him, seeing that she'd had the desired effect. "See, Josh, how great this place is? You can be anybody, anything. It's like a big props room." She tossed the hat off, rooted around in a rack of clothes, pulled out a lacy black slip, draped it across herself, shook her hair back. "Ain't nothing more determined than a cat on a hot tin roof? Is there, is there, baby?"

"Maggie!"

"Good, baby, good." She was still in character.

"How do you do that?" He wasn't sure if he was addressing Maggie or Libby. It was almost scary. It was as if the real Libby, his Libby, had vanished. He gently took the slip from her. "I like you as you the best."

She wrinkled her nose. "*That's* pretty boring."

He glanced around. There was no one. He put his hands on either side of her face and tilted it toward him. "Not to me," he said, and kissed her softly.

She rested her head against his chest. "You're nice," she murmured, leaning into him for a moment, then pushing off. Not meeting his eyes, she wandered aimlessly toward the door. He wondered what she meant by that, by "nice." He wasn't sure he wanted to be "nice."

She stood at the entrance, looking out at the gray street, where it was beginning to rain. "Ready to go?" She seemed somehow deflated, and he cursed himself for whatever he'd done to change her mood.

"Don't you want to look a little longer?" he asked.

She shook her head. "We've got places to be, remember?" Her voice was strained and flat, and her eyes, when she turned away from the window, as opaque as the sky.

***

Josh had a headache by the time they pulled up at Good Shepherd. They muttered goodbyes, then Libby spun off, rushing to get the twins. He'd slammed the car door harder than he'd intended to, and he wondered if she'd noticed.

He didn't understand women, that was for sure. It was still raining, and by the time he got to the building, he was streaming puddles. He squeaked into the lobby on wet sneakers.

Marbry bustled through. "You're late. Better wipe up that

water before someone slips," she called over her shoulder. He went into the boy's bathroom and grabbed the paper hand towels and was squatting down, wiping up the floor when Ms. Jones found him.

"Ah, Josh, there you are," she boomed above him.

He straightened, the dripping towels still in his hand. "Sorry I'm a bit late," he stammered.

She waved him off. "You're fine." She flashed him one of her brief, bright smiles. "You know, you've been doing such a fine job with Marius. I just wanted to let you know that I know it isn't always easy."

He looked up at her, unsure of what she was getting at.

"Honestly, Ms. Jones, I wish I felt like I was getting somewhere. But it's hard to know if things are sinking in with him."

"He's beginning to get letters, numbers. Even Marbry has noticed it."

Josh shrugged, flushed. But it was so slow, so painstakingly slow.

Ms. Jones was looking at him with her searchlight gaze. "I know you want more, Josh. More connection. But it will have to wait. Everything in its own time."

"Yeah, I guess so."

She turned to go, but Josh called out after her.

"I forgot something." He patted his jacket pocket. "I brought this disposable camera for him. I thought, y'know, the way he's always looking out windows and looking around, that maybe he could take pictures and then we could make stories about them together."

Ms. Jones looked startled. She paused, frowning. He was

afraid she didn't like the idea. Then she said, "It might be a very good idea. There could be a problem with the other children wanting one, but in that case, well, I guess we'd just have to buy one for all of them. Sure, see how it goes." She smiled again before moving off briskly.

Josh hung up his soaking jacket in the hallway and went to the activity room to meet with Marius. The boy was at his appointed place by the window, looking small and fragile in his wheelchair. Josh thought with a pang what it would be like to lose your mother so young. Sometimes other relatives visited him, and he perked up. Josh thought it would be better in some ways if he could be with his family instead of at Good Shepherd, and wasn't sure why he wasn't. He thought of his own mother, how she had always been there for him. Until recently. But he was old now; he could take care of himself. He wasn't six.

Josh cleared his throat to get Marius's attention. "Hi," he said.

Marius turned his head from his intense examination of the bare oak branches outside the window. "You wet," he observed.

Josh laughed. Marius just gazed at him with that deep, uninflected look that seemed to take in everything. Oh, he was smart, all right. There was a lot going on behind those eyes. But *what* was an entirely different question.

"What we doin' t'day?" Marius asked, sighing. As if this was yet another task to be gotten through in the endless gray tasks of his day. But it was improvement. He was talking. Josh just wanted something else, a smile, a laugh, anything that would identify the creature in front of him as a child.

Josh remembered the camera then, and had to run out in the hall to get it out of his jacket pocket.

"Look, Marius," he said. "I got you a camera. You can take pictures with it."

He handed the cardboard camera to the boy. Marius turned it over in his small hands. "I seen this."

Josh nodded, encouragingly.

The boy examined it, frowning. "How it work?" he finally said.

Josh felt a flush of hope. He showed the boy how to look through the viewfinder, how to depress the button and shoot the picture. He explained that there were only twenty-four pictures, and they counted up to twenty-four using all their fingers and toes and four pencils. "So just take pictures of things you think are really interesting," Josh said, "and next time I come, I'll get the pictures printed for you, okay?"

The boy nodded gravely. Josh wasn't sure if he really understood. Maybe it didn't matter.

They went on to work on letter recognition in the reader, Marius reverting to his normally lethargic participation, although he occasionally glanced at the camera. Still, by the time they had finished, Josh had the same deflated feeling he always had at the end of a session with Marius, of not really making much of a difference.

Just before Marbry was due to march in, Josh leaned down and looked into Marius's eyes. "Take all the pictures, okay, Marius?"

The boy nodded again, and then a ghost of a smile crossed his face. "Twenty-four," he said.

As Marbry brushed past Josh on his way out, she whispered, "Why d'you have that shit-eating grin on your face?"

Marbry looked from him to Marius.

"No reason," Josh said, going out in the hall to put on his still-damp jacket.

Marbry made a *humph* sound and squinted her eyes at him. *Ha, got her,* Josh thought, and left, whistling.

FIFTEEN

Helen still broke out in a cold sweat on the drive over to the art class. It was the third week, she thought, surely she should be over her fear of the class by now. It was fine once she got in there, once she found her chair and took out her materials. Olaffson usually had a still life set up or other people's work tacked up; there was always something to engage her, take her out of herself.

So far, she'd had very little interaction with the other students, which was the way she wanted it. She didn't want any cozy exchange of intimate details, the kinds of pseudo-intimacy that sprang up in classes of this sort. The other people seemed just as private and focused on the work as she was. There was a shy young girl who worked at a grocery store, a retired drama professor, an acerbic retired elementary school teacher, and a woman a little older than Helen, who seemed to have taken Olaffson's course before.

Olaffson was worth it all. After only two lessons, she had found a place in herself that was freer, more willing to take risks. He talked about killing the critic and gave them stretching exercises to start off with. He had them paint with their non-dominant hand, then paint the worst painting they were capable of. He could be goofy, a little inane, but then he'd zero in on exactly the thing that needed to be done. He made her care and not care at the same time. He talked about nonattachment even as he taught them how to really see. It was about seeing, she had learned from him, not technique. She'd always had it backward, getting so uptight about technique that she hadn't really seen. But now she caught herself looking at everything, noticing the sweep of a tree's branches or the voluptuousness of clouds piling on the horizon like whipped cream.

She'd abandoned herself to painting, and in two weeks had produced three small pieces. Now he wanted her to work large and fast. She was scared, didn't think she could do it. To work large seemed a physical impossibility, made her shoulders ache thinking about it. Walking down the hall to the classroom, clutching the unwieldy canvas under her arm, she found herself muttering resentfully to herself. This would be it, she thought, this would be the moment of truth. He'd see she was a fraud.

She stopped and lingered in front of a large oil, a still life of sunflowers in a tin can, and tried to analyze it for its compositional qualities as Olaffson had been teaching. She put her blank canvas on the scuffed linoleum, inhaling the smell of oil and turpentine still clinging to the canvas before her.

As she stood there, she slowly became aware of voices drifting out of the classroom. The sounds resolved themselves into words that, at first, she didn't pay any attention to. Then she heard the word *Masters*. She snapped out of her pleasant reverie and strained to hear. Masters? About David Masters? How could they know—it had been months since anything had been in the papers. No. She was being paranoid. And yet. People were mean and bored, always ready to pounce on a person's vulnerability.

She leaned against the wall, paralyzed.

Just then, Olaffson came down the hall, his arms swinging energetically, his face beaming like a child's. She could not greet him. She stared at him and lowered herself to the floor, where she sat crossed-legged, her head in her hands.

She felt him lean over her, put his hand on her shoulder.

"Whoa, what's this? Helen?"

She fought for breath, finally took her hands away from her face. He was squatting down, looking at her, and holding out a water bottle.

"Are you sick?" His blue, direct eyes burrowed into her. And yet he looked so kind.

She shook her head. "No. I, uh, I can't go to class today." All she wanted to do was get out of there.

"You look like you saw a ghost."

"He's not a ghost yet. Oh, god, they know."

"Look, is there something you need to talk about? I don't want you to leave. You are doing good work."

She stared at him. "I think they know about me." Her words came out in strangled gasps.

She could see him suppress a smile. "Know what?"

She looked away. Did she want him to know? Better to leave before anyone knew. But then she looked at him, and it came out. "You know the boy that hit David Masters? You know the accident, in August?"

He looked confused for a moment, then she could see that he had fixed on it.

"Well, that boy was my son. And I heard them talking in there. I heard the word *Masters*, and now they know and now I can't go back in there. I knew this would happen." She pushed against him, frantic to just get up and run.

Olaffson grasped her arms and gently shook her. "Helen, you heard the word *masters*? Look, could it be they were talking about getting a master's degree? In art?"

She looked at him dumbly, aware of his strong grip on her arms.

"You mean?"

"Debbie has been talking to me about it. Don't you think that is what they would be talking about?" He nodded encouragingly.

She began crying. It had been so long since anyone had touched her, so long since anyone had looked into her eyes, and the relief that maybe she could stay in the class and not have to give it up were all too much for her. With disgust she realized that snot was running from her nose. She fought to regain control, but couldn't. All the while he continued to steady her with his arms, and when at last the gasping subsided, he pulled out a clean white handkerchief from his back pocket. It was soft and smelled like Ivory Snow. She blew her nose noisily in it and handed it back to him.

"I didn't know anybody carried these anymore."

"Old habits die hard. There now, you'll paint better tonight." He patted her back once more and stepped away, his eyes now more distant.

A peace settled over her. She felt spacious and empty and relaxed.

"I'm going to wash up—I'll be right in."

He put his hand up in acknowledgment and turned and walked toward the classroom. She went to the lavatory, splashed water on her face, found an old compact in her purse, and managed to cover the red splotches. Then she quietly retrieved her canvas and slipped into the back of the classroom.

Olaffson was right. She painted better than she ever had before. Her brush seemed to find the color of its own accord, and all her careful deliberations about color theory vanished. She began to trust herself. It was as if a door she hadn't known, a door inside her, had opened, and she had walked through to find an exotic garden.

Everything about her painting changed after that lesson. She abandoned her timid still lifes. Now she felt more like an explorer than anything else. She felt the way she remembered feeling as a kid, spending hours in the woods, collecting stones and sticks and pinecones, bringing them home to make ant castles in her sandbox. She had spent hours absorbed in her ant castles, urging the insects through tunnels, up drawbridges. She still could feel the warm sun on her back, the shadows of leaves shifting on her hands, the cool feel of the bottom layer of sand.

Painting now seemed as visceral to her as that early play. Her studies and paintings were lush, bold, strange things, filled with organic shapes that first appeared to be flowers or trees but resolved themselves into figures. She experimented with monotypes, enjoying the serendipity of chance images. She collected Japanese papers, layering the prints so they became collages, sometimes painting over those and scraping away the surface layer. She often didn't know what her subject was until it revealed itself. Many of the paintings were dark, with haunted faces behind crumbling walls: she did a whole series of

Walmart paintings with tattooed arms and product labels and strange animals lurking under florescent lights.

She was often angry when she painted, she sometimes cried. She did a collage with old pictures of Hal and Josh, with her charcoal face changing into a gargoyle, a harridan. She did one of a boy's figure, seen from behind, walking through a desert, a tiny figure, and across it were prison bars and her hands grasping them. But then she left those, too, and went into what Olaffson called her "lush phase."

She didn't know where those paintings and drawings came from. She would start with a charcoal sketch of dishes piled in the sink and end up with a female form suggestively draped over them. She'd begin a painting as a still life with homely objects from her bedroom—a chair, a clock radio, a pile of clothes, but it would end up with the suggestion of two figures intertwined. She would intentionally try to make her work as stark as possible, pick a grayed palette, and then lushness would sneak in—curves, and flashes of orange or red or purple. It made her feel the same way dreams of finding herself naked in public places made her feel.

Often, when she was painting, she was thinking of Olaffson, as if the act of painting brought that warmth, the sense of support and steadiness that she felt whenever she was around him. She dreamed of him, too, sometimes, and when that happened, she resisted waking up, lying in bed, lingering between waking and sleeping, trying to hold on to the last sweet remnants of her dream.

And sometimes, in a semi-erotic lather, she found herself painting male nudes, thinking of him all the while, yet the lines of the bodies she painted were never Olaffson's short, wiry ones, but depicted a body more like Hal's long, stolid one. Even when she consciously tried to vary the contours of her male bodies, they still ended up reminding her of Hal, the planes of his face, the way his long limbs took up space, knees folded in a chair, or his back hunched over as he worked on something. It was something that puzzled and annoyed her, as if all those years of living together had imprinted his very form indelibly on her mind, so that even when she was trying her hardest to get away from him, he was there with her.

SECTION 7:
CHANGE PARTNERS
AND DANCE

SIXTEEN

Meg got the call from ClockWorks that her clock was ready. It was the call that she had been eagerly awaiting and yet dreading at the same time. When the caller asked for Valerie Tate, Meg completely blanked out. Then she remembered her ruse and was overcome with a kind of vertigo.

"Yes?" she stuttered.

"Your clock is ready."

"Were you able to get it running?"

There was an aggrieved sigh at the end of the line. "It wasn't easy, let me tell you. People need to treat these old clocks better."

Meg felt scolded. She was aware of an intense dislike for Hal. She would go and pick up the clock and that would be it. Any ideas she had of helping the family, of trying to help the boy, were gone. It would hardly be worth dealing with such a dislikable character. No wonder the kid was screwed up.

She drove over to the shop, anxious to get any encounter with Hal over with. She pushed the door open hastily and strode up to the counter. It wasn't until she was halfway across the room that above the myriad of ticking clocks, she became aware of another sound, the sound of angry voices.

A man—not Hal—behind the counter peered intently

through his magnifiers at the workings he was fixing, apparently trying very hard to tune the fight out. Meg stood, stunned, in the middle of the room. Through the glassed-in office she could see Hal and Josh, shouting and gesturing. Hal had his back turned to her, but Meg could see Josh's face. It had the same stricken look on it that she remembered from the accident. The door was open, and she could hear every word.

"—can't handle it alone, Dad. She sleeps all the time, and she doesn't even cook anymore."

"I'm sorry, Josh, but I can't help."

"It's my fault, isn't it? You left because of me—"

"Your mother and I had a fight—"

"But it was that night. It was a fight about me, wasn't it? Wasn't it, Dad?"

Hal thrust out his arms and let them fall helplessly at his side. "I just needed to get away for a while—"

"You've been away, Dad, for a long time."

Josh's eyes, which had been fastened on his father, flickered away and fastened briefly on Meg. She saw him register that she had overheard, then rush past his father, by her, and out of the store. Meg stared at a large grandfather clock and remembered, oddly, the time when she had come in. The whole exchange she had witnessed had taken less than a minute.

As if released from a trance, Meg proceeded to the counter and cleared her throat. The assistant looked up, his jeweler loupe still in his hand, and blinked myopically at her.

"I'm Me—Valerie Tate. I'm here to pick up my clock."

The man tipped up his chin and called to Hal. "That was his job. He'll want to talk with you," he muttered, then turned back to his gears and tools. The clocks seemed to tick more loudly now that there were no human voices to compete with them, and Meg got the feeling she had the first time she came here, of an insular, airless world. The clock hands moved relentlessly around the faces. It was somehow depressing, as if time were reduced to the mere markings on the clock faces, emptied of texture and movement.

Hal appeared before her all of a sudden. His face was taut and flushed, and there was a glazed, feverish look in his eyes. "Yes?" he said brusquely,

"I'm here to pick up my clock—Valerie Tate?"

He tapped his fingers on the counter. "Oh, yes. Yes." His demeanor changed—suddenly he was at attention. "Here it is." He reached down and brought out the small package swathed in cloth. He set the clock lovingly on the counter and unwrapped it. Meg hardly recognized it. It had been cleaned, and the wood oiled, the metal fittings were buffed to a high sheen.

"It's, it's beautiful," she stammered.

He looked up at her with piercing blue eyes. "Yes, it really is. Look at this—this is very unusual, these shaped stepped pillars with helical gearing and matching stepped shaped gear…"

Meg noticed that as he talked about the clock, his whole face took on an animation and relaxation she had not seen before. His voice grew quietly authoritative, not harsh and irritated. He looked up at her then and caught her looking at him.

"Are you listening?" he asked.

"Oh, yes," Meg replied, "but could you go over that last part again? Just to make sure I've got it?"

"I've got it going now, but in one hundred twenty days, you'll have to start it again. You must be very careful when you do this—forcing anything could potentially break the mechanism. It is equally important not to neglect the clock." Again, Meg chafed at the scolding tone in his voice.

"My goodness, Mr. Lovejoy, it's not a child!"

Hal looked up at her, confused, and flushed again. "What do you mean? What are you talking about?"

"I'm sorry, it was a joke. I meant only that the use of the word *neglected* seemed a bit strong, as if you were talking about a child."

"But this clock *is* something very precious, miss, something irreplaceable. It actually could be valuable. I haven't been able to discover if it is a very good reproduction or an original. It is quite old, I think. If it is an original—" He gave a low whistle. "Most important clocks have been discovered. But a few have fallen through the cracks. It's not probable, but it could be one of those." He looked at her with frustrated intensity.

Meg knew she should let it go, but something in her couldn't. "I see. I appreciate your educating me. It's just that it is an inanimate object, that's all. I guess I'm sensitive to the word *neglect*, because I work with neglected kids all day."

Hal was blinking at her, his eyes glazing over again. There was a long silence. Finally, he said, "Do you have any kids?"

It was Meg's turn to flush. "No, I don't. Why?" She could hear the defensiveness in her own voice.

"Just wondering. I do."

"Was that your son I saw in here a few minutes ago?" *That was reckless,* she thought, but she was being compulsively reckless today.

Hal looked down at the counter, then away. "Yes."

"He's a good-looking boy. What's his name?"

"Josh." There was another pause, as if Hal was struggling to know what to say. Then, "It isn't easy you know. Kids. It's easy when they are little, but it gets harder. It's like they become strangers, then they become enemies. And it is somehow your fault." He stopped abruptly, as if just becoming aware of Meg. "I'm sorry. Don't know where that came from. Okay, so here's the bill, Ms. Tate, and if you ever have any problem with the clock, please bring it back. The work is unconditionally guaranteed." He wrapped the clock up tenderly in brown paper before handing her the bill. She glanced at it and pulled out her checkbook, then realized that her name on the check would give her away. Panicked, she scrounged around in her purse for loose bills, finding barely enough. He stood there holding the clock, as if reluctant to let it go. "I would be happy to research it for you."

Meg, shaking with anger at the man's clear ineptness with his son, had trouble controlling her voice. "Don't go to any trouble." She gazed at the mummy-like package. "It's important to me because of my grandparents. I plan on using it in my class to teach about gears, about analog time."

A look of horror came over Hal's face. "I would advise against that."

Is the man deranged? Meg thought "I'll take it now, please."

Hal hesitated, then gently placed the package on the counter. Meg shivered, anxious to be out of there, away from all the swinging pendulums, the ticking faces, the smell of Tung oil, Hal's intense eyes. She stepped out into the street and was glad for the breeze and the sunshine filtering through the leaves. She would, she thought defiantly, absolutely use it in her classroom.

She had to grudgingly admit that he had done a beautiful job with the clock. Still, she was angry with him. People with children didn't realize what damage they did. It wasn't fair. The fact of her childlessness always crept up on her like this, when she least expected it, filling her with a familiar ache. How longingly that man had looked at her clock; how longingly she had looked at his son. Well, they could trade, she thought, just the way her kids traded sandwiches and chips at lunch. *Here, Mr. Lovejoy, have my clock.* Only you can't, can you, trade children? They belong, somehow, even to the sorriest of parents.

***

He felt Meg lie down beside him. He wanted to tell her to climb in, take off her clothes, for Pete's sake, but she lay on top of the covers. She was talking about a boy again, some boy she wished was their son. He felt again the old sadness and guilt. She'd wanted children so badly, and he'd let her down. He wanted Meg all to himself; he wanted to be free to do his work. There was only room for those two things in his life. He knew that he wasn't up to parenthood. Not up to the guilt. No, he knew himself. He wished he could have been able to give Meg what she wanted, but he couldn't.

She had fought him for a long time. It seemed to have gone on for years, each of them in their corners, unrelenting, hurt, angry. He had come close to giving in a few times, but it felt too much like giving in, and he knew he'd resent the kid that came from that kind of compromise.

Then suddenly, it was over. Had she finally let him off the hook because deep down, she knew he didn't have it in him? She threw herself into her teaching then, and home seemed like home again. She'd sometimes bring it up wistfully, as she did now, but never reproachfully.

Now he reproached himself. Now he had time. Maybe if she had kids of her own, she wouldn't be picking up strays.

There had always been this tension in him, between wanting to be free and wanting to belong. When he'd gone "up north," he thought he'd left Milledge behind for good. What had he been fleeing? What had he been so anxious to shake off? He remembered how light he'd felt as the road unwound under the wheels of the car, remembered the feeling of sloughing off heavy layers of a skin that wasn't really his, his what? His history, he supposed.

He felt Meg leaving, and he wanted to call her back. He hadn't meant to drift away from her. "Meg, Meg," he called, but then he knew she was gone.

Out of the emptiness, Peggy began to sing, "Little boy lost, in search of little boy found. You go wondering, wandering, stumbling, tumbling round, round…" He listened to the notes rise and fall. Then she was there, leaning over and kissing him, her dress glowing in the dimness. David wondered if it was made of silk. His mother had had a dress that shimmered like that once.

"Don't leave me," he said, out of a sudden anguish that threatened to obliterate him.

"Would I leave you?" she said. "Hey, I have a question for you. I've been around a bit. This place is better than some, worse than others. It's okay, but nothing to write home about. I can understand why you left. What I can't understand is why you came back."

David laughed. "Anyway, it's a place like any other, with its good and its bad. But in the end, it was my place."

His history, the South's history, the damn town's history. He'd always wanted to get away. He'd been "Jew boy, nigger lover, nerd." When he was young, he dreamed of reinventing himself. He could taste his future life, more real in anticipation than any life could be. He would be a successful lawyer, live in a brownstone in Boston or in a high-rise in Chicago. He would go to museums and concerts, and everyone he knew would be sophisticated and civilized, no small-town jocks or bleached-blond beauty queens there.

"And so, darling, did you?"

"Did I—?"

"Did you reinvent yourself? I did, you know. Quite successfully, if I do say so myself." She smiled that slightly rueful smiled and sipped her drink. "I didn't do too badly for a bread slicer from Fargo… but we were talking about you."

"I didn't do too badly. I came back—"

"So you've said. But why?"

David looked at the light shining off Peggy's platinum hair.

"So—what was so bad? It was the life you dreamed of." Her leg kicked out girlishly from under her skirt.

"I don't know. I was restless. It all seemed too—easy. Like I was playing a role. I felt like an imposter."

171

"Ahh," Peggy said in that low, seductive way. "'Little boy false in search of little boy true, will you be ever done traveling, always unraveling you, you?'"

"When I came back, it seemed that my past reclaimed me in some way I can't explain exactly. I met Meg, she seemed grittier, more real, and—"

"And—?"

"I guess that's it. When I met her, I felt I had come home."

David waited for Peggy's reply, but there was none. Only a deep and resounding silence.

SEVENTEEN

Helen reached her brush toward the yellow, then hesitated. Something was missing. Olaffson had said last night not to think about it too much, but to feel what comes next, and go with the feeling. She found this irritatingly vague, like so many of the things he said, but now she tried it. She scooped some yellow and then some blue and, holding her breath, let the colors mix on the canvas. Her homemade tripod teetered on the decaying picnic table as the brush glided over the canvas. She stepped back and looked. A not unpleasing effect, she decided. *Breathe,* she heard Olaffson's voice say in her head. *Where in your body do you feel? Move from that place.* She was trying to do that, too. All these new efforts felt awkward, uncomfortable. But she persisted for those rare moments when everything came together in unexpected ways.

A slight breeze moved through the bamboo hedge, shifting the shadows on the canvas. The air felt good on her skin, and she could feel it drying the sweat that had begun to collect between her breasts, under her arms. The unseasonable late-October warmth had tempted her outside. She knew she looked hardly decent, her belly and thighs barely squeezed into shorts, nothing on top but a sports bra. But no one ever came by, Josh was at school, and besides, she didn't care how she looked—all she cared about was the glorious, clear light, the sun on her back, the painting.

Josh. She frowned, losing her focus. He had stomped out of the house that morning in a foul mood, and when she tried to ask him if anything was bothering him, he just yelled "Nothing!" in that emphatic way that told her it was something. She suspected girlfriend trouble, or he'd been to visit Hal. He always came back in a bad mood after seeing Hal, but she still encouraged him to see his dad. They had spent a tense, awkward day together for her birthday. What had she been hoping for? That one day would make it all better, like some cheesy Hollywood movie? All it had done was highlight how fragmented they were. It had been as if everyone was just waiting for the day to end.

It was better, she thought, if she just didn't think about her family. Just live in the moment. Her heart was breaking for Josh. There was nothing she could do to reach him, to comfort him. He had changed. They'd lost the old easy playfulness, the bantering. The veil of his innocence had been violently torn away. In its place, he had put an impenetrable wall around himself. He was dutiful, responsible, anxious for her. But he wasn't there. The light had gone out of his eyes. She felt the loss of him as keenly as if he'd been kidnapped, stolen from her. Because in a way, he had.

She missed Hal, but she'd been missing him for years. And it was easier without him. She could live in her own rhythm, not have to tiptoe around his irritations about every little thing, his constant harping about the state of the world.

She was trying to let them go. For the first time in a long time, her every waking thought wasn't about them. It was about her, about her work. She squinted now at her painting, trying to discern whether there was too much shadow in the left-hand corner, when she heard a crash and curse come from the house, then the sliding glass doors opened and there stood Hal, gaping at her.

"Helen?"

"Yes?" She turned so that she was facing him, goose bumps of surprise prickling her skin.

Hal stepped outside onto the lawn. "What are you doing? And what are you wearing? My god, Josh was right. You and this place are just falling apart." He hesitated, then came toward her, his shoulders hunched, his finger waving at her wildly, his face red.

She felt her own shoulders tense. Felt the old hopeless feeling in the face of his rage, his inexplicable, take-no-prisoners anger. *Breathe,* she told herself.

And then the strangest thing happened.

She laughed. She couldn't help it, it just rose up from inside her involuntarily and burst out. He looked ridiculous.

Hal stopped short. "You are laughing at *me*?" His finger came at her again, then he jabbed it at his own head. "You are crazy. You are seriously losing it."

Helen wiped the sweat off her face and noticed that paint came off of it. She must look a mess. Hal hated messes.

"I guess we both look pretty ridiculous right now. Don't you think?"

It seemed for a moment he would stop and think about that,

but then he barreled on. "What if someone comes?" He looked anxiously at the next-door neighbor's house.

She laughed again. "Who? No one ever comes here. It's hot, and the sun feels good on my skin. Besides, I always make a mess when I'm painting, and it's easier to get paint off skin than clothes."

She turned back, considering the painting.

It was as if Hal saw the brush for the first time, then took in the painting.

"Jesus, Helen, the house is a mess. There are dirty dishes in the sink and laundry spilling out of the hamper, and it smells."

"Yes," she said languidly, "that's why I'm outside."

She hadn't meant to antagonize him, but she didn't mind that she had. He shook his head in disgust. She saw then that he, too, had lost weight, that he looked unshaven and haggard. She felt an urge to put her hand on his face, to kiss him, but she suppressed it. She dabbed her brush in the water, dried it slightly, then dabbed it in red paint.

"All the clocks are wrong, Helen. How can you keep track of time? You do still care about knowing the time, don't you?" He said this almost pleadingly.

She held up her wrist with the watch on it. "This still works." She shrugged, and continued painting. She was not going to get caught up in his welter. He stared at her in disbelief, then turned and stalked back into the house. She heard him moving around inside, noisily cleaning up dishes and vacuuming, and imagined him puffing and self-righteous. In the old days, she would have been ashamed, would have scurried in and apologized and cleaned and made a pot of fresh coffee so that he could critique her in comfort. *Let him clean,* she thought. *It is his mess, too.*

He came back out and sat down and watched her. She glanced at him, then refocused on her work. If he had something to say, let him. She wasn't going to stop and draw it out of him. Finally he said, "Why... why is Josh so angry with me?"

She turned to look at him then. *Why indeed?* she wanted to say, her own anger ignited now. *Because you so totally don't get him, because you've abandoned him and me, because in his worst hour of need you punished him? And since when do you care what I think?*

Instead, she carefully put her brush down. "Why don't you ask him?" she said slowly.

"I just thought you'd know. You two are so much alike, you understand him better." He fidgeted, looked nervously at the ground.

Why, he's afraid of Josh, Helen thought. *Afraid of his own son.*

She looked at him then, at the warm afternoon light modeling his high cheekbones, at his strong neck, his shoulders sloping forward dejectedly.

"I can't run interference for you, Hal," she said softly, and felt an old, piercing tenderness. "You and Josh are going to have to work this out on your own. I'm sorry." Against her will, her body yearned toward him.

Hal sat there, rubbing his chin, looking hard at her as if trying to penetrate into her mind, as if she were keeping something from him. Finally, pushing up wearily from the chair, he squinted at her work. She felt suddenly exposed, wanting him to both comment and to refrain from commenting.

"I reset all the clocks," he said with a sigh, not meeting her eyes. "Try not to let them run down."

Helen watched him walk away, and sat down, trembling. He'd upset her hard-won equilibrium. She tried to summon up her earlier contentment, but it was gone.

***

Hal unlocked the shop door, turned over the Closed sign, and shut the door behind him, leaning against it for a moment. It was a relief to be inside the cool shop, away from the sun and away from Helen. His shoulders ached, and he realized that he'd been holding his breath. How could she live like that? How could anyone? Apparently she got up when she wished, ate when she felt like it, and painted anytime at all. He realized with horror that probably he'd been what had stood between her and this chaotic life she was living.

He breathed in the familiar scent of Tung oil. The clocks created a velvet hum of ticking, and he looked with pleasure at them—the beautiful quartered oak grandfather clock, the walnut-and-maple Victorian gingerbread clock, the German cuckoo clock he'd found at an auction, the schoolhouse clock a dealer had brought in, and his favorite, the Seth Thomas regulator, its mahogany case gleaming. They were like old friends whose inner history and workings he knew intimately. They were more transparent to him than any living person.

He sat down at his bench and picked up the #89 movement

that he'd been overhauling. He peered at it, pushing the gears to try to find the problem. At first he couldn't find it, and then he saw that the mainspring was jamming. He looked around to see if he had a .017 mainspring somewhere to replace it. He found the last one, made a note to order more, then sat down to work. As he worked, the tightness in his shoulders lessened. His hands began to take over, tightening a gear here, loosening a screw there. It was detailed, delicate work, getting clocks to run precisely. People just didn't have enough respect anymore for clocks, for analog time. Hal had often thought the decline of civilization had begun with digital clocks. All the beauty, all the physicality, especially of the pendulum clocks, had been lost. Time had become the simple flip of a number on a screen.

Was there anything more comforting than the ticking of a clock, the slow majestic ringing of the hours? The sense of order imposed on the day as it unfurled? Let the rest of the world have their clock radios, their cheap plastic digital watches. Here in this shop, there would be order, the stately progression of hours marked properly by the singular tickings and strikings, each one as identifiable as birdsong.

Order. His thoughts drifted back to Helen and the mess he'd found at home. How could she have let things go like that? Every clock stopped or showing a different time. Now he saw why Josh had been worried about Helen. And yet she hadn't seemed the least upset—out there painting as if all were right with the world. Watching her from inside the house, he felt as if he were watching a stranger. He didn't recognize his Helen in her deep concentration, in the energetic gestures of brush to paint to canvas, or in her ludicrous getup. For a moment, he found himself grudgingly respecting her for her diligence. For a moment, she seemed wholly apart from him, someone he had no connection to.

Any respect, though, had been quickly replaced by rage as his eyes became accustomed to the dark kitchen and he saw dirty dishes on every surface. Rage he was much more at home with, and it gave him the energy to do something about the house. Not that Helen seemed the least grateful, or even upset by his anger.

He tried to focus on the regulator he was fixing. They thought he was against Josh, but that wasn't it. How easily they judged him. He just wanted Josh spared, that was all. Not to dither his youth away, then come to middle-age unmoored. He needed something substantial to go into—physics, engineering. Something with a future in it. He was good at math and science, why the hell couldn't he focus on what he was good at? Helen didn't see it, didn't see the shipwreck Josh was headed for. Didn't see how a man had to measure up in the world. And now she was next to useless, playing away with her paints. It was up to him now, to try to steer Josh in some way. To try to get him on track.

Hal finished fixing the gear and looked up, surprised to find that it had gotten dark. He made notes on what he did, tidied up his desk, and fished around for the unread *Horology Today*. Then he carefully turned off the lights and headed down to the Huddle House for his customary omelet.

He liked the routine at the Huddle House. His waitress knew what he wanted, just said "The same?" when he came in. He always sat in the same back corner, where he wouldn't be disturbed. And it was cheap.

Tonight someone was at his table, which caused in him a vague disturbance. He slid into the booth in front of it. There was a new waitress there, someone he didn't know. Well, it was destined to be a day of disappointments, he tried to tell himself philosophically, but he still felt itchy, as if he'd rolled in poison ivy.

He consoled himself with his new magazine. He'd finally succumbed to the ads for *Horology Today*, a pricey British journal, because they had a great deal for new American subscribers. He plunged into it greedily. Here was his own tribe. He knew no one locally who cared about clocks, and although he had some Internet colleagues, he wasn't really one to spend a lot of time chatting at the computer.

He thumbed to the table of contents and glanced at the offerings when one title caught his eye about skeleton clocks. Aha! Just what he hadn't been able to find in all his stacks of journals. He flipped it open and began reading.

For many years, skeleton clocks were largely shunned within the horological community. It was not until F.B. Royer-Collard published his Skeleton Clocks in 1969, to be later followed on by two books by Derek Roberts in 1987 and 1989 that collectors began to take notice of these masterpieces of the art of clock making. Today, they are much sought after, and those examples that have rare complications (special features or functions, such as calendars, moon phases or astronomical functions) or display extreme skills in the presentation of the frame, dial or wheelworks command premium prices, some into the six-figure range.

As with any other popular type of antique, one needs to guard against fakes. There are a great many modern copies of classic skele-

ton clocks coming currently from China, and there are a number of reputable firms who sell these as what they are: modern, low-priced and attractive decorative pieces. Over the years, the Chinese copies have become better, and unfortunately, unscrupulous resellers, especially within online venues like eBay, advertise these as antique. I've even seen some mainstream auctioneers who have "unknowingly" sold these as genuine antiques. Selling copies as authentic or antique is inexcusable as a careful look at the brass frames should show signs of the small casting flaws that were present in any cast frames made prior to the 1920s. Many good American reproductions were made in the early twenties and thirties when there was a renewed interest in these clocks; however, it is important nevertheless to make sure you do not mistake a good reproduction for an early 18thc clock.

On a side note, several early skeletons, including a small number based on the Royal Pavilion, Brighton, which may be safely attributed to Smiths of Clerkenwell, were reported missing from several great British houses in the years immediately following World War II. It has been speculated that these clocks were either traded for rations during the war or taken by unscrupulous soldiers during the chaos of war. The mystery remains intriguing, and horologists are always on the lookout for these clocks.

Hal's coffee grew cold at his elbow. *That woman's clock must be an early American reproduction*, he thought, trying to quell the excitement he felt stirring in his gut. There was no way one of the actual clocks would wash up here in this Southern backwater.

He shook his head to clear it. He had to be careful, not get carried away. He thought back to the clock, wished mightily that he still had it. That delicacy, that intricacy, the fineness of it. *That kind of thing doesn't end up at flea markets*, he thought.

Wherever those originals are, they are locked up in European great houses, in museums. He was sure of it. He knew this world. Still.

If that woman's clock was actually one of a small number of clocks produced by the Smiths of Clerkenwell, he'd be on the map. He wouldn't just be an obscure clock repairman in some Podunk town, he'd be recognized as a horologist. He imagined himself talking in London about his unlikely discovery, an article in *Horology Today* with him holding the clock, the clock spinning in all its golden glory. The leaden cloud he lived in lifted for a moment. Then it would all be worth it, all the years of failure. Then they'd see. All of them. And Helen would be sorry. And Josh would be proud.

He threw some bills on the table, opened the glass door, and stepped onto the busy street. He stopped at the corner, the magazine tucked under his arm. Tomorrow he'd do more research and probably find it was as he thought, a good reproduction. But tonight, looking up at the cloudless sky, tonight he believed anything was possible.

EIGHTEEN

Meg sat behind her desk. She didn't think she could move. It had been quite a day, even a worse day than usual. She had had to endure the visitation of one of the educators from the state superintendent's office—a tall, glamorous woman smelling of expensive perfume and aglitter with diamonds. She had been there to observe and to "remind" the faculty of the new state standards. Meg felt exactly like a grunt in the trenches—sweaty, covered with dirt, inarticulate—being visited by a general who never saw real action, someone puffed up with theory. She felt a resentment she did not, as a Quaker, approve of.

To top it off, she had needed desperately to go to the bathroom all day. Her aide had been sick, and with the visitation, there had been few chances. It was against the law to leave the kids alone; she had finally asked the secretary to come and watch them for a few minutes. She could feel herself getting a bladder infection—she felt feverish and sick and it hurt when she walked.

She made her way gingerly to the parking lot. She might have to call in sick tomorrow. The only thing propelling her toward her car was the promise of a hot pad and a prescription called in to the pharmacy. She reached for her cell phone and dialed her doctor. Blessedly, they knew her and would send in the prescription. As she drove home, she kept seeing the administrator's patronizing smile, her flashing diamonds. She gripped the wheel tighter, passed a truck meandering down the left lane, her foot heavy on the pedal. She'd like to see Ms. Diamonds try to last one week, one day, in her classroom. She wouldn't look so petal fresh at the end of it. *No Child Left Behind, my ass.* All those standards, the deadly curriculum, were designed for some fantasy child, not her children. She began to think of how she would tell David about Ms. Diamonds, of how he would relish the ironic details. But then she remembered where he was, what he was. She could still tell him, she thought defiantly. He was still there. He'd hear her even if he couldn't respond.

The doctors were now talking about David being in a vegetative state—they weren't sure how much more they could do for him. Meg felt certain that David was still there—sometimes he seemed to squeeze her hand, and she felt he heard her. His doctor said he could do little more than wait to see if David woke up. There was new research going on, the doctor said, and there was a center David could be sent to eventually, where they had had some success in reviving people, but it was too early for that now.

Waiting was not one of Meg's virtues. She was good at being proactive, at planning and doing. David used to tell her to "wait for the right time," a piece of philosophy he had gotten from a fortune cookie somewhere along the line, and which he loved to quote. But for Meg, the right time was always now.

It was never easy now, coming home to an empty house. Sometimes she'd forget David was gone, and still called out to him as she threw her keys on the front hall table. She had taken to leaving the radio on so there would be voices when she came in.

Today, she opened the door to a cacophony of sound. The radio was playing, and the phone rang shrilly. She needed to just turn the phone off and let the message machine take it, she thought. So many people called, oftentimes expecting her to simply replace David in their lives. She didn't speak much Spanish, but she spent many hours trying to direct clients to resources, all in Spanish.

The ringing stopped, then started again. *Oh, drat,* Meg thought, and then, *What if it's about David? What if he has woken up?* She ran across the living room and tackled the phone.

"Hello."

"Mrs. Tate? Mrs. Tate?"

She was about to tell him he had a wrong number, but then she remembered. The clock shop. That man.

"Yes?"

"This is Hal, from ClockWorks."

"Yes?" Meg found she was shaking.

"Well, I did some research on your clock..." He paused.

"Yes?" Meg heard the note of impatience in her voice.

"It's about your clock."

"My clock?"

"I stumbled across an article about clocks like yours. I, uh, thought you'd be interested. You see, there is some small, very small, possibility—"

Meg couldn't follow what he was saying. Impatient, she cut him short. "I am not that interested, really, Mr. Lovejoy, I believe I told you. I'm going to use it in my classroom—it's there already."

There was a long pause. Meg thought perhaps they'd been cut off, then he said, with a heavy sigh, "But... I told you, your clock is a delicate thing. In your classroom?"

"Yes."

"Ms. Tate, that is very fine of you. It's important—people have no sense of timekeeping these days, no respect for real clocks, it's all just little phosphorescent numbers flipping on a black background." Meg heard a deep intake of breath on the other end; he was really getting worked up. "But, ma'am, you might want to use another clock. Your clock, well, there is a very slight possibility that it is an original. If it is, it could fetch up to twenty-five thousand dollars. Maybe more. But the important thing is, it would be historical. It would be significant."

Meg sank down on the kitchen chair. This was surreal. She just didn't have the psychic space to take it in.

"Ms. Tate? Are you there?"

"Yes, I'm here." She paused. "Significant to whom?"

"To the world of horology. To, to history. You do care about history, don't you?"

"Mr. Lovejoy!"

"I'm sorry. I get excited about these things. I didn't mean to come at you like that. At least"—there was a long exhalation of breath—"at least you should get it insured."

"Well, yes, I suppose."

"And I want you to know I think it is terrific that you bring real analog clocks into your classroom."

"It has all those gears and things—it fascinates them."

"I'll bet you are a good teacher."

"I'm all right."

"I'm no good with kids myself. Well, I guess you saw that."

Meg felt exposed, as if he'd read her disapproval. "Please, Mr. Lovejoy…"

"No, it's true. I've totally screwed up things with my son. I don't know, I…" There was a long pause. Meg hoped he was done. "Well, anyway, you were there that day. And I want to apologize for that."

"These things happen."

She just wanted to get him off the phone. "Listen, thanks for calling me about my clock. I appreciate it. I, uh, I guess I'll get it insured. But I have to go now."

Again there was a long pause. "All right, then. Sorry to take up your time. Good-bye."

"Good-bye."

Meg's hand shook as she hung up the phone. What a strange, obsessive guy. She wondered if she should have ever brought that damn clock in to begin with. Curiosity kills the cat, indeed. She really didn't have the energy for the whole Valerie Tate charade tonight. She put on the kettle for ginger tea, scrounged some aspirin, and got into her pajamas. She was just pouring her tea when the phone rang again.

"Mrs. Tate?"

Meg stared at the phone. She had to get caller ID.

"Yes, Mr. Lovejoy?"

"So sorry to bother you again. Um, this is very awkward. I, well, I just couldn't forget the thing you said about my treating a clock like a child. That day. When you came into the shop. I don't know, it just sort of stuck in my head. Then this clock thing came up, and I thought…"

What was he on with? Meg thought, sipping her tea, fervently wishing she hadn't picked up the phone.

There was a sharp intake of breath. "Okay, here goes. I could really use some help with my kid. Could we meet sometime for coffee or something? I mean, I'm sorry if I'm intruding. I don't even know you." There was a long, expectant silence at the other end.

Stunned, Meg put down her tea, then said guardedly, "I honestly don't know if I can be of any help. I don't know either of you." She hoped this would put him off the scent. Did the man have any emotional intelligence? You can't suddenly ask a complete stranger to be your therapist.

"Oh, but that sort of makes it better, don't you think? You might have a fresh perspective. And you work with kids. I mean, you're a professional."

"But I'm not a therapist."

"That's another point in your favor, as far as I'm concerned. All that psych stuff, all that mumbo jumbo, pseudoscience. I need to talk to a real person."

Meg was about to protest, to set this Luddite straight, when she flashed on Josh's tear-streaked face that day in the shop. He had looked so raw, so vulnerable, so lost. *Oh, what the hell,* Meg thought, and she didn't know if it was pity or curiosity or her own loneliness and exhaustion or some combination of all of them that kept her on the phone, that found her agreeing to meet with him.

"Look, I'd be glad to listen. But there are no magic formulas. At least that's what they tell me."

There was an audible sigh. "When can we meet?"

"Well, as a matter of fact, I'm taking the day off tomorrow. How about we meet at nine a.m.—would that suit you?"

"Sure, that would be great. We don't open up till ten. There is a place near here, the Mayflower, do you know it?"

"That would be fine."

"Great. I'll see you there, and I'll bring the information about the clock. And thanks so much." He hung up.

Meg held on to the phone, the dial tone buzzing, then slowly replaced it in its cradle, regretting the meeting already. She saw again Josh's his pale, anguished face. But what could she do for him? For Hal? She doubted that whatever the trouble was between them could be ameliorated by a childless, discouraged elementary school teacher who had exchanged her righteous anger for a perverse and misplaced interest in the boy who put her beloved David in a state of limbo.

What could anyone do for anyone else, really, in the end? She'd gotten suckered in by her own wayward heart.

She'd meet Hal this once, and that would be the end of it.

***

Josh didn't quite know what to make of his mother lately. Some days she never got out of her bathrobe, never turned on the lights. Her voice would be tired and whiny, and her apathy and unwashed hair irritated him. Other times she'd be up, with music playing, sitting in a clean kitchen, sketching away madly, hardly noticing if he was there or not. That didn't irritate him so much as frighten him. There was almost an unnatural brightness to her then, as if she were wired, on something. She seemed alien to him then, untouchable.

He just wanted her to go back to being his mother. He missed her nagging him to pick up his clothes, and the way she always watched him eat her food with such pleasure, urging him to eat more. He missed the way she joked around when his friends came over, the way she fussed over them, too. It was as if she lived to be his mom, and it had made him dismissive and irritable then.

Now he was angry with her, something he'd never felt so strongly before. He'd been angry with Hal for a long time, it seemed, but he and Helen had gotten along. He kept tripping over his anger at her, being surprised by it. Now he wanted to shake her and yell at her to *get herself together!* Yet somewhere in the pit of his stomach, he felt her disintegration was his fault, so that his anger mixed with guilt and made him avoid her all the more.

Part of him wanted to tell her—his old, regular mom—that he'd seen Hal, and how awkward and weird it had been, but now he didn't know how to broach it. He didn't know how to talk to her anymore, and especially didn't know how to talk about Hal. It was weird, like they'd silently agreed to erase Hal altogether.

The other thing that made him feel weird was reading the papers, looking for updates on David Masters' condition. David was still in a coma. Josh didn't know what that meant. He read everything he could about comas. He learned that people sometimes came out of comas intact, sometimes stayed in them indefinitely until someone pulled the plug. Sometimes people just died. Sometimes they woke up and became like the kids Josh worked with, damaged, unable to communicate except through grunts.

Alive. David Masters was still alive. Josh reminded himself of this, especially after waking up, drenched in sweat from nightmares of Masters hitting the windshield or of him dying in the hospital. Sometimes in these dreams everyone in the town came after Josh with torches, ready to string him up, like a mob out of a spaghetti Western. But other times he dreamed of David Masters rising out of his bed, whole and intact. In these dreams David took Josh under his wing, saw something special in Josh. These dreams were thrilling, fast paced, momentous. Sometimes in these dreams, Josh learned that David Masters was his real dad.

He never told anyone about the dreams. He went to therapy every week and endured a well-meaning, nervous little man's invitations to reveal his inner life, but he didn't trust him. He did, however, like and trust his parole officer. Dale was a large African American man with a shaved head and a deep baritone. He and Josh had quickly sized each other up; Dale knew Josh wouldn't give him any trouble, Josh knew that Dale didn't care about his inner life as long as he checked in. Ironically, Dale probably knew more about his life now than anyone else did. Josh found himself telling Dale about Libby, about the kids at Good Shepherd, about his mom, about Hal. Maybe it was easy to talk to him because he never asked too many questions. He just sat there behind his desk, his black, muscular arms crossed, his gold chains draped around his massive neck, and simply regarded Josh. Dale was cool.

Tonight Josh was meeting Libby at the indie film festival downtown. They had seen each other almost every day since the day she picked him up at Good Shepherd. He caught himself feeling happy. Ever since Libby had come into his life, he wasn't as depressed. He had thrown his antidepressants down the drain. He didn't want to be like his mother, didn't want that glazed look in his eyes. When he was on the pills, he felt like his head was wrapped in cotton. Now he got down, but he got up, too. Mostly he could stand things because he was with Libby. He loved her mouth, her kisses, the way she curled up next to him, and how strong and protective he felt with her. It felt as if the two of them were in a bubble made of their future, the future they were heading to, the one only they could see. Their secret future gave him strength, buoyed him.

He took a shower, changed. He felt sorry for his mother, all alone in the house. He wished she had some friends. He felt like he was escaping while she was stuck there. He felt slightly guilty, yet he couldn't wait to get out. He wedged on his Nikes, bounded down the stairs, and listened for Helen. He almost didn't want to see her, was tempted to quietly leave. But he should check in, let her know what he was doing. He stood in the front hall, hesitating, then turned toward the kitchen. He sighed, felt all the lightness and anticipation leave him.

He heard the tea kettle go off, heard the rattle of cups. He gingerly pushed open the door, preparing himself for what he might find—a dark, dirty room, his mother still in her robe, her hair a tangle. Instead, he was shocked to see the lights on, that she had dressed and brushed her hair. She looked up from the sketchpad on her lap when she heard him, and smiled at him, a real smile.

"What ya doing, Mom?" Josh blushed, afraid she might guess his surprise at finding her seeming so sane.

"Drawing. You know, for my class."

"Oh, yeah. I forgot about that." He wandered over to her, glanced at the sketch of the teapot, a cup. "Hey, not bad. Anyway, got to go…" His voice trailed off. He didn't want her to ask what he was doing, didn't want to see the shadow of worry cross her eyes, didn't want to explain to her that she could trust him, and he didn't want to mention Libby. He found himself bouncing on his toes like Andy.

Helen leaned back, held the pencil up to the pot as if measuring something, then began sketching with quick, sure strokes.

"I thought you said you had to go," she finally said.

"Uh, yeah."

"So go." She looked up, and leaned over to kiss him. "Have a good time," she said, then turned back to her drawing.

It wasn't till Josh was halfway downtown that he realized his mother hadn't asked him where he was going.

The realization brought him to a standstill. It was the oddest feeling, as if a weight on his leg had been removed and yet he really didn't know how to walk without it. He was used to his mother fretting about him. Did it mean she didn't care? Or that finally, she was getting her own life together and he didn't have to worry about her anymore? Maybe she was going to be okay?

He contemplated the possibility. Maybe it was better that

Hal had left, after all. They could all have their separate lives, which they'd pretty much had before. They could stop pretending they were a family. Maybe it was the pretending that had worn everyone out, especially Helen. Now she could do her art thing, put her energy, such as it was, into that.

Still, it felt odd to think he wasn't at the center of her thoughts, that other things had supplanted him. He knew he should be glad, but he felt distinctly uncomfortable.

He pushed his way up the last hill. It was dusk, and the new streets lights glowed. He quickened his step, hearing now the music coming from the square, caught up in the ferment of smells from busy restaurants. He took in the shop windows, with their fanciful Halloween decorations, the wares of the street vendors, the bright faces of the people anticipating a night of fun. All thoughts of Helen melted away.

He saw Libby before she saw him. She had her profile to him, and he couldn't tell from that angle whether her expression was one of rapt attention or dismay. She leaned against the concrete fountain, hemmed in by a ring of people watching and listening to some entertainer. There was always some entertainer on the square, especially on weekend evenings, picking up loose change. Sometimes it was a kid on a guitar or a fiddle and a banjo, but often it was a violinist and a soprano or a percussionist and flutist, all serious musicians from the music school. Tonight's offering seemed to fall into no category he could think of—a drum, a harmonica maybe, then talking, laughter. He rose up on his toes to peer over shoulders and heads, and there was Scary Harry. Of course. He was the perfect entertainer for Halloween.

Harry was dressed like an old vaudeville act—spats and a

bowler hat, a loud tie and baggy jacket. A drum hung from a strap on his neck, and a harmonica was held in place by a wire. A tarnished brass trumpet languished at his side. His face was intelligent, feral almost, its features fine—a mobile mouth, aquiline nose. It was almost eerie now to see Libby's features—weathered and worn, but still hers—on the man's face.

He sought her face now in the crush, but she was obscured by the gathering crowd. Josh got closer, couldn't make out what Harry was saying, but picked up the acid tone. Harry was famous around town for his cynical, edgy political views, neither right nor left, just his. Josh had sometimes thought he had good things to say, but that his tone was over-the-top, self-serving, and outlandish. He shivered involuntarily. He was everything Libby had described and so much more. Poor Libby!

He spotted her again, and making his way over to her, tapped her shoulder. She started, spun her head around. There was something almost fierce in her expression, a kind a fury and wariness. But she smiled when she realized it was him, and shrugged.

"Let's get out of here," he whispered, leaning down to her and taking her hand.

She hesitated, looking back over her shoulder at Harry.

"Come on, don't subject yourself to this." He tugged on her hand.

"He's got the kids with him," she whispered. "Look, that's what I used to do." And then he saw them, two little waifs about eight, scurrying around with hats, collecting money.

Harry blew a riff on the trumpet, followed it with a loud drumbeat.

"Okay, all you yahoos out there, now that I've got your

attention, who can tell me the difference between Dick Cheney and Beelzebub?" There were laughs, murmurs, an angry shout, boos, and several muffled answers Josh couldn't make out, with Harry's retort—"No, but nice try. The difference between Dick Cheney and Beelzebub is that when the devil swipes your soul, you get to name your terms. With DC and company, you don't even notice that your soul has been swiped until it is all gone, and just look at the lot of you zombies." Another drumbeat, scattered applause, a few more boos.

"Come on, Libby, the kids will be okay. Let's get out of here. He's making my skin crawl."

Libby shrugged, but didn't move.

"Soulless, that's what we've become." Harry's voice was rising in a frenzied pitch. "No better than fodder for corporations. Everyone out for himself. No loyalty. Take my daughter over there, yes, there"—he pointed, and the crowd opened—"hiding from her old dad, her brother and sister. Too good for her old man now." He holds his nose, prances like a dandy. Some nervous laughter, people drifting away. Josh looked down at Libby. She was frozen to the spot, her face flaming.

"Ladies and gents, an ungrateful child is sharper than a serpent's tooth." And his eyes bore into Libby, exposed now in the thinning crowd.

Josh grabbed Libby's upper arm, put his other hand against the small of her back, and propelled her forcefully away, out of the park. They escaped onto Main Street, then down a few side streets, neither of them saying a word. Josh guided them into Jumpy Joe's, a small, dimly lit coffee shop. Libby wiped tears away with the back of her hand while Josh steered her toward an empty couch.

"Why does he do that?" Libby asked after they were settled. Her nose was red, her eyes swollen. "He'll be fine, and then, he just goes off. No warning. He was so nice this afternoon—I almost believed it. For a while, I believed he was okay, himself again. What a fool!"

Josh gazed helplessly at her wrecked face. He couldn't think of anything to say. He patted her arm awkwardly. He got up and got two coffees, and handed her one.

She wiped her face again and blew her nose into the napkin, looking away. Then he blurted out, without really thinking about it, "My old man's a dick, but nothing like yours." As soon as the words were out of his mouth, he regretted them, would have stuffed them back in if he could have.

Libby raised her head up. "I told you, didn't I? Sometimes when I tell people, even when I try to be really accurate, I think, no way, he can't really be that bad, but then something like this happens. Jeez." She let out a heavy sigh. "I'm glad at least that you get it."

Josh was relieved that he'd said the right thing—he was never sure what the right thing was with Libby. She sipped her coffee and gradually came out of her funk, began to look less pale, to talk more. He put his arm around her. They decided to skip the film festival—Libby was afraid that people would spot her, laugh at her.

Later, walking out into the night, the air grown sharp, Libby huddled into Josh. He liked the way her body felt next to his, warm, supple. "Don't go home, Libby. Stay with me. My mom won't know. You won't have to see him."

"Oh, Josh." She turned into him, kissing him hungrily. He wanted her so much, wanted to protect her, to take care of her. "If you knew how I wanted that, but—"

"No buts." Josh stroked her hair. "No buts."

"When he gets like this—the kids. He could hurt them. He could hurt her. There's nobody else, Josh. There's nobody else between him and them."

"Jesus!" Josh slammed his hand against the wall behind her. "I should go over there and punch him out, something. He needs to be put away."

"Shh, no, shh, don't talk like that. You're already on probation. Josh, listen, I'll be okay. I can call nine-one-one. He's a coward. He may bully me in a crowd, but not alone. I'll be all right. Okay? You'd only make it worse, believe me. He loves an audience."

Josh knew she was right, but still didn't want to let her go.

"You need a lift home?" She was suddenly in charge, dispassionate.

"No, I need to walk. Walk it off. Go on."

She hesitated, then left, going toward the parking garage. He watched her go, suddenly tired and defeated. What good was he to her? Then he turned and headed down the hill, back to his house where he was no longer at home.

NINETEEN

Meg circled the block several times before she finally found a parking place. It had been years since she'd been to the Mayflower, and she was surprised that it was still there, the same faded gold lettering on the grimy window. She parked a block away and walked slowly to the old eatery, feeling a strange mixture of elation at being out of school and yet apprehension at meeting Hal. She had decided that day in the shop that she really didn't like him, and she had determined that she would get her clock and that would be then end of it. Now her duplicity had come back to haunt her.

Meg passed the newsstand and browsed the magazines, biding her time. She picked up the local newspaper and looked at the headlines. There was a picture of Garnett Ridge and a painting of Our Lady of Guadalupe that had been painted on the side of a duplex. The headline read "Another Gang Shooting Rattles Neighborhood." Meg shivered; she had several students from Garnett Ridge, and she knew chances were good that they would end up in gangs. That was what happened when people were rendered invisible and powerless, David would say. He'd have hope and a plan, but all she felt was the relentless bearing down of large, impersonal forces. So many of her kids' lives were already compromised.

Meg put down the paper and rounded the corner to the Mayflower. The smell of frying bacon and coffee assailed her as she opened the door. Inside, it was dark and cozy, with a cheerful cacophony of clinking silver and lively chatter, the waitress skimming through with her coffee pot, bantering with the regulars.

Meg stood in the doorway, suddenly frozen. This was the kind of place she and David always frequented on vacations, indulging in long leisurely breakfasts with sinfully rich omelets and hash browns.

"Ms. Tate?" Meg blinked, forgetting as always her assumed name. Hal stood in front of her—he must have been watching for her. He loomed over her, his shoulders hunched. She noticed how thin and pale he was, his face etched with anxiety.

"Yes. Hi." She put out her hand to him, not knowing what else to do.

He shook her hand and led her over to a booth. The waitress came by, and they ordered coffee and looked at menus silently for a long, awkward time.

"Thanks for coming," he said at last.

Meg looked up from her menu. "You're welcome."

They ordered, then sat in awkward silence, neither of them knowing what to say. Hal played with the salt and pepper shakers, moving them like pawns in an invisible chess game. He said, finally, as if he had rehearsed a speech, "My son is a good kid, he really is. He's gotten into some trouble lately, though, and I can't seem to get through to him. He's always angry." He paused, as if unsure how to go on. "I know it is strange to talk to a stranger about all this, but I don't know who else to talk to."

You could try your wife, Meg thought, irritated.

"Lots of kids his age are angry."

Hal swept away the salt and pepper shakers, knocking them over. "Yeah, but he never used to be." He looked out the window and sighed. "Everything was going along fine, you know, just going along. I thought we had a pretty good life, a pretty good family. I mean, lately, we've had some trouble communicating. But the usual stuff. I thought we were reasonably happy. Not TV happy, just ordinary. Josh was my world."

Meg felt a mean streak niggle at her, prompting her. "And then?" She steeled herself for what was coming.

Hal really looked at her then. She saw his eyes empty, his long face grow slack.

"He did this really stupid thing." Hal's fist was on the table, white knuckled. Meg started, afraid he was going to hit the table. "He got in with the wrong crowd, fancied himself an artist. Those crazy kids. He smoked some dope and hit this guy—you probably saw it in the paper—Masters. He was jogging late at night. He's some sort of local hero. I don't know. I don't keep up with all this community stuff. I have a shop to run. Figures Josh would hit someone like that. Now we're all waiting to see if the guy will pull out or not."

Meg's mean streak was getting wider. She wanted to make him say it, feel it. "Pull out of what?"

Hal looked startled. "Out of a coma. We're waiting to find out if Josh is a murderer."

For a minute, the room began to swing around Meg. She thought she should go outside, get some fresh air, run away. She gripped the underside of the table to steady herself.

"Here y'all are—one Western omelet and one two-egg scramble. Cranberry juice for the missus, orange juice for the gentleman." The waitress stood back and admired her handiwork. "It's so nice to see couples coming out for breakfast. Law, most of these men here just grunt and read the newspaper. Well, y'all enjoy."

Before Meg could stutter out a correction, the waitress had turned on her heel and was off.

Hal looked down at his omelet. "That was embarrassing," he muttered.

"Well, it's an understandable mistake. Anyway, you were saying—about your son? It's a very sad story. I'm sorry. Your son must be going through a terrible time." She was taking refuge in her professional role now, the only way to stay in one piece. And she meant it, did he see how hard this was for Josh?

Hal stared at her. "I'm trying to get him to understand that he has to take responsibility for his actions. My wife, she always coddles him, everything he wants to do is great by her. She encouraged him to do this filmmaking business. It's just a distraction. He's wasting time. Sooner or later he has to deal with the real world."

Meg said, as gently as she could, "It sounds like he's having to do that now."

Hal rubbed his chin. "Yeah, I guess. He's doing some community work. Except now, it seems he's just angry. Always defending his friends, still hanging on to this idea of becoming a filmmaker. As if that is something you can do and still put food on the table. It's crazy! Better he get straight with reality now before he wastes too much time." Hal looked glumly off into the distance. "On top of it all, he seems to blame me for everything that has gone wrong," he said, plaintively.

Meg turned over a forkful of egg on her plate. Her dislike of Hal surfaced again, expanded. No wonder the kid was angry. But she could see that Hal was really at a loss. What did he want from her? Absolution? Validation?

"You know, what I tell my parents who are having problems with their kids is first of all you need to just spend time together having fun. Not talking about the problems, but just hanging out. Not parenting. You know, like you said, you once were very close to your son. What did you do then?"

Hal's face lightened. "Well, we made things, you know. Model airplanes. We played a lot of games. We went camping. Fishing."

"Well, why not go camping now? Or fishing?"

Hal shrugged. "He won't do it. He can hardly stand to be in the same room with me."

Meg felt drained and needed, suddenly, badly to leave. "Well, it might be worth a try. I guess that's about all I can offer you in the way of advice. Look, I need to be getting home. I'm sorry if I haven't been a lot of help."

Hal lost his preoccupied look and stood up. "Oh, no, no. You've been a lot of help. Thank you. Thank you so much. You know, you just had such a kind face, when you came into the shop, I thought, that's someone I could talk to. And then you said you were a teacher—" He groped for her hand and squeezed it. "Thank you. Can I let you know how it goes? With Josh, I mean?"

Meg hesitated. "Yes, of course. I wish you all the best." She grabbed her coat and fled outside. Her heart beat fast, and she felt as if she couldn't get a breath. Waiting to find out if Josh was a murderer. What a thing to say.

***

Josh glanced around nervously—he didn't want anyone to see him waiting for his father. But no one seemed to notice him—not the kids eating out on the picnic tables, not the kids smoking on the front steps. He leaned against the warm brick wall, trying to breathe. A flock of black starlings alight on the bare oak branches. It all was so ordinary, and yet it seemed surreal.

Josh still couldn't figure out what Hal wanted with him, but whatever it was, it couldn't be good. Hal's voice over the phone last night had made Josh jump. It was well-known that Hal never talked on the phone unless forced to.

"Son, how 'bout we go out for lunch tomorrow?"

The oddness of the request had taken Josh by surprise. Lunch? With his father? Why? There was some reason, some undisclosed agenda.

"Well, okay, I guess. Why?"

There was a pause on Hal's end. "Well, look, I just want to spend some time with you."

Time? Spend? Who had Hal been talking to? Josh was surprised he didn't say "quality time." It all sounded so phony.

"I'll pick you up at twelve at school."

"I don't get lunch period till twelve forty-five."

"Okay then, twelve forty-five." There was an abrupt click. *That* Josh expected—not "good-bye" or "see you, buddy." No, just business. In a way it was more comforting than this other Hal who wanted to "spend time."

There had been enough time between last night and this noon for Josh to grow increasingly suspicious and uncomfortable. He was sure there was a lecture on the way—whatever it was, it wouldn't be good. He shifted his weight impatiently to his other foot. He wished Hal would get there so they could get this over with.

Hal's old dented truck pulled up to the curb in front of Josh. Josh thought with fleeting despair that he wished his dad had a newer, nicer car. He pushed hard with his foot off the wall, picked up his book bag, and swung it into the backseat, then climbed in the front, slamming the door behind him.

"Planning on doing homework during lunch?" Hal smirked.

His idea of a lame joke, Josh thought, buckling himself in. "No, Dad, it's just easier than climbing up to the fourth floor lockers."

"Not much point in paying locker fees, then, I guess."

What was the point of trying to get Hal to understand anything about his life? Josh looked out the window and willed himself somewhere else—anywhere.

"Guess not," he muttered. As usual, Hal was concentrating on minutiae, on how much things cost, on what Josh did wrong. Oh, it was going to be a fun lunch.

Hal pulled into the Grill's parking lot. He drove in an irritatingly slow and deliberate way, as if it took all his concentration, staring straight ahead. His profile looked to Josh as if it were carved in stone. Impenetrable. *My dad belongs on Mt. Rushmore,* he thought.

Hal found a parking space, eased into it slowly, and shut off the engine. Josh hopped out of the car, got to the door, and went in without waiting for Hal. Inside, the place was crowded, almost all its red booths full. A girl he knew from yearbook two years ago was serving tables, and Josh turned away from her, suddenly intent on counting the yellow gumballs in the gumball dispenser. Behind him, his father talked with the hostess, who led them over to a booth by the plate glass windows. Josh tried to hide his face between his hunched shoulders.

Thankfully, they got another waitress, not the girl Josh knew. After they ordered, Hal began the interview.

"So, you going out for drama club this year?"

Josh watched Hal's fingers arrange and rearrange his silverware into patterns, but he didn't raise his eyes to his father's face. "Like I have time!" he sniffed. A jet of anger burned him. What was Hal thinking? Didn't he know how Good Shepherd took up all his time? Were they not going to talk about *it*? Were they just going to pretend they were normal?

Hal didn't say anything. Josh noticed his father's fingernails were smudged with grease. His forefinger pressed on a fork, making it jump. He wasn't going to make this easy for Hal.

Hal finally spoke. "Mom says you've got a girlfriend these days—that's the rumor, anyway, since Mom's never laid eyes on her."

It may have been meant as a joke, but it sounded like the same old stuff his dad always spouted. So, he was being criticized for not bringing Libby home? Home to what? A half-crazy mother and roaches crawling over dirty dishes? God only knew what mood Helen would be in, what weird painting she would have set up in the living room. Josh felt like punching something.

Thankfully, their orders came.

"Son, I asked you a question." Hal was staring at him. Josh could read no expression in those eyes.

Josh held his father's gaze. "What home? It's more like a pit stop these days." He didn't have to add—"since you left." He could see he'd finally penetrated Hal's controlling exterior, saw a flicker of anxiety in his eyes. *Good*, Josh thought. *Let him suffer a little for once.*

"Well, anyway," Hal said, contemplating a French fry, not really looking at Josh, "I'm glad you've got a girlfriend. It's good." Josh watched Hal eat the French fry, waiting for the qualifier, but none came. It jolted Josh, this awkward positivity. What did it mean?

"Do you remember that girl you had a crush on in fourth grade? What was her name? Linda? Louise? That cute little brunette kid?"

"Lindy." How did his dad remember crap like that? A memory, of walking home with his dad after school, telling his dad about Lindy, their shoes crunching on acorns, Josh pouring out his heart to his dad and Hal listening. There was the wrought iron fence he'd dragged a stick across every morning and every afternoon, the satisfying sensation it gave him. Josh felt himself begin to soften, remembering those long walks home, how the two of them seemed so in sync.

"You were crazy about that kid. I think I remember she

spurned you, and you were inconsolable. That's when we joined Indian Guides, to kind of take your mind off things."

"I never put that together," Josh said, feeling deflated. He was having a hard time with this trot down memory lane. It felt unfair, somehow, as if Hal were taking advantage. *That's not the issue!* he wanted to scream. *The issue is now. Don't invoke the past to make up for your colossal betrayals.* He steeled himself against his father's voice.

Hal was warming to his memories now, he was actually becoming animated. "Then there was the time we lost the trail, do you remember…"

Josh shook his head. "Dad, I've got to get back to school. I really can't be late." He was already sliding out of the booth, shrugging his shoulders into his backpack. He pushed through the glass doors and leaned against his dad's car, taking deep breaths, trying to steady himself. What was the use? It always ended this way, Josh always felt worse when he saw his dad, not better.

Hal hurried over to the car, unlocked the passenger side, and put his arm briefly around Josh. "We'll have to do this again, son. Keep up with each other a bit more."

Josh got in the car, muttering something noncommittal. He would do everything in his power to avoid that.

TWENTY

"Ah, Eros," Olaffson said one evening after class. Helen flushed to the roots of her hair. Everyone else had left. Helen had stayed late, unable to leave her painting. "I'm sorry," she said to Olaffson, "What?"

"Oh, nothing. Sorry to interrupt. Take your time," he had said. Now he regarded the painting thoughtfully. "Good, good," he said, finally, chomping down on his pipe.

"But it isn't what I intended, Andrew. I had a very clear picture of what I wanted, and then this crops up." She shook her hand derisively at the nude redheaded woman with the heavy breasts, right in the middle of a garage full of paint cans, old furniture, and rusty bikes. "She just appeared, and what is she doing there anyway? It's cold in there!"

She tried to laugh away her nervousness. The truth was, when she painted, she was often more aroused than she had been for years with Hal. And Olaffson, with his constant odor of turpentine and tobacco, elicited the same response. She was afraid he'd know that. He seemed to know everything about her.

He was looking at her with his large blue eyes. "That is what painting is. It's discovery. You start with one idea, but something mysterious enters. That's the way it's supposed to be."

"It's a little scary."

"That's true. You aren't painting if it isn't a little scary." He stood back from the painting, squinted his eyes.

"Do you think it's done?" he asked.

She looked at it carefully. "I don't know. I don't know where to go with it, but I don't know if I'm ready to leave it, either."

"Then maybe it isn't done. Maybe you should leave it a while, and come back to it with fresh eyes." He turned to her, and gently reached out and tucked a strand of hair behind her ear. "You often hide behind your hair. What is it you are afraid of?"

Helen caught her breath. She was aware of the ticking wall clock. Through the plate glass windows, it was twilight, and the day was finally succumbing to night, the hills and warehouses washed in violet. A crescent moon shone faintly in the sky, and Venus.

Finally, she looked up at him. "I don't know," she whispered.

"What in this painting bothers you?" He turned again to the painting, contemplating it.

She looked at the painting, at the redheaded woman who looked back at her with such sadness, at the woman's yearning, fleshy body, so alive amidst the detritus of suburban life.

"She's sad. And it is as if she's not living in the main house, but in a place where all the old junk is."

"And look," he gestured with his pipe. "All the junk is in grays, purples, blues, but she is pink and peach. Look at the voluptuousness of her, yet as you say, the sadness of the eyes. There is a contrast there that is intriguing."

"It embarrasses me to make her so, so naked."

"Yes, she's naked in every way, not just her body. Her soul, too. But does it embarrass you at the time you are painting, or afterward?"

"Afterward, really."

"Good. So, why do you think it embarrasses you now?"

Helen felt herself flushing. "Because I don't think of myself as having that in me—it frightens me."

"That's what we are all afraid of," he said, "all the parts of ourselves we've stowed away in the basement, in the garage."

Despite the soft ticking, Helen felt time stop. Her terror melted away, and a spaciousness opened around her. What he said was true. It didn't seem so frightening now. Suddenly, she felt she could not live without him, that if he left her, she would die.

"But," she continued in a whisper, "your paintings are so calm, so open. Mine are so fraught."

"I've had my fraught periods. I'm in a good place now. You will get there. But there is no substitute. You can't skip it. You have to go through it. I'm sorry."

A cool breeze came through the open window. She closed her eyes, and when she opened them, she was leaning into him, noticing the tufts of gray hair sprouting behind his T-shirt, the day's growth of his beard. Their lips met, and his arm came around her for a moment and pressed her to him briefly, before pushing her away.

"I'm sorry." She held her hand up to her mouth. Her legs felt as if they might give way.

He was looking at her intently, but she couldn't read his expression.

"Helen, you're not in love with me—"

"You could have fooled me." She turned, busied herself with organizing her paints. Her hands were shaking now with anger, not shame. She wanted to say, *Oh, yeah, what about Eros, buster? Did I call your bluff?*

"Who am I in love with, then?"

"With yourself."

He leaned over and kissed her fleetingly, chastely, on the forehead, and left, his sneakers squeaking on the tile floor. She listened until it was silent, then began violently washing her brushes, cursing Olaffson and all men.

***

Josh held Libby's hand on his knee and stroked it tenderly. The faces of Anthony Quinn and Giulietta Masina flickered across the screen. Libby had wanted him to see *La Strada*, one of her favorite movies, but he was having trouble taking it in.

He'd been alarmed when he met Libby outside Flicker and saw her red eyes and her pale face, yet she had refused to explain, saying she didn't want to miss the movie.

In the blue light from the screen, Josh searched Libby's face for clues. Her face mirrored Giulietta Masina's sad childlike clown face: When Giulietta smiled, Libby smiled. When she was despondent, Libby's eyes drooped. Tears slipped down Libby's cheek as Anthony Quinn once more deserted the little waif. But the haunting music with its spare, insistent trumpet notes was getting increasingly on his nerves. Josh wanted to enter into the movie as Libby did, but all he could think of was what had upset Libby. He was impatient for the movie to end, to find out. When she was like this, he felt so distanced from her, and it frightened him. Without her, he would be in free fall.

Finally, the lights came on. Libby gave him a weak smile and blew her nose into a Kleenex. She pulled out her compact and cringed at her reflection. "I look awful," she said, wiping her glasses on her shirt before putting them back on. With a firm push to the bridge of her glasses, she sighed. "Well, come on, let's get out of here. I just want to go somewhere where no one will see us."

He put his arm around her and pulled her close to him. Her hip jutted into his thigh, her head barely cleared his armpit. He bent down and smelled her lemony hair. She put her arm around his waist, holding him tightly, so that as they left the theater, they walked with the gait of three-legged racers.

They passed through the outer lobby. The scent of slightly rancid popcorn hung in the air. On the walls were posters of old classics and new indies; at the tables were, thankfully, only a few unknown people, all declaring their fraternity in the avant-garde with their flea market clothes and piercings. Libby burrowed into Josh, letting him lead her outside.

It had been raining, a cold, bitter rain. It was just dusk. They walked through the moist air laden with the odor of French fries and pizza, not speaking, for a block. People passed them in clusters, talking excitedly, students laughing. Josh was happy just to be holding Libby. He hated that she was upset, but he liked how yielding she was, how much she seemed to need him. He felt he would do anything to make her happy then, slay any dragon that was besetting her. He felt manly, protective.

Then Libby pulled away, pushing her hair from her face. "Okay," she began, as if answering a question, "you know how I told you that we were staying with my grandmother?"

Josh nodded, afraid to say anything that would make her stop talking.

"Well, I guess I could have predicted this. My dad got into this real big fight with Gram, and well, so she's kicked us out."

Josh felt as if someone had kicked him in the stomach. "What do you mean, kicked you out? You can't kick out relatives."

"Yeah, well, you can, actually."

"But why?"

Libby wheeled around to face him. "Because we're freaks, that's why," she shouted. Josh was aware of people passing by, of curious glances over shoulders.

Josh put his hand on her shoulder, to quiet her. She shook him off.

"You're not a freak," he said.

"Oh, but I am. The apple doesn't fall far from the tree."

"Your grandmother must be a bitch."

Libby looked at him with an expression of total defeat and sighed. "No, she's not. She's just... normal. She just expects us to pay our bills. She doesn't understand that artistes are exempt from all that." Her voice was bitter.

"What about your mom?"

"She huddles in the back room and cries while they fight."

A pain started in Josh's stomach, like a small rodent gnawing there.

"Look, Libby, you said you were going to leave. Maybe now is the time." His thoughts rushed ahead, to him and Libby living together, away, far away from here, pursuing their own art, unimpeded by their families.

"It's not so easy, Josh. I still have my little brother and sister to think about, and with Mom the way she is, I'm not sure she can take care of them."

Josh stared at her, openmouthed. Where was the fiery, passionate Libby, bound and determined to get away?

"You're right," he said, "I don't have brothers and sisters. I don't know what that's like." He paused, leaned his hand on the rough brick building for support. "But"—he groped for words—"but you don't want to end up like your mom. You've got to get away sometime."

Libby shook her head, letting her hair cover her face. "I knew you would say that."

"You could stay at our house. My mom would love someone to take care of." Although as soon as he said it, he regretted it. He was referring to the old version of Helen, his real mom.

Pulling her hair over her shoulder, Libby tilted her face up to him. "I know you mean that, Josh. You are so good. But I can't. I'm afraid of what might happen to them if I'm not around, see? I told you, I can handle my dad, but no one else can."

The rodent in Josh's gut became a crocodile, eating him from the inside.

"What are you going to do, then?" he asked hoarsely.

"I'm going with them, Josh. We'll go back to New York. I came to say good-bye tonight."

The crocodile broke through. Josh hit his fist against the wall, letting the rough bricks tear at his skin. "No, no, no!" he bellowed.

Libby let him yell, watched him with a resigned passivity.

Finally, he turned to her. "I thought we... well, I guess our relationship means more to me than to you."

"No, Josh, no. How can you say that? It's, just, now, I have to go. It doesn't mean I won't come back. Or that we can't text and stuff."

Josh rolled his eyes. "Great. Text."

Libby stepped closer to Josh. "Hold me, Josh."

He put his arms around her and felt her struggling not to cry. It dawned on him that he really didn't know that much about her life, that he had always seen her only in relation to him, as if she dematerialized when she was away from him. And now she was leaving, and taking all that unknown life with her, so that now he felt doubly bereft—of the Libby he knew and the Libby he didn't know.

She sighed and pulled away. "Walk me to my car, okay? And here, I wrote down all my information for you—I'll keep my email address, so you can always get me there. This is the school. I'll have an email account there. I don't know how long I'll be able to pay for my phone."

Josh looked down at the paper. The snail mail was a motel address.

"We always go there, till we find other digs." Her mouth pursed in an expression of disgust. "It's not so great, but it's cheap."

They walked apart now. When they got to her car, Josh opened the door for her. He felt stiff and self-conscious, as if this were their first date, not their last. She hesitated, then kissed him gently, cupping his face in her hands. "I'm worried about you, Josh. Are you going to be okay? I mean, with your folks and all." She seemed so grown-up, and her concern seemed almost professional. As if she had morphed from his Libby already, morphed into someone he hardly knew.

He felt his eyes blurring with tears. No, he was not going to be all right. He was in free fall again.

TWENTY-ONE

Josh threw his backpack into the corner and threw himself on the bed. On his computer screen wallpaper, a picture of Libby gazed serenely back at him. The picture had been taken under a tree at Good Shepherd, and Libby was backlit, her hair diffused with light. Her eyes had that dreamy look she had without her glasses, and her mouth curved as if she were about to laugh at him, which was probably what had happened.

Josh had texted or emailed Libby almost daily. Her phone was spotty, depending on whether the bill had been paid. She emailed less often—between school and work and her family, it seemed she didn't have time. When she did write, it was so descriptive that he felt as if he were with her in New York. The apartment sounded seedy, with a showerhead that merely trickled water and mold growing in the bathroom. She slept on a pullout couch, her parents and the younger kids had the two bedrooms. Her father had gotten a job on a soap, and the kids were already doing ads and making pretty good money.

She almost never mentioned her mother; it was as if Libby wanted to forget about her. Did her mother scrub the mold, make supper? Or just languish in her bed, cowering, waiting for the next blow? He thought sometimes that as much as Libby complained about her father, he still was the force that held the family together. Or Libby was. Or the two of them together. It depressed Josh to think of her parents, to think of his. He and Libby would be better parents, they'd have to be.

Her father had gotten her a transfer to the Professional Performing Arts High School. She worked at night in a deli on Broadway. She described the old-timers who went there; she had actually spotted Alan Alda, but didn't get to wait on him. She said she didn't mind waiting tables; it was exercise and almost a sport, because you couldn't lose concentration. "Everything here is so fast," she said. "It makes me feel alive."

Josh was racked with jealousy. He imagined all the sophisticated guys she was meeting, actors and directors. He imagined them ogling her as she leaned over to serve a plate of pastrami on rye. She assured him that most of them were gay, and she would never get involved with someone in the "business." She said she was so sick of the business, and yet, Josh knew, it was in her blood. She was as ambitious as anyone he had ever met. Despite all her assurances, all her protestations to the contrary, Josh couldn't shake the feeling she really enjoyed being there, in the thick of things.

He turned over and punched the pillow, burying his face in it.

When he wasn't emailing Libby, Josh continued researching David Masters. He read articles in the local paper about how Masters had championed the cause of a group of African-Americans with an unusually high rate of cancer, managing to get a federal investigation of the cluster. Another series of articles showed his tireless efforts to expose a local paper plant's noncompliance with federal emission standards. Masters had also been one of the movers in creating the East Park Community Center, which had become a model for low-income neighborhood centers.

Accompanying the articles were pictures of David Masters—often grinning, his round face animated. He often seemed caught in movement, so that his features were never quite clear to Josh. Josh couldn't help thinking of how different Masters was from his own father. When Josh thought of Hal, he thought of him with his jeweler's loupe, hunched over a recalcitrant gear. His dad, hiding away in his shop, was a nobody, Josh realized. Hal wasn't a man that accomplished things in the real world, Josh thought with a mixture of pity and bitterness.

When he thought about his father, Josh always got a headache. He didn't know how to be with him. He almost preferred their old pattern of fighting over Hal's recent awkward attempts at some form of relationship. He felt guilty now for having been so resistant to Hal's luncheon overture, but he hadn't known how else to be.

He heard his mother moving around in the kitchen. It didn't necessarily mean she was going to cook supper, he knew from experience. The other night he had gone into the kitchen only to find her staring at her face in the mirror, drawing a self-portrait. When he'd asked if they were going to have supper, she waved toward the pantry. "I think there is a can of beans in there, maybe some hotdogs in the fridge," she said, never taking her eyes off the mirror. It was spooky. Since his license was suspended, he couldn't go shopping and had been reduced to eating grilled cheese most nights or eating at Good Shepherd. He had thought he hated the way Helen used to fuss over what he ate, but now he would have been delighted to put up with any amount of fussing for a square meal. He figured his Thanksgiving would be spent with Marbry and Marius. Anything would be better than being home for the holiday.

Josh sat up, looked out the window, where the sky had become gray and cloudy. He thought about doing his homework, but it didn't seem worth the effort, somehow. He checked his email, but there was nothing from Libby, and he had written her a long email yesterday. He thought about going into the kitchen and talking to his mom, maybe cooking something for both of them. He never knew exactly who Helen would be on any given day—depressed, distractedly painting, or his old mom, the one that treated him like he hung the moon and never ate enough. Exhausted at the prospect of trying to talk with Helen, he kicked off his shoes, and without changing, he turned off the lights. The hot, stuffy air of his room sat on his chest like a cat. "Something," he whispered into the dark, "something has to change."

***

Would she ever get used to this alias? Meg, as always, was taken aback when Hal asked for Valerie Tate. *I need to give this charade up,* she thought. Then she thought of Josh, the same image that always came to her mind, of him standing over David, his eyes staring in disbelief, of his father yelling at him.

"Yes?" she said.

"Hi, Hal here. I just wanted to report that I did what you suggested."

"Oh?"

"Yeah. I took my kid out to lunch."

"How did that go?"

"Well, ya know, not too bad." There was a pause. "Not great, but it was start, anyway. It's so hard to talk to him. I mean, it was awkward. I'm not very good at communicating."

"But you made the effort. I know it is hard, but even if they don't act like it, kids are happy to get the attention."

"Yeah, well, if you say so. Okay, gotta go, got a customer—oh, hey, thanks a lot."

He hung up before Meg could say, "You're welcome."

Meg hung up the phone with a sigh. Why was her every encounter with this man so frustrating? She was going to have to come clean or at least discourage him, that was for sure. She wondered how Josh really was, how he was with his mother. She wanted to ask Hal if he thought Josh was in any kind of trouble or depression—but that would entail getting in deeper with Hal. Poor Hal, so clueless. She wondered if she were actually making things worse.

It was Saturday, and the empty hours lay before her, a desert of loneliness she had to traverse. During the week, her job kept her so busy she sometimes forgot to be lonely. But weekends were hard. She structured her time like a general, wary of leaving any chink in her defenses. She would see David first of course, then go to the open-air market, buy something delicious for dinner. She'd drop by her friend Susan's house and maybe persuade her to see a movie. She'd ask Susan for supper. Meg quickened at that idea, afraid to admit to herself just how much she dreaded eating alone on the weekends.

She dressed quickly, putting on a green dress she knew David liked. She brushed her hair and left it down, quickly put on mascara and lipstick. Like a date, she thought grimly. But it cheered her up. She grabbed her purse. David would not want her to give in to despair, she was sure of it.

She parked in her usual place at the hospital, the first floor of the parking deck. *Funny how quickly we form habits,* she thought. *Like pews in church.* She left her gloves on the seat and put the parking ticket in the car and ran up the stairs. When she got to the lobby, Sister Antonette was passing through and came over and gave her a big hug. Meg had known her from various charitable organizations she had been involved with, and when David came to the hospital, Sister Antonette had taken special care of them.

"My dear." Antonette gave her a big hug. Tears started in Meg's eyes. She felt she could stay in the sister's bosomy embrace for a good long time. She pulled away, wiping the tears with her knuckles.

"How are you?" Antonette asked, looking at her searchingly.

Meg shrugged. "Okay, I guess. Weekends are hard."

"I've been saying special prayers. We can never lose hope."

Meg nodded, looked away, hope eluding her. How to tell the nun that sometimes she didn't want to come, didn't want to face the silence, her chatter dropping like pennies into a wishing well.

"I'd better go up and see him," she said, kissing Antonette on her powdery cheek.

"Yes, dear," said the nun, briskly moving on to her next task. *How does she do it?* Meg thought, getting on the elevator. *How does she face illness and death every day and still maintain such peace?*

Meg was on automatic, her head down, still musing on Sister Antonette when she noticed someone sitting in the hall outside David's room. A boy with his head down, his hands between his knees. He was thin, wore scruffy jeans, had a thatch of unruly dark hair. She could only see his profile, but the boy looked somehow familiar. The boy looked like Josh.

Meg caught her breath. She must be imagining it. Her wistfulness had conjured him. She stopped, her hand against the wall. The boy lifted his head and looked at her. He was as she remembered him, only paler and thinner, with a scraggly beard. The eyes were the same, though, dark and deep and brooding.

He looked confused for a moment. Then he rose unsteadily and stood in front of her.

"Are you Mrs. Masters?" he said, his voice barely a whisper.

She nodded.

"I had to come see you. I wanted to see him, but they wouldn't let me."

"They only allow family."

They stared at each other. Part of Meg wanted to slap the hapless boy, the other part wanted to hug him.

"I, uh, I want you to know that I'm sorry." The kid seemed to shrink into himself. "I know you probably hate me. But—"

She shook her head, cut him off. "No, not really." No, she felt many things, but not hate.

"Look," he said, "I've just got to get this out. I've been reading about him, about David, I mean. I know he is someone special. I wish I had known him… I wish I could be like him. But he can't die, okay? Not because I'll go to jail or anything, it's just that he can't die…" The boy's voice rose an octave, and his face crumpled. He looked at her pleadingly, as if she somehow had the power to save David, the power to absolve Josh.

"Come on, now," she said, feeling light-headed and at a loss. She gestured toward the elevators. "Let's go down to the cafeteria and talk. I think that's what we should do."

They stepped into the elevator, and he regained control of himself. "I'm all right," he muttered. "You probably think I'm nuts."

Meg thought, *Well, you have the right to be.* "No, I…" They both stared at the reflective elevator doors. "I'm glad you came. I've wanted to meet you, too." And she blushed, staring at the image of the two of them in the door. Both of them skinny, with dark hair and eyes. They could be taken for mother and son. *If I had a son,* she thought, *I wouldn't be so alone with this.* Meg indulged the fantasy for just a moment, but when the elevator door opened, she shook herself out of it.

In the cafeteria they got some Cokes and sat down. Meg still felt at sea, flooded by too many emotions. She'd thought so much about Josh, now here he was in the flesh, complicated and real and kind of stale smelling, as if he hadn't had a shower in a while. Not really the fantasy Josh she'd fashioned for herself. But still, the courage to come! She wanted to ask him, *What do you want from me?* But she waited, letting him take his time.

Josh stared into his cup, his hair almost grazing the rim. She felt the urge to brush it back. Finally, he looked up. "What's going to happen to him?" he asked.

Meg shook her head. "I don't know. I thought at first that he'd be out of it pretty quickly, then he wasn't, and now they say he could just stay in the coma indefinitely. Sometimes people wake up spontaneously, there was a case in the paper recently, someone just started talking… anyway, the doctors don't know. There is a special clinic he might be sent to in Texas."

Josh perked up. "Oh, yeah? Could they cure him?"

Meg stared at Josh. *Cure.* That seemed an almost medieval concept, too close to *miracle* to be entertained. He had a *miraculous cure.* Another fantasy, she thought grimly. "I don't know. They have had some successes. Not cures, exactly. But improvements." Then she saw it, David learning to walk again, to talk again, and she wasn't sure she could cope with it, deal with David so diminished.

"Why don't they send him now?" Josh's voice had an artificial brightness to it, a strained hopefulness.

"Time has to pass, a certain time, a benchmark before they can send him there."

Josh deflated, his face drooping, his eyes turning in on himself. "But he could die, right? That's what my dad's focused on, because that will make me a murderer. But I already feel like a murderer," he whispered.

Meg's eyes filled at the anguish in his voice. She felt as if she were drowning in sorrow, hers, Josh's, Hal's. Was there no end to it?

"I wish David had been my dad. My dad sucks," the boy muttered into his cup.

"At least your dad can walk and talk, Josh. Maybe you should give him a chance."

Josh looked away, embarrassed. "If you knew him, you wouldn't say that. Him and his fucking clocks. Everything has to be just right or he flies into a rage. Nothing I ever do is good enough. If I get a B, he's mad it's not an A. He hates my friends. He doesn't get me, y'know. He doesn't get that filmmaking is as important to me as his stupid clocks are to him."

Meg looked down at her hands. Hal's awkward eagerness at the Mayflower flashed through her mind.

"I'm sorry you feel that way, Josh. I'm sure David would have liked a son like you. We never had kids." She cleared her throat, tried to steady the quaver in her voice. "Don't be too hard on your dad, though. It is tougher than you know to be a parent." She was in character now, Valerie Tate.

Josh hung his head again, drank down the rest of his Coke, and got up. He put his hand out awkwardly to Meg. "Thanks for talking to me. You could have just told me to get lost." He was agitated again. "Can I call you to find out how he is sometimes?" Josh stood up to go.

Meg swallowed. "All right. I suppose that would be all right. Do you have my number?"

Josh had already started toward the exit. "Yes," he called back, then turned the corner and disappeared.

Meg looked down at the Formica table. Why had she agreed to him calling? Now she'd have both of them calling her. The light from the windows was fading. The cafeteria was long deserted. It suddenly seemed an empty and sterile place, and Meg felt more alone than she had in months. She got up wearily and returned to David's room.

Dwindling late-afternoon sunlight left David's room dim.

The air was warm and too close. Meg fervently wished she could open the windows and let in some fresh air, but of course, the windows didn't open. *Might be too healthy,* Meg thought bitterly.

The sparse sunlight fell on David, and in the light, she saw the way his face had settled into a sort of chiseled rigidity, his face, which had always been so mobile and expressive. Every so often, he would grimace or even smile faintly, but whether these were any more indicative of an interior life than a baby passing gas, she didn't know.

She had, for the first weeks and months, real conviction that David was there, intact. It wasn't so easy to believe that now. Hope was something you worked at, she found.

She took off her sweater now and straightened the blanket, folding the top of the sheet down over the blanket, smoothing it. These things had become rituals, something to do to bring movement into the still room. Then she sat on the bed, tucked her legs up under her. David had thinned, so that there was more room for her than there might have been at one time.

She picked up his limp hand and squeezed it. She could still tell him her stories and, in telling them, pretend that nothing had really changed. She could tell him about Hal—who else could she tell? "Imagine," she said to David, stroking his bony shins under the blanket, "having a father like Hal! He seems to want to connect with the boy, but he's flat-footed." And she paused, forgetting there would be no reply. She described Josh as best she could, from what little she had glimpsed. "If we had had a child, David, I can imagine Josh being ours. He seems sensitive and spirited. I wish I could get to know him better." She paused again, thinking of the three of them living together somewhere in the country, David whole and such a good father to Josh, Meg making supper, watching the two of them out the window, playing ball. They wouldn't have made the mistakes Hal and his wife had made with Josh.

It was so unfair! People thought she didn't want children, that she was so dedicated to her work. Which became the truth, after a while. It was only now, thinking of Josh, that it stung her afresh.

Looking at her beloved adversary now, she longed for the days they battled each other. At least then he was strong, vibrant, alive. She lay down on the bed, put her head on David's chest, and carefully arranged his arm around her.

She listened to his steady heartbeat. Tears slowly seeped out of her eyes. David made some sort of sound, but when she looked at his face, there was no expression there.

***

David felt Meg against him, her arm around his neck. As if they were dancing. At last.

Much later, Peggy Lee's smoky voice enveloped David. "Is that all there is? Is that all there is? If that's all there is, my friend, then let's keep dancing…" He felt a letting go of something, a project or a worry. It made him sad to let it go, something he was supposed to do, but Peggy was right. Just keep dancing. She was always right, in her way.

Meg didn't like to dance. David had taken her a few times, but she always froze, became self-conscious. He tried to tell her to feel the music, to go with it, that the music would tell her how to move, but she simply didn't understand it. She counted the beat, needed to know the steps, made it a head thing. She was so dear, so loving, that he finally decided he couldn't put her through any more dancing attempts. It was with regret on his part that they stopped going. So now when Peggy asked him to, he eagerly accepted. He felt a slight degree of betrayal toward Meg, but rationalized that in the end, she wouldn't mind. Not really.

Now his parents were dancing in the front room. He was supposed to be in bed. He and his brother had been bathed and read to, lights had been turned off, but he hadn't been able to go to sleep. The music drifted up, and he heard their nighttime voices—whispering, laughing—and smelled the cigarettes. He crept down the stairs to just below the landing, where he could see them, but they couldn't see him. Not that they were looking for him. He felt as if they had severed any thought of him, that they had become different people altogether. He wasn't jealous so much as fascinated. His mother swung her hair around and looked up in a strange, teasing way at his father; his father's tie was loosened, and he spun her around, making silly faces, then suddenly kissed her.

Peggy Lee's voice drifted up to David, caressing his ear as he gripped the banister.

He stayed glued to the step. If he didn't, he was afraid that the man would dance the woman out of the house and his parents might never come back to him.

The next thing he knew, his father was lifting him in his arms. His cheek was nestled against his father's damp shirt, and he felt his mother stroking his head, the two of them murmuring softly as they tucked him into bed. He settled comfortably down into the sheets, secure now that his parents had returned.

Had it been the next day, or was he just confusing things again? The next day, walking to school, his morning reverie was interrupted by a stinging sensation in his leg. Stopping to see what it was, he bent over, and zing, another sting, coming now fast and furious, so that he was skipping and hopping to avoid the rocks being pitched at his legs, running now, unclear where it was all coming from. "Dance, nigger lover, dance," he heard from the behind a tree, the voice harsh but familiar somehow, and he ran from the voice, but he wanted to scream at the kid, *What do you know about dancing?*

SECTION 8:

ALL SHOOK UP

TWENTY-TWO

Hal found himself whistling as he ironed, badly, his best shirt. He hadn't really expected Valerie to see him again, but she had agreed. He wanted to pay her back for her good advice. He was feeling a little better about Josh. At least he didn't feel so desperate. Surprisingly, Josh had agreed to go to lunch again next week. He had hedged a bit, but in the end agreed. Hal felt the merest hint of hope brush against him, but that was enough for now. He felt lighter somehow.

He hadn't talked with Helen about this. He'd wanted to, initially. He'd wanted to tell her that he thought things were getting better, that he and Josh were getting better. He wanted to tell her that maybe it would be all right, that they would be able to go back to being a family again. He'd reflexively picked up the phone, then put it down. He'd thought of what Helen might have said, of the bitter look around her mouth. He thought of the sort of abstracted way she looked at him these days, and it unhinged him. As if they hadn't spent twenty years together, as if he were a stranger. No, it was better to do this on his own. All Helen expected from him was failure. And when he was with her, that was all he expected from himself.

Anyway, he liked Valerie. There was something about her

that drew him, some calmness. She was comforting. He didn't really think he was being unfaithful to Helen just to go out with the woman. It was hell being alone all the time, and he bet it was for Valerie, too. He had no idea when he moved out of the house how hard it would be, this solitude. He hadn't realized that he could be alone all day with his clocks because he had someone to come home to at night.

Valerie had agreed to meet him downtown at Trapeze. He was anxious to show her the article about her clock, to make a believer out of her. He was halfway there when he realized he had left the journal behind, and had to turn back to get it. When he finally pulled up to Trapeze, he saw she was already seated outside. He watched her a moment, the way she smiled and nodded at the waiter, her small head delicate on her long neck, her gray-streaked dark hair brushing her shoulders. He hadn't really thought of her as attractive, but he realized suddenly that she was. And the thought made him waver. What was he doing? And then she caught sight of him, and she put up a hand in a gesture of greeting.

He found his heart thudding as he made his way over to her, found that he felt awkward, like a geeky kid who'd never been on a date.

"Hi there," he said with false heartiness.

She smiled. "Hi. How are you?"

He let out the breath he'd been holding and pulled out a chair. "You know, not bad." She smiled and nodded her head. She seemed different than before, more remote, and this made him anxious. She didn't ask him about Josh. Then he said quickly, remembering his manners, "How are you?"

Valerie dipped her head, looked up at him. "About the same, I guess."

She was already sipping a glass of wine. Hal ordered a beer, and some nuts. He hadn't had a beer in so long he wasn't sure he would handle it.

"Well, you said you had something to tell me about my clock. It seemed rather urgent."

She said this rather primly, and Hal wasn't sure again whether she really was interested in the clock. He wanted her to be, badly. He wanted someone to share his excitement.

"Well, good. I've got the article right here."

He opened *Horology Today* to an article showing a clock similar to her clock. She put on her glasses, took a long time studying it.

"I've had to dig, but there is a small possibility that your clock could be an actual early nineteenth-century clock, not simply a very good reproduction. How one of those could have ended up here, with your family, is anyone's guess. And if it is authentic, it could be worth up to, well, thirty thousand dollars."

"My goodness." She looked up at him in amazement. "Surely my little clock isn't worth much. I mean, I have no idea where my grandparents got it, but they came from modest means."

Hal took a deep breath. "No, you're right, it is highly unlikely. I've looked and looked for a signature. But if it is old, then the engraving may have rubbed off, or been filed down so that it couldn't be identified. Especially if it was stolen."

She stared at him for a moment. "It just complicates things, in a way."

"Complicates things?"

"I really like the idea of using it in my classroom. I don't like the idea of treating it like the Hope Diamond."

"But, I mean, well, of course, I understand wanting to use it. Although not, heavens, in a classroom." He imagined again the travesty of sticky fingers touching the delicate works. "But you should at least know the value to have it insured." He heard himself pleading. She just didn't get it. His excitement turned to irritation.

She laughed as if he were a foolish child. "Maybe I'll list it in my homeowner's insurance. If you want to give me an estimate?"

"That's just it. I think I need a second opinion before I could give that to you."

Valerie shrugged. "It all seems like a lot of work, and right now I don't have the energy for it."

"Well, I could get the second opinion, and then take a small commission if you decide to sell it." He hadn't planned on saying this.

She looked at him over her wine glass, considering. "Yes, I suppose I could use the money, I really could, for medical bills—"

"You're not sick?" Hal said with alarm.

"Oh, no, I mean, the bills that my husband accrued—he was sick a long time."

Hal hung his head. "I'm so sorry. I didn't mean to pry."

"But the clock gives me such pleasure... it would be like losing a piece of my childhood." She shook her hair back decisively.

Hal nodded. "I can understand that. But think about exploring this further. It's just exciting for me to find it. So—unexpectedly. And wouldn't you really like to know?"

Valerie regarded him again with what Hal was beginning to learn was a habitual considering gaze.

"So, something like this is really important to you, to your career? Sort of like an explorer discovering a new continent or something?"

Hal looked down, embarrassed. "Well, not quite like that. But yes, I guess, you know, I never thought anything like it would wash up at the shop. In Europe, maybe, or New York… and it takes some skill to recognize these things. I'm always studying up on clocks, but mostly classic American clocks—regulators, banjos, things like that."

"It must be fascinating—a whole world unto itself."

"Oh, it is. I can hardly keep up with it, there is so much to learn. Although most of the important clocks have been accounted for already—there are very few discoveries left to be made." He looked down at the article, unable to take his eyes off the clock pictured there.

"You know," she said after a while, "I can't take it in, really." She sipped her wine. "And—I almost didn't come tonight. It felt odd. But now I'm glad I got out. A chance to learn something new."

Hal lifted his gaze from the article. "Yes, me, too."

She fiddled with her glass. "How is your son, by the way?"

"Oh, I wanted to tell you. I'm feeling better about him. He agreed to go to lunch with me again next week. I had thought after our first try that, well—I didn't feel like it was such a success. But maybe you were right, maybe they're glad to get the attention but just don't show it."

"Well, I'm happy for you. You are really lucky, you know. Lucky to have him."

Hal looked down. It had been a long time since he'd thought that, but yes, he supposed he was. When he looked back at Valerie, she was staring at him again with large, sad eyes. He groped for a reason. Surely she should be happy about the clock?

"Are you okay?"

"Ha," she laughed, then sighed. "I don't know." Valerie pushed a few strands of hair away from her face, and he saw that her eyes were unusually bright. "I need to go." She scooted out of her seat.

Hal hastily gathered up the journal, his heart sinking. Why did he always put his foot in it? Valerie was at the cashier's desk.

"Let me take care of it," Hal said gruffly.

She put on her coat. "They've already split it." She signed the receipt, thanked the lady behind the desk, and started walking toward the street.

Hal quickly paid his bill and caught up with Valerie. "Look, hey, I'm sorry. I don't know what I did to upset you."

"It's not you. I'm not usually like this. It's just—I'm not myself right now." She turned away from him, and he could see her shoulders shaking.

He hovered behind her, feeling helpless and stupid. He never could deal with women's tears. He knew women expected some act of tenderness or understanding, but it had to be the right one, and hell if he knew what that was supposed to be. He was baffled. They had been talking about a clock, for god's sake.

Valerie opened the door to her car and turned to him, holding out her hand. "Thank you for taking the time researching my clock," she said stiffly. "I'll let you know if I decide to get a second opinion or sell the clock. Right now, I really don't think so, but that could change. Good-bye."

He shook her hand, mumbled something, and watched her pull away from the curb. Her taillights disappeared around the corner, leaving Hal riveted to the spot. What had gone wrong? Groups of laughing young people wove around him, he heard music coming from a nearby bar. He felt again his unfitness for life, his awkwardness. He had thought he'd found a friend, someone who understood him. He was wrong.

Bereft, he walked slowly to his car.

***

"What shape are you? Marbry is a triangle. You're a circle."

Josh was beginning to understand Leticia, the little girl with CHARGE syndrome. She saw the world, including people, in shapes. Not literally, but as if someone's "aura" could be translated into a kind of shape. And she was right, Josh thought, there was something pointy and angular to Marbry.

He looked at the tiny oracle. Nine years old, but you'd think she was six. Her pale, translucent skin showed her blue veins, and she had a squarish face with short, wide ears and large eyes magnified by her glasses. She looked like an elf. She blinked at him, then began her frenetic running in circles. Marbry swooped down and picked her up, securing her so that the child suddenly became limp in her arms.

Sometimes now, going back to the "real world," Josh missed the colorful, quirky textures of life inside Good Shepherd. He'd hated the place at first, but now he found himself looking forward to coming to work. In a way, if he stopped to think about it, it was the only place he felt real. At home, at school, it was as if he was just going through the motions. Here, he felt he had a purpose. The kids didn't seem like freaks anymore; if anything, they were more trusting and open than "normal" people. Sometimes when he was out in the world, he had to adjust to how closed and suspicious people were. Sure, the work was hard, but now the more physical the work, the more he liked it. He liked to go home exhausted. That way he didn't have to think about anything.

It was time for him to work with Marius. He picked up his book bag and took out the photos he'd had developed. Twenty-four. They had, surprisingly, all come out. Ms. Jones had told Josh that Marius seemed to consider every shot, and he would report to her gravely on how many were left.

Looking at the shots at Rite Aid, Josh had been surprised at how many good ones there were. Some of the shots cut off people's heads, some were at crazy angles, but lots of them were quite good. There was one of Chondra, grinning lopsidedly, her hair sticking straight up from her head. There was one of Marbry, taken close up, with her characteristic mocking expression. There was one of Big James, the teenage boy with DMS, flashing a peace sign, his wheelchair thick with political and joke stickers. There was even one of Josh, looking kind of earnest and strained. It wasn't how Josh saw himself, pale and scrawny with too much hair. He felt kind of sorry for himself.

Now he was excited to show them to Marius. He tried not to get his hopes up too much. Marius was still, for the most part, unresponsive. Most days Josh left feeling that he wasn't doing much good. Taking a deep breath, Josh clutched the package and entered the activity room. Marius was parked by his usual window. Marius turned to look at Josh when he entered. He didn't smile, just fastened his almond-shaped eyes on Josh's face. Josh forced a smile, knowing it wouldn't be returned.

"I've got something for you, Marius." He handed the folder to Marius.

The boy slowly turned the folder over in his hands, just like he had with the camera.

"Open it, see, here," Josh said, trying to keep the impatience out of his voice.

Marius opened the flap and slid out the photos. He examined each gravely, carefully putting them aside, one by one. Josh wanted him to say something, but he bit his tongue. Finally, Marius looked up.

"Twenty-four," he said.

Josh nodded. Was that all he was going to say?

Finally, Marius said, "I made them."

"Yes, Marius, you did!"

And then Marius smiled. It began as a slow upturn of closed lips and expanded into a full-fledged grin. Even his eyes turned up. And then, he laughed, a short chuckle, but still a laugh. He picked up the picture of Marbry and waved it at Josh. "Funny face," he said.

Josh held his breath. He felt if he made the wrong move, it would all be over.

"Yes, she sure does. How about some of the other pictures? What stories can you tell me about them?"

Marius looked through the stack and picked up Chondra's picture. He flapped his arms and made a caw-caw sound.

Josh said, "Use your words, Marius. You have good words."

The smiled faded a bit, but then came back. "She a bird." He pointed out the window.

"Good, Marius. What's her name? Can you make a complete sentence?"

Marius nodded, "Chondra like a black bird. She a *Chondra bird*." The boy looked at Josh slyly, then broke out in a grin.

Josh stared. Marius had been silent, but he hadn't been blind or deaf.

Marius smiled again, and picked up Josh's photo. "This *you*," he said, jabbing his finger at Josh.

Josh looked down at the picture. "What story can you tell me about that photo, Marius?"

Marius gazed at the photo for a long time. Slowly the smile faded. "Josh sad."

Josh shivered. He wasn't sure he liked this game anymore. "Go on, Marius. Can you tell me a story about it?"

Marius shrugged his shoulders. "Maybe Josh's mother died."

"No, oh, no, Marius."

Marius looked puzzled. "Why you sad?"

"Why *are* you sad?" Josh corrected him.

"Why *are* you sad, Josh?" Marius put his hand on Josh's shoulder and looked at him with his steady gaze.

I don't know, Josh wanted to say. *I'm not sad, don't be silly.* But he was sad. And he knew why.

He tore his eyes away from Marius's gaze. "My best friend moved away, Marius. I'm lonely."

Marius nodded gravely. He looked back out the window.

Boy, now I've done it, Josh thought. *Ruined everything, as usual.*

243

Then Marius turned back. "I your friend," he said, and a small hint of a smile flickered across his face. Then he looked up abruptly. Marbry had appeared in the door.

"Uh, oh. Funny face."

Josh looked up at Marbry, then back at Marius. Marius flashed him a grin, then turned his customary poker face to Marbry.

"Well, don't you two look thick as thieves," Marbry said, then whisked Marius around and headed toward the door. "By the way, Caitlin is looking for you, Josh. You seem real popular today."

"Bye, Marius," Josh called. But they were through the door already.

Josh sat back in his chair. Wow. Did that really happen? He looked around the activity room, and it seemed an entirely different place. It seemed cheerful and friendly instead of drab and dispirited. He beat a rhythm on the table. *Oh, yeah, Marius smiled, oh, yeah... and I did it. I got through to him.* Josh felt like doing a Chondra and crowing himself. He'd tell Ms. Jones later, but for now he wanted to hug it to himself.

TWENTY-THREE

Peggy kicked off her shoes and tucked them under her, then sprawled at the foot of his bed. "Tell me a story, David. I'm so damn tired. What ever happened to that boyhood friend of yours, anyway? The one you rode bikes with?" She took out a pack of cigarettes and tapped one out, offering it to him, but he shook his head.

"You mean Anthony?"

She nodded, blowing out smoke in rings. David watched them float up, break apart.

"When Anthony came home from Vietnam, he came back with one arm. But it was more than that. He came back dulled, fatalistic. I tried to evoke our past, but Anthony wasn't having any. The only time he came alive was when he was angry, and that would come unexpectedly. Rage storms. Once Anthony's mother called me at college and asked me to talk to Anthony over the phone. But Anthony just vented his fury on me, pointing out that I was a white boy in college, and what did I have to do with a goon-killing nigger anyway?

"I was hurt, so I gave up. But sometime later—I can't remember it all—I did try. On a whim. I happened to be near his mother's house and thought, what the hell. I went up to the

245

front door. It was the same as I remember it—gaudy hydrangeas in full summer bloom, the porch weathered and unpainted as always. A little kid I didn't recognize opened the door and glared at me suspiciously. 'Grandma!' he called.

"Anthony's mother came to the door and squinted at me. She hesitated. 'David? Come in, hon. Jason, get your toys outta here. Come on in. I'm glad to see you.' Then she started crying.

"I stood uncomfortably in the middle of the room. It was much smaller than I remembered it, but the familiar praying-hands statue was on the bookshelf with the Bible and the comforting smell of yams and collards and vinegar still hung in the air. 'Anthony?' I stammered.

"She motioned for me to sit down, and she sank down next to me, shaking her head. 'We don't know where he is. Lord, he just took off.' She sniffed and wiped her nose. I realized that she was a pretty woman, and younger than my mom, but she looked so tired. She shook her head again.

"'He been driving me and the kids crazy. He's so mad all the time. But I don't want him out on the streets.' She grabbed my arm and shook it. 'You find him, David. You find my Anthony. You're smart. He'll listen to you. You were such good friends.' I saw that she attributed powers to me I didn't have.

"'I'll try,' I said. But as she led me out into the blinding sunshine, I felt very little confidence.

"After that, I searched for Anthony whenever I was home. It became an obsession. I went to all the likeliest places. The bars, Wilson's Soul Food, the pool hall. Sometimes I'd get a lead, but by the time I followed it up, Anthony would be gone. They told me at the Salvation Army that he'd been there, but had been kicked out for brawling. Someone thought they had seen him on the street, but I never found him. I always went back to school with a vague feeling of failure.

"Then, one winter break, I glimpsed Anthony outside the pool hall. I pulled Dad's Chevy station wagon over and parked. It was snowing, wet sloppy flakes, and the neon light in the window cast a pink glow on the huddle of men smoking and laughing outside. I hesitated, suddenly shy or frightened, I don't know. The men had caught sight of me then, so I couldn't back away. Anthony didn't seem to have seen me, though. His head was down. I took a deep breath and walked closer and called out to him. Anthony's head jerked up. He just stared at me, then said, 'You calling me, white boy?'

"I felt slapped. The others tittered. I tried again. 'I just want to talk to you, okay? Can we talk for a few minutes?' Anthony didn't move, then pushed off the brick wall with his foot. 'All right,' he muttered.

"Anthony came up to where I was standing. 'Let's walk,' I said, glancing back at the others. 'I need a little privacy.'

"Anthony shrugged as if it didn't matter to him one way or the other, turned, and called, 'Later,' to the others. They nodded nonchalantly, and as Anthony and I walked in silence, I could hear them talking and laughing again.

"It was cold, and I shrugged my shoulders inside my coat to get warm. Anthony smelled of Wild Turkey and cigarettes and unwashed, acrid flesh. I glanced at him, trying to find my old friend in the scowling features. I was still startled by the folded up sleeve.

"'Anthony,' I started, 'look, I'm sorry if I've done anything to offend you—'"

"'You can stop with that shit right there, white boy. This ain't about you. It's about me and this fucking country and getting screwed by old white men.' There was a pause, and we stopped walking.

"I faced him then. I felt small and helpless in the face of Anthony's anger. I felt on the verge of sissy white tears. I wanted my friend back but had no idea how to reach him. Plus, Anthony was right, what did I know about that hell? About Vietnam? About being black and armless? Still, I thought there must be some way to get through.

"'Okay, you win. You're right, you've been screwed. I'm sorry, okay? But I didn't do it.'

"Anthony threw his butt down on the ground. 'No, you didn't. But you can just go along in your life like nothing happened.'

"'No, I can't. Not when I've lost my best friend.'

"I thought I saw something flicker behind his eyes. Then, dropping his homeboy accent, he said, 'David, you might as well think of me dead.'

"I shook my head. 'I can't. Man, you can beat this thing. You have the VA loan. You can pursue your dreams.'

"Anthony held up his stump, 'With this? Hey, man, maybe a one-armed white man can do it, but a one-armed black man? Fantasy land, man. 'Sides, I couldn't be retrofitted for the kind of job I'd want…'

"'Hell, do you think you're the only one wounded in this war?'

"Anthony looked pissed. 'Why don't you leave me alone? Huh? You and your high and mighty ideas. You're just like your dad, a bunch of white Yankee do-gooders.'

"I heard my voice shake. 'That's right, we are. And I'm not going to leave you alone, do you hear me? I'm not going to leave you alone!'

"Anthony was already walking away, shaking his head. The snow fell thickly between us. I couldn't move. It was as if I had frozen there. I watched him walk away, a dark ragged figure, slowly covered by snow, finally disappearing. And the boy in me did not believe it could have come to this."

David looked down at where Peggy had sprawled, looked for her smoke rings, but she, too, was gone. It was only now, now that he had time—endless pools of time in which to dip—that David realized that everyone he'd ever tried to save was Anthony.

***

Meg carefully lifted the lizard out of its glass cage and into the box she'd prepared for it. It curled its tail around her wrist, and its tiny claws clung to her hand. She had to work to pry it loose. She shook the droppings onto newspapers and put the cage in the sink, squirting Joy into the bottom and blasting it with hot water before scrubbing it down, and then drying it with paper towels.

She usually enjoyed these calming housekeeping chores, but today, the after-school silence descended on her like a blanket. It was the same silence that plagued her at home, a thick, syrupy quiet. It brought, unbidden, clear memories of David, memories she tried to evade, but couldn't. She tried to focus on the lizard as it swallowed a cricket, but even that primal scene couldn't pin her to the present.

She put the rocks back in the cage, taking a minute to enjoy the warm smoothness of each one, the weight and different textures. She brought one to her cheek, and her feet remembered the feel of the stones in the Broad River, the shallow water gently washing over them, David taking her hand, guiding her into the canoe. She felt his warm, strong hand and saw his grinning, sunburned face. "Think you can manage the left, right thing, honey?" he teased her. And she wanted to stay there with him, but then he was gone and she was alone.

And it was that, that there was nothing to look forward to anymore, that it had all changed and she could only feast on memories—that she couldn't believe. A paltry feast—a feast that just whetted the appetite and left the stomach empty. Like a trickster, her memories mocked her.

She heard the delicate shifting of gears as she passed by the clock, perched on its high shelf above the shell collection. She stopped a moment, watched the minute hand move around the clock face. Every second was taking her that much farther from David.

She couldn't get used to this living without a future, this limbo, this not knowing if David would be restored. She was as suspended as he was between life and death. She thought about amnesia and whether it would be better than those sweet memories that pricked her. No, then she would lose all of David forever.

She shook her head, wanting only to stop thinking, and reached down to pick up a memo that had fallen off her desk. As she looked up, she realized there was someone standing in the doorway, blocking the light—a tall man with a stoop to his shoulder, someone she thought she knew. A father of one of her students, perhaps?

She straightened up. "Can I help you?"

He came in, and she was stunned to realize it was Hal.

He walked into the room diffidently. *If he had a hat,* she thought, *it would be in his hands.*

"I'm sorry to surprise you like this."

Meg sought the comfort of her desk chair. She thought maybe she was having hot flashes. It was too much, too much.

"I need to talk to you. May I sit down?"

She gestured to one of the small chairs. He sat, his long stork-like legs drawn up so that his knees almost touched his chin. He looked comical, and it made her feel more competent, in control of the situation.

"Yes?" Meg said, apprehensive.

Hal shrugged. Then he said, "I know your name's not Tate. Or Valerie. I called earlier and described you, and they told me your name. Why did you lie to me?"

By the measured way he spoke, Meg knew he was trying to contain his anger. She felt herself flush from her feet to the roots of her hair, as guilty as a child. "Would you have wanted to talk to me if you had known who I was?"

Hal frowned. "I guess not. But why—? Why come into the shop? Did you know who I was?"

Meg nodded. "At the trial, I wanted to hate Josh. I was so angry. But then, there he was, a kid. I could see it had been an accident. I could see he was a good kid—he wasn't a tough, destructive jerk like I'd imagined. Then I thought, if it had been my kid—"

Hal stared at her. "So you really didn't care about the clock at all?"

"No, it was a pretext. I was curious, and lonely, I guess."

He looked around, exasperated, as if he couldn't find the words. Then he saw the clock. He frowned.

Meg held her breath. Guilty again.

"Well," he said resignedly, "it seems to be intact."

"I told you I wanted to use it here." She hated her own defensiveness. "Is that why you are here, for the clock?"

He raised his hand in a gesture like someone erasing a board. "Well, not entirely. I do want you to strongly consider getting another opinion. But that's not the only reason." He took a deep breath. "No, it's Josh."

"Has something happened?" Meg could feel her pulse speed up.

"I had such hopes, but he seems worse now. Mooning after this girl who left town. He shuts himself in his room. He canceled our lunch. He was angry with me but didn't say why. And he insists he is going to study film. In New York. I don't know how we'll pay for that. He lives in la-la land." Hal got up and started pacing. "He's got to wake up and get practical. I just don't want him throwing his life away."

Meg swiveled in her chair to see him better. "Hal, he's young. He's confused and he's in love. It doesn't seem that hard to understand. Weren't you ever in love?"

Hal stopped pacing and blinked at her. There was a silence, and he turned his face away, then turned around. "It's just hard to remember what it feels like to be that young."

"Oh, come on. It's not that hard."

Hal opened and closed his mouth like a fish coming to the surface to feed. Then he said, "Well, maybe it's too painful to remember."

Ahh, thought Meg, *maybe we are getting somewhere.*

"I wasted too much of my life daydreaming. And now look at me—a nobody, a failure. I never even got out of Milledge. I don't want my son to wake up in twenty years and realize he frittered his life away."

Meg gripped the edge of her desk. The sharpness of it bit into her hand and grounded her. Who were these people? Why were they in her life?

Meg stood up and faced Hal. "For Christ's sake, Hal! Get over yourself. How dare you come whining to me? My husband is lying in a hospital, we have no children, and you are worried about being a *failure*?" She was shaking with rage. Hal, stunned, opened his mouth to speak, but she held up her hand. "No, you listen. Josh needs a father. He needs you."

Hal stood in the middle of the room like an overgrown second grader, his arms hanging awkwardly at his sides, a look of disbelief on his face.

Meg walked over and took the clock off the shelf. "Here. Sell it for me. I could use the money."

He took it numbly. "Are you sure?"

She nodded. Suddenly the clock seemed tainted. She just wanted to get rid of it, get rid of the whole skewed relationship with Hal. And she did need the money.

He stood holding it, looking awkward and abashed. "I have a dealer in New York."

"Hal, I don't care."

"Well, I'll get back to you about it as soon as possible."

She nodded and he left.

Meg watched him dragging down the hall, his head bowed. She sat down, still trembling with rage. Good riddance to Hal, good riddance to the clock.

Then she put her head in her hands and cried.

***

Like a bad fairy sent to ruin his mood, Caitlin poked her head into the activity room. He couldn't stand Caitlin, the new "volunteer" at Good Shepherd. She roared up to work in her souped-up Pinto, a black hula dancer bobbing on the dash, heavy metal blaring. She dyed her hair pink and black and sported gothic tattoos on her arms and back and hip, which he knew because she wore her pants down around her pubic bone. Although she had started working long after he had, she was officious and treated Josh as if he didn't know anything. She was loud and rough with the kids, too, but effective, he had to grudgingly admit. She was strong and could hoist the kids on and off the toilets like nobody's business. Still, he didn't like her.

"Hey, Josh, want a ride home?"

That was a new one. He always wanted a ride home; he hated riding the bus. Still, he didn't know how much time he wanted to spend with her. She must have something up her sleeve.

"Why are you suddenly altruistic? I thought we didn't like each other very much."

Caitlin grinned. "Speak for yourself, Josho? I like you fine. You're a bit of a dweeb, but hey, I like dweebs."

"Gee thanks."

"Oh, c'mon. I'm just joshing you. I'm joshing Josh."

She was looking at him as if she would burst into hilarious laughter. He wished he were in on the joke.

She tapped her foot. "A simple yes or no will do. I've got things to do."

"Well, it would get me home faster. And it is bloody cold out."

"Okay, then. Let's go."

They straightened up the activity room chairs and tables, turned off the lights, and left the building. It was a beautiful, clear night, with a cooling breeze gently moving through the leaves. Josh lingered for a moment at the oak tree, seeing Libby there.

"Hey, c'mon, Josh."

He slid into the front seat. The car reeked of cigarette smoke, sweaty clothes, old gym shoes. Caitlin stepped hard on the gas and peeled out of the parking lot. Josh hung on to the seat belt. She reached over and groped in the dash and withdrew a roach and a lighter and handed them to him.

"Here, light up for us."

Josh looked at the paraphernalia in his hand. "You know I'm on parole. I can't do this." He began to sweat, knowing that if they were pulled over, no one would believe he'd gotten into the car innocently.

"Yadda, yadda. You really are no fun. As I suspected."

"I guess so." Gingerly, he put everything back into the dash. But the smell of the weed brought it all back. It brought back

Libby's kiss, Susie and Libby's fight, Andy's antics. It brought back the drive home, the thumping in the night, the creak of the door as he got out, the body lying there, the blood oily in the streetlights. It brought back his father's face twisted in rage, and the cold, bright lights of the jail that night.

"Pull over, I think I'm going to be sick."

She swerved the car over to the side, and Josh stumbled into ironweed and goldenrod and retched and retched until he was sure he'd bring up his own gut.

Then the spasms subsided, and he was left emptied and weak.

He made his way back to the car, wishing with every shred of energy left that he didn't have to face Caitlin. He put his hand on the roof, braced himself to get in. When he did, the smell of cigarette smoke assailed him, and he thought he would lose control again. But he mastered himself, lowering himself carefully onto the seat.

He didn't speak to her, just turned and looked out the open window. She started up the car and eased into the traffic. He glanced at her and saw that without her bravado, underneath the pink hair and tattoos was a pudgy, glum kid. She threw her cigarette out the window.

"Better now?"

"Yeah. Sorry about that."

"Hey, it happens. Just tell me where to turn."

He directed her, and she left him on the corner near his house. He hadn't wanted her to know where he lived. They said awkward good-byes, and he began walking.

Alone now, the scene of the accident came back to him again. He was left with the raw and unbuffered knowledge that he had indeed put David Masters in the hospital, that the whole scene in the hospital, Meg's sad eyes, the smell of disinfectant, the grim prognosis, all of it was because of him. He had treated it like a movie, and had distracted himself with Libby, but now there was no distraction. He was drowning, sinking deeper into a cold darkness where it was harder and harder to breathe.

***

When Josh got home, still shaky from his ride with Caitlin, he found Helen sitting at the kitchen table, sketching feverishly. She didn't seem to notice him when he walked in, even though the screen door slammed behind him. Josh marveled at how intent she was. He looked over her shoulder at charcoal chairs and dishes, all fluidly and loosely rendered. The sight of them irritated him. She gave them all her attention, and there was nothing left for him.

"Mom," he said softly.

Her lips pursed in concentration. She didn't answer.

"Mom," he said more firmly.

She looked up at him then, squinting. "Hi, Josh," she said, sighing, putting the sketchpad down, looking suddenly tired.

"Mom, are you okay? Have you had anything to eat? It's almost seven o'clock."

She looked around blankly as if for an answer. "Well, I, no. I could fix us something…"

He cringed at the weariness in her voice.

"No, Mom, look I just got paid." Even though he was still technically doing community service, they had found a way to hire him for extra time over the holiday break. "It's a Saturday night. Let's go down to that new place at Beechwood, that Italian place. Let's live a little. My treat."

"Oh, no, no, Josh, you need to save your money." She started to get up, to clear away some dishes. He put his hand on her arm. He needed her attention, all of it, tonight.

"Forget this. Leave it. Get dressed. We're going out."

She put down the coffee cup she'd picked up and looked at him, startled. A flush came over her, and she smiled. "Well, all right, Josh. How nice. I haven't been out on a date with a handsome guy in a while." She paused, looking at him as if finally seeing him. "I'll just get changed. Do something with my hair. It won't take a minute."

He began to pick up the kitchen. He put the dirty dishes in the dishwasher, wiped down the counters. He was pierced with a keen longing for the old Helen, the one that took care of him, the one whose kitchen was always orderly and full of good food. Well, maybe tonight, over a real meal, she would relax, turn back into her old self. And maybe he could tell her about Caitlin—he would make it funny, leaving out the embarrassing part—and she'd laugh like she used to. Maybe he would even tell her about seeing Meg. Maybe.

Helen emerged with her long brown hair freshly brushed and down to her shoulders, fresh lipstick, and a black knit dress he'd never seen. He realized that there were gray streaks in her hair, streaks he'd never noticed before. Her face was thinner than he remembered it, more severe, but also more beautiful.

When he was little, he had thought his mother was pretty, but as he grew up, he'd stopped noticing. Now, she looked unfamiliar, and he felt a sudden uneasiness.

"You look nice, Mom," he said.

She gave him a small, shy smile.

At the restaurant, Helen looked around appreciatively. "This is nice. You are very thoughtful, Josh." She frowned slightly, shook the menu. "Anyway, I'm starved. What about you?"

They ordered pasta and salads and had garlic bread, and Josh pressed wine on her. They both ate as if it were their last meal. Josh waited for her to ask him how he was, to maybe lean over and stroke his cheek with the back of her hand, the way she used to always do. But she didn't. She chatted on about her paintings, her art teacher. It was as if he were watching his mother in a play, one in which she played the housewife turned artist. He almost felt she were striking a pose for an imaginary audience.

"He's an amazing artist, Josh. I'd love for you to see his paintings."

Her blatant admiration for this man made Josh uncomfortable again. It occurred to Josh for the first time that perhaps his parents might not get back together, that this separation might be permanent. And it would be his fault. For the second time that day, he felt as if he couldn't breathe.

"You sound like you're in love with him or something." Josh heard the petulant whine in his voice and despised it, but couldn't seem to stop it.

Helen's animated face crumbled. "Josh—no. He is a wonderful man. I love his class, that's all. Besides, he's married."

"Well, so are you."

Helen's eyebrows shot up, and she opened her mouth but closed it again.

"I know that, Josh," she said.

"When is he coming back? When is Dad coming home?" Josh noticed the aggressive tone of his voice, but he couldn't help himself.

Helen sighed, put down her fork.

"He walked out on me. On us, Josh. I don't know when he'll come back. Or if. I've been trying not to think about it."

"Isn't there anything you can do? Don't you think you should do something? Try to get him to come home? You know how he is—he's probably just waiting for a word from you."

"I don't know what the word is, Josh," she said quietly.

"How can you let him go like that, Mom? Like you don't care?"

Helen looked past him.

"I'm tired, Josh. I've spent years trying to reel him back to us. It's up to him now. I can't do it anymore."

"He doesn't know how, Mom."

Helen picked up her fork and looked into his eyes. "I know."

"You mean we won't ever go back to being a family?"

"Do you think it is what I want, Josh?" Helen whispered urgently, leaning toward him. "But I can't control your dad. I realize that now. There's very little I have control over."

Rage flooded in waves through Josh. He didn't believe it, didn't believe his mother had no control over the situation. She was his mother, for god's sake.

He asked for the check and paid silently. Helen was looking

at him lovingly but dispassionately, as if considering a stranger. She reached over to touch his cheek, but he shrugged her away.

"I'm sorry, Josh. I know it's hard on you."

He looked at the ceiling. Didn't she get it? Hard on him? He was drowning here, and there was nobody—not her, not Hal—nobody reaching into that cold black water and fishing him out.

"Ready to go, Josh?" She reached over for her handbag.

"Look, Mom, I want to go to Barnes and Noble and listen to some music—I'll walk home later, okay?"

She frowned. "Is it safe?"

"Oh, sure, yeah."

She cocked her head as if to argue, then shrugged. "Thanks for dinner, son. It meant a lot to me." She hugged him lightly and turned to go.

He was furious at her composure, at her willingness to let him go.

He stood outside the restaurant and watched her pull out. She didn't even give him a backward glance.

TWENTY-FOUR

Josh walked to the bookstore, stood outside the door for a moment and stared at the window bright with tinsel and twirling snowflakes. When the door opened, he could hear Christmas music and smell coffee. He stood there a moment, oddly paralyzed. He gazed at the display in the window, but it all seemed the same—the brightly colored blockbusters, the how-to books. It left him feeling flat.

He turned away from the window and began walking. He found himself walking downtown. He felt impelled suddenly, as if some unseen force was pushing him from behind. He had no plan, only an urgency to be gone, away from his hurtful and disappointing family, away from himself. Only Libby was real for him.

The air smelled of rain, and the trees whipped around overhead, but not a drop fell. The cold air was charged with minerals and ozone and change. *Yeah, why not leave this lousy town?* He quickened his pace. *Yeah, leave it all behind.*

He was on Broad Street, and the Friday-night revelers were zipping into town. Gusts of exhaust blew around him. Cars poured into Peaches Fine Foods, and the usual group of winos was hanging out at the So Fine liquor store. He pushed up the hill, passed the projects, ducked under a large mimosa tree, crossed Pulaski, and saw the brightly lit Greyhound station like a beacon on the hill.

He had almost four hundred dollars in his pocket from the overtime he had been putting in at Good Shepherd, enough, surely, to get him to NYC. He'd surprise her, maybe slip into one of her classes and watch her before she saw him. He envisioned the look of disbelief on Libby's face, followed quickly by joy, and her throwing herself into his arms. Maybe she'd introduce him to some film people, and he could get working again. They'd find a loft apartment. They could start their real lives.

He rounded the corner and was enveloped by diesel exhaust. Inside the station, he bought a ticket for sixty-two fifty. He stuffed the remaining bills in his billfold while the clerk wearily told him that the trip would take eighteen hours, but the next bus would not depart until 6:00 a.m. Irritated that his forward momentum was stymied, he slunk down in a chair and tried to block out the squalling of a nearby baby. The stench of stale cigarette smoke hung in the air. He checked his phone—only one stripe left. He'd have to buy a charger somewhere. He turned it off, jammed it into his pocket. He didn't want to know if his mom called him, anyway. He felt sleepy, but resisted sleep. There were a couple of tough-looking white guys with tattoos sitting across from him, and he had all that cash in his pocket. He had to be careful.

Despite himself, he dozed lightly, though, full from the big meal. He woke in starts, shifting uncomfortably in the hard plastic chair. Through half-shut eyes, he imagined the scene around him as a movie: he saw the station in black-and-white, and himself in a black leather jacket. Of course, the bus station would be a *gare* in Paris, the hicks across from him Nazi soldiers. He himself would be a spy or in the resistance. In his reverie, his mother came in, a double agent in a trench coat and fedora, mysterious and not wholly trustworthy, wearing red lipstick. Then David Masters, his contact, came and sat by him, slipping him the information he needed for the next leg of the journey. Josh drifted in and out of sleep. He was aware of the young mother murmuring to the now-quiet baby, aware the shuffling of feet as people moved around, settling their packages around them and sighing. Finally, the bus for New York City was announced, and Josh shook himself. He got up stiffly, got in line, and stepped up into the frigid bus. Hugging himself, he found a seat by the window, and watched as the bus pulled out and the lights of his town grew dimmer and dimmer.

***

Hal sat at his desk, waiting for the call from the "webmaster." He hated that he had to rely on someone else, but the truth was he wasn't good at computers. Business was slow, so he had finally succumbed to Mike's urging that they put up a website. While he waited, he worked on repairing a fine old Omega watch. If someone asked how he did it, he wouldn't have been able to say. His hands simply knew what to do. When he was working, the work seemed to flow from the tools on its own.

The phone rang, and startled out of his trance, Hal grabbed it. "Yes?"

On the other end he heard ragged breathing. "Hal?"

It was Helen. Hal's first reaction was irritation. She sounded like she had been crying. Why was she always such a mess?

"What is it, Helen?"

"It's Josh." He heard her struggle to gain control. The first image Hal had was of Josh dead.

"What? Calm down, Helen, and tell me what's happened." It was like that night. The feeling of dread pouring down on him, obliterating him. His own heart beat faster.

"He's not here. I looked in his bed. It hadn't been slept in." She started to cry again, her breaths becoming choked and ragged.

Hal's head spun. "When was the last time you saw him?"

"We went out to eat last night." Her pitch, high and strained. "He said he was going to the bookstore to listen to music and would walk home. He never came home. I didn't realize it."

Hal put his head on his desk.

"Hal?"

"What?"

"Did he contact you at all?"

"Me? Are you kidding. I'd be the last person he'd call."

"I had to call the police. The police are questioning his friends now. Oh, god, Hal, what if something happened to him? What if someone mugged him—or worse?"

Whether to just calm her or whether he believed it, he said, "I don't think that's it."

"Hal, he wouldn't skip out, would he? That's not like him. I mean, he's been so good on parole. His officer said he doesn't believe Josh would skip out."

"He might, though. But where would he go? I'll bet those damn friends of his know."

Helen was silent.

"Helen?"

"Why do you always have to blame his friends? Besides, he's pretty much lost them all by now."

"Look, Helen, let's not get into it now? Okay?"

There was another silence.

"Helen?"

"Can you come over?" Her voice was small, pleading.

For the second time that morning, he felt an almost physical shock. He looked around his shop, at the orderly ticking clocks, and he panicked at the thought of leaving them.

"Yes," he said, "of course I'll come."

***

Helen sat at her kitchen table, her sketchpad on her knees, her fingers covered with charcoal. She had been trying to distract herself with drawing. A policeman, Lt. Marks, sat across from her, looking at her with exasperation.

"Mrs. Lovejoy, could you please, please just put that down for a moment. So we can talk?"

Helen tilted her head, made a few more strokes, then sighed and reluctantly put down the pad. "I don't get new models very often," she said.

Lt. Marks was an older man, pockmarked and at least thirty

pounds overweight. He looked to Helen as if everything exasperated him and nothing surprised him. He took off his cap and ran his fingers through thinning gray hair.

"So, now, let's go back to last night. Did he seem particularly upset about anything? Did he talk to you about anything in particular?"

Helen tried to remember. "It was such a pleasant evening. He wanted to take me out. He was very proud to be able to do it. We just chatted about this and that—nothing heavy that I can recall."

Lt. Marks looked as if he expected her to elaborate. Helen squinted, trying to recall the evening in more detail.

"Wait, there was something... I think he was upset about his father's and my separation. Yes, I definitely think that bothered him."

Lt. Marks leaned forward. "So he was a little upset?"

"Yes, but only a little. He really seemed, basically, fine." Tears welled up in her eyes, and she lost hold of her studied composure. "You don't think something bad happened to him, do you? I mean, he's been so responsible, just ask his parole officer. This is just not like him."

Lt. Marks reached back and took out a clean ironed white handkerchief and handed it to her, grimacing regretfully as the hanky became smudged with black.

Helen wiped her eyes and blew her nose. "Thanks," she murmured and was about to hand it back to him, but he shook his head and smiled.

"Part of the job description. Ma'am," he continued, "now, these kids can be impulsive, as you know. We'll follow up with his friends. We'll keep trying the phone company. Do you think he turned it off?"

"I think it ran out of power. He was always forgetting to charge it."

The detective gave her a considering look. "He'll turn up. Bad for his parole, though."

Helen sighed. "He's a good boy, you know. This whole thing—it was just one moment of bad judgment, it was just bad luck." She sounded beseeching, and hated herself for it. Always this need to defend Josh.

"I'll need you to fill out this missing persons report." He handed her a form.

He sat forward in his chair, wearily pushed his cap back, and clasped his hands in front of him. "Ma'am, lots of kids get into trouble at this age. It happens. It doesn't mean his life is ruined." He sighed. "Now, do you think he'll contact you if he has skipped out?"

Helen stared at him. "I have no idea. Yes, maybe."

"And you'll let us know as soon as that happens?"

Helen nodded docilely.

"Okay then." He stood up, put out his hand. "Thanks very much. We'll find him. I guess we've missed your husband, but we'll try him at work."

The man shuffled out. Helen had not told him about Libby, not that she knew very much about her. She hadn't consciously held back any information, she simply hadn't thought of it. Lt. Marks had said he would be sending their tech guy over to get Josh's hard drive. Now Helen wandered in and turned on the computer. The screen came up and a picture of a pretty young woman with pale skin and a cloud of soft curls. She looked straight into the camera with a grave expression, not the usual four-cornered smiles most of the kids faced cameras with.

Helen sat in Josh's chair and stared at the girl. There was something arresting about the child. She looked both world-weary and waiflike. Helen regretted suddenly her self-involvement that had kept Josh from bringing this girl home. It would have been nice if they had met before—when Helen had kept a clean house, when Hal lived at home, when Josh wasn't on parole. She imagined for a moment getting to know the girl, sharing an interest in books or clothes or art, imagined gaining a daughter, not losing a son.

But then she asked herself if she would really want to go back. And she knew the answer. She had been to hell, but for the first time in her life, she had befriended herself. No one else could save her, and she could save no one. It was a cool, calm thing, this knowledge. After a lifetime of pouring herself into others, it was a relief.

She read Josh's emails to Libby and hers to him. It became clear that Josh was deeply in love with this girl. She read all about his work at Good Shepherd, his anger at his father, his anxiety over her, his fears of losing his way, of never making anything of himself.

It was this last that hurt her the most. He sounded so like Hal: in Hal was the full flowering of a bitterness that was only incipient in Josh's letters. But it was there, unmistakably.

Libby's replies to Josh's emails were briefer, cooler. Helen wondered if Josh even noticed, or if he was so consumed with his ardor that he inflated any sign from her.

Poor Josh! He was so like her in this, this willingness to love. Her hand at her throat, Helen read on, becoming more and more convinced that this was a lopsided love. By the time she finished, her heart ached for her son.

If this is what he's gone to, it will crush him, she thought.

Then she did something the old Helen would never have done. She trashed all the correspondence. She knew that the police would be able to read his hard drive, but she didn't want to make it easy for them.

She heard Hal come in, slamming the door behind him. She felt herself tense.

"Helen? Helen!" he called.

She sat silently in Josh's darkened room. Then, as he approached, she called, "I'm in here."

He stood in the doorway a moment, then flipped on the light switch.

Helen squinted her eyes.

"What are you doing in the dark?" he muttered. He looked around at Josh's room, at the model airplanes hanging from the ceiling, at the swim trophies on the bureau, at the film noir posters on the walls, all mixed up with Josh's early drawings. He picked up a Star Wars figure that lay on its side on a shelf and set it upright. Then he sat on the bed and looked at Helen.

All her defenses went up. She was about to blame Hal for Josh's disappearance before he could blame her. She was trying to formulate the right tack in her mind. But then she noticed Hal's slumped shoulders and the deeply drawn lines in his face. Maybe it was because she had practiced seeing that she noticed. And so she stopped herself from saying the same old tired things.

"What are we going to do, Helen?"

Helen was taken aback and pleased, strangely, by the *we*. "I don't know."

"Do you think he's gone to the girlfriend?"

She nodded.

"Did you tell the police?"

She shook her head.

Hal looked alarmed. "That's withholding evidence."

"I know."

"Why did you do it?"

"I didn't really think of it till they left. I thought we could use it, maybe get a head start. Find him."

Hal looked hard at her. "Do you know where she lives?"

Helen looked down at the scribble notes she'd made. "In New York City. I don't know where she lives, but I know where she goes to school."

"Maybe I should fly up there and try to talk to him. This is serious, leaving the state. Maybe we can get him back here before they realize where he's been. Oh, god, Helen, what was he thinking?"

Helen shook her head. "He wasn't thinking, he was feeling."

Hal looked at his hands. "Yeah, that's what Valerie said."

Helen felt herself jerked out her usual lethargy. "Valerie? You didn't waste any time." She was shaken, jealous, but also, curious. Hal? "You know, I never expected you to find someone else... I thought we would work on this..." For the second time in one day, she lost her composure.

Hal reached out and touched her arm. She shook him off.

"It's not like that, at all. Really, Helen. Look, you shut me out, I just needed someone to talk to."

"Since when are you the great communicator?"

Hal shook his head. "I'm not. Look, I know I'm not. It's all so crazy right now, I'm trying to figure things out. Okay? Let's focus on Josh right now, okay?"

"All right." Helen still felt pricked, wounded.

"I think I should go. If we both go, it would be suspicious. I actually have a dealer in New York I need to contact. So it could be a business trip. Maybe I can find Josh, talk some sense to him. The police won't be looking up there yet. I could get him home before anyone knows he left the state."

Helen looked at him warily. "Your track record with Josh isn't so great."

Hal put his face in his hands. "I know, I know." He sighed heavily. "I know I'll have to be different. I know I can't just yell at him, okay?" He sounded as if he were pleading with her.

This was something new, something fragile. Helen held her breath, not wanting to say the wrong thing.

"I think you should go, Hal. I think you should."

He looked at her, unsure if she were on the level.

"I'm really scared, Hal. I'm scared we won't find him, or they'll find him and put him in jail forever, or he'll be dead." She started crying then, didn't hold back the tears.

"I know, Helen." He got up and bent down and hugged her awkwardly. She inhaled his familiar scent, let him hug her. It was comforting to have his arms around her, amazing that he came over to her. Wasn't this what she'd always wanted from him? Why then did she feel almost frantic, as if she couldn't breathe? She gently pushed him away.

"I will find him, Helen. I promise. I won't let you down."

"I know you will, Hal," she said without conviction. She pulled out Lt. Marks's hanky and blew hard.

***

Josh dozed on the bus, until the freezing AC roused him. He regretted his thin hoodie, wished he had a warm jacket. Well, he'd buy one when he got to New York. He hugged his arms, rubbing them to warm them. He had slowly gotten used to the stale cigarette odor that clung to the plastic seat, but he remained slightly nauseated. Someone was talking loudly in an overbearing voice, some woman. In a gravely country drawl, she described the intimate processes of her body and their slow disintegration. Josh tried hard not to listen. In his mind, he hummed to himself "Your Body Is a Wonderland," but her words—"fallen uterus, irritated bladder..."—drummed like a bass line to another song.

He shifted in his seat, easing his cramped legs into yet another contorted position. Outside, the sun was already beginning its westward descent, and the road was striated with the long shadows of trees. He dimly remembered the bus stopping and people getting on and off. Now he was anxious to get to a station and stretch his legs, get a bite to eat, a cup of good, strong coffee, and plan the rest of his trip. Signs for Washington, D.C., began to appear, and Josh found himself as excited as a little kid. He had never been to any city except Atlanta, although he had always wanted desperately to go to LA. Here he was in the nation's capital, and yesterday, it had been the furthest thing from his mind.

The bus merged with increasingly heavy traffic, and slowed down as it entered the city. Josh's heart pounded. He spotted the Washington Monument, the Jefferson Memorial. He looked out at the city sidewalks, covered with people looking purposeful, walking briskly, carrying briefcases and purses. For a moment, he imagined being one of them—being someone ordinary, someone whose family was ordinary, someone who was productive and directed. Not a wannabe. Not a loser. Not someone who might be a murderer.

He shook his head. He wasn't going to think about that.

The bus swung into a large concrete island with a refueling station and food court. The loud-mouthed woman, having told all her stories, now snored loudly. Josh jiggled his knee, impatient to get off, and as soon as the bus stopped, he jumped up to the door.

"Half-hour stop, folks," the driver announced, pushing his hat back from his forehead. "Make sure you have your ticket when you get back on board."

Josh patted his breast pocket, felt the flimsy slip of paper that was his ticket to freedom. He jumped out into the fresh air and gulped it down. He wondered if he should call Libby now, make sure he didn't miss her when he got in, make sure he knew how to get to her place. Maybe surprising her wasn't the best idea after all. But first, the bathroom and coffee.

He could smell the coffee as he came out of the men's room. It had that slightly burned, acrid smell that coffee had at places like this. Still, it would wake him up and fill him up. He realized that he was starving and, although he didn't want to waste money on food, decided he'd have to eat something.

He stood in line to get his coffee and a biscuit and reached around to his back pocket for his wallet. He patted his left pocket, then his right. A slow, sickening realization began to nudge at his awareness. Josh tried to resist it, but it expanded. Gone. No. It couldn't be. He checked again. His money and wallet were gone. He felt sick then, his heart beat too fast. He broke out in a sweat.

"Okay, ready for your order." He looked blankly at the woman behind the counter, taking in her elaborately styled hair and pudgy, fat face. Her heavily lined eyes stared back at him with a look of bored irritation.

"Hey, you—what do you want to eat?"

Josh shook his head. "Sorry, I've changed my mind."

She rolled her eyes at her partner. "Next!" she called, and Josh slunk out of line.

Maybe it dropped out in the bus, Josh thought, quickening his steps to where the bus was being refueled. Hunger bit into him, and the smell of the diesel made him queasy. He found the bus, but the driver was nowhere to be seen. He tried to get on the bus, but he couldn't get in.

"Hey, you, what ya doing!" a guy in a uniform yelled at him.

"I left my wallet on the bus." Josh turned to him, knowing his face was red and the guy probably thought he was lying.

The guy looked at him suspiciously.

Josh felt the blood leave his head. "I'm sorry, sir, I just panicked, that's all."

They man gave him a hard look, then tilted his head toward the bus. "Okay, kid—go in for a minute and take a look. Make it snappy." He opened the door.

Josh ran up the steps. He found where he'd been sitting and felt in the seat, looked under the seat and all around. Nothing. His stomach clenched. Nothing. How could this have happened?

He got off the bus. The attendant said, "Nothing?"

Josh shook his head.

"Better call your folks," the man said, then turned his back on him.

It wasn't any use, anyway. He remembered those two tattooed guys eyeing him when he came in last night—was it only last night? They must have pegged him from the get-go. They probably had his pocket picked before he ever got on the damn bus. Or maybe it wasn't them, maybe it was some quiet unassuming character that slipped by like a shadow. Almost three hundred bucks! His cell phone was almost out of juice, and he hadn't thought to get a charger. He turned it off to save the battery. He felt weak and, for the first time, scared. It dawned on him that he might have done a very foolish thing. He found a bench to sit on, watching the bus to make sure that didn't get away from him, too. Hot, tarry air rose up around him. He watched the other passengers sitting at concrete tables, smoking and eating, laughing. Why couldn't he just be normal, like them?

He patted his pocket again. He still had his ticket. He'd get to New York and walk till he found her. They'd figure out what to do together. The thought of Libby, of her soft hair, her downy skin, her slightly unfocused eyes, gave him hope. Once they were together, everything would be all right.

SECTION 9:
BLUE CHRISTMAS

TWENTY-FIVE

By the time the bus got to New York, Josh was faint from hunger. He hadn't been able to sleep well on the bus. He had shifted around in his seat, trying to get comfortable, but no matter how he crossed or uncrossed his legs, hunched his shoulders, or turned his head, he couldn't relax. The frigid air-conditioning seeped through his hoodie, and hunger gnawed at him. He'd never been so hungry, and he was amazed at how painful and insistent a feeling it was. He tried to trick himself into thinking of other things—of living with Libby in a loft in the city, of Oscar night, dressed in a tux, the camera panning as he lightly jumped to the dais to receive his Oscar, but even these well-worn fantasies failed him. The meal with Helen came back to him, the pasta drowned in red sauce, the buttery mozzarella. He groaned.

It had dawned on him that his mother would be worried about him, and that had made him feel even sicker. He thought of calling her, but what would he say to her, anyway? How would he explain himself? He imagined her anxious, tearful voice or, worse, her newly distanced voice. He couldn't face it. He had to stay focused on Libby right now, get his bearings. But when he tried to conjure Libby, he couldn't get her in focus, either. He knew he shouldn't use his precious cell phone battery to sneak a look at her picture, but he did. She stared back at him in her myopic way, her hair tumbling over her shoulders in waves. Josh took in her image as if it were food itself, and it braced him. He switched off the phone and looked out the window.

He watched the Manhattan skyline grow closer and closer with a strange sense of déjà vu. He had seen that skyline in countless movies, and yet, here it was, real, and he was heading toward it. The buildings sparkled like ornaments against the inky sky. Josh imagined at any moment he would see King Kong hanging from the top of the Empire State Building. The bus crossed the Hudson, and then they were in the city itself. The brackish smell of the river seeped into the bus, and for a moment, Josh forgot his hunger in his excitement.

The bus swung into the Port Authority. The brakes squeaked, the bus jolted to a stop, and the doors opened with a hydraulic sigh. People around him got wearily to their feet, pulling suitcases off racks, shaking crumbs off of themselves. Josh felt a curious lethargy, a momentary unwillingness to leave the safety of the bus, and he sat and waited until the bus had almost emptied. Now that he was here, he wasn't sure what to do. Outside, the smell of diesel turned his hunger into nausea. He looked around, disoriented. Most people seemed to be heading toward a large, mall-like building. He put his head down and followed them, trying to look as if he knew what he was doing.

Inside the Authority it was cool again, and noisy. He stood, arrested, not sure in which direction to turn. The voices echoing off the walls, the sound of clipped footsteps, the squeak of suitcase wheels, and the bright lights hanging from the ceiling dazzled him; the odors of pizza, coffee, and sugar taunted him.

Still, he was quickened by the energy, the movement of people striding purposefully around him, by the sheer audacity of having gotten himself here.

Following a group of people, Josh realized he was heading toward the subway. Panicked, he turned against the crowd and tried to retrace his steps to the main hall. A small, twisted man with a limp blocked his way. Confused, Josh tried to go around him. The man glared at him, holding up a sign saying he was deaf and mute and needed money for food. Josh tried to get past him again. The man tapped him again, pointed to the sign, and rubbed his stomach. Josh shuddered at the man's aggressive, almost sneering face. He felt like rubbing his own stomach in response. But when Josh gestured and mouthed, "I don't have anything," the man angrily brushed past him. Shaken, Josh ran up the nearest stairs. He had never in his life been treated like that, and it frightened him as much as if someone had drawn a gun on him.

He found the terminal again and an information booth, where luckily the map was free. He asked the woman behind the desk to show him where the Professional Performing Arts High School was located, and she pointed indifferently to the map and went on talking on her cell phone, tapping her long red acrylic nails impatiently on the desk. He wanted to ask her how to get there from here, but decided against it.

Pushing through the plate glass doors to the street, Josh momentarily forgot his hunger and anxiety. He was in New York, the city he had dreamed about all his life. It was a beautiful day, cold and crisp, and the sky he could see above the tall buildings was a Technicolor blue. He was cold, but his excitement kept him from feeling it. He had never seen so many people on a street: business men in suits, tourists with cameras, mothers pushing strollers, teenagers roving in groups, laughing. He felt a pang, wishing suddenly that he had his friends with him. People had cell phones attached to their ears, and he caught intriguing snatches of conversation: "I don't care if he said we could take the loss… ," "That's right, she said she found a Prada purse at Filene's… ," "And then, oh my god, this gorgeous guy came off stage…" He stood there, the city swirling like a kaleidoscope around him, and breathed it in. Here it was, New York, a place of movement, a place where things happened. Not like Milledge, where nothing ever happened.

He wandered, following the crowds. Everyone seemed to be going toward a teeming intersection, bright with glittering neon signs. Above him, on a digital billboard, an incredibly buff man and gorgeous woman in a bikini kissed and grappled on the sand, then a photo of a bottle of Perry Ellis cologne appeared as the couple faded away. He stopped to look at beautifully decorated storefronts. The Gap store sported male and female mannequins dressed in bright sweaters and jeans, holding ski poles, their scarves flying out behind them. Josh jammed his fists into his pockets, superimposing his face and Libby's on the plastic dolls. He would ski, of course, in his new life, just as he would wear only the freshest clothes. Moving on, he stopped in front of Skagen, his mouth watering at the sight of the sleek minimalist watches displayed in a case minimally decorated with silver and white glass ornaments. No watch like that had ever found its way to ClockWorks; the watches his father repaired were often large, clunky things with worn bands. Josh shivered, whether with cold, excitement, or a feeling of betrayal, he wasn't sure.

He looked down at the map. He was at Times Square. Broadway, the Great White Way. He stopped, stunned, while the crowds parted around him. He was here. He didn't care now if he looked like a rube as he gawked up at the opulent buildings, at the stores, the street vendors. He was a rube. But it was a good sign, to stumble on Times Square first. It was confirmation. He was going to be part of this someday.

But for now, he had to find Libby. It was Monday, so he'd try to find Libby at school. He consulted the map again. The school wasn't far: 328 West Forty-Eighth Street. He was tempted to use his phone GPS, but didn't want to waste the power. Libby would make everything all right. She would take him home and feed him, and they'd figure things out from there. He'd tell her about how strange his mother had been, how his father had taken him out to those awkward, embarrassing lunches, and, mostly, how lonely he felt without her. He would tell her how he tired of waiting for his real life to begin, his life with her. He'd go to film school. They'd live together, work hard, very hard, and make their marks. He'd leave all that mess behind him—his dad, his mom, David in a coma. He'd shake off Milledge the way a dog shakes off water. He'd change his name, his appearance, maybe. He'd disappear; people disappeared all the time. He'd start over. Everything would be different. Everything would be perfect.

***

Josh stood outside the black iron gate surrounding the imposing nineteenth-century gray stone facade of the school. Unsure whether he should go in or just wait on the sidewalk, Josh hesitated indecisively. But there was nowhere to sit, so he took a deep breath and went in. Inside, the crowded halls were reassuringly like any high school halls, except that students wore leotards and tights or carried instrument cases. He heard a distant piano and someone singing scales. No one seemed to notice him, which was a good thing. He could pass here. He deserved to be in film school; he was good enough. These kids, half of them were just rich kids on a lark. But he was the real thing. He knew it. And he'd show them, all of them.

He scrutinized each girl he passed, looking for the familiar glasses, the long curly hair. He thought he saw her from the back—that was her way of tossing her hair—and went up to the girl and tapped her on the shoulder. "Libby?" he said as the girl turned and shrugged away from him, giving him a dirty look.

The halls suddenly emptied, and he was left alone. He spotted a half-empty package of cheese crackers on a bench, and sidled over to it, picked it up, watching to make sure no one saw him. He shoved the crackers into his mouth and thought he'd never tasted anything so delicious. But the morsel intensified his hunger, and so he began roaming the halls, hoping to find more. What he really needed to find was the office, he knew.

A middle-aged, portly man came down the hall and stopped when he saw Josh. "May I help you?" he said in a slightly British accent.

"I'm waiting for a, uh, friend," Josh stammered.

The man squinted his eyes in a very theatrical way. "And his or her name *is*?"

Josh cleared his throat. "Libby. Libby Starkweather."

"Hmm. Oh, yes, Libby. I think she has my class next period. Why don't you follow me, and we'll see if we can't get you two together." He gave Josh a long, considering look, and Josh could feel himself flush. What did he look like to this man? He was suddenly aware that he hadn't combed his hair or washed in a very long time. Maybe he did look out of place.

They came to a large, almost filled classroom. Josh stationed himself at the door, watching as the last students trickled in, but none of them were Libby. He was beginning give up hope. A thin girl with spiky hair and multiple ear piercings hesitated as she passed him, then circled back.

"Josh?" he recognized the voice, but nothing else. Her eyes were heavily made up and her lips pale. She looked like she had the part of a ghost or vampire in some play. He could not put her together with his Libby.

"I, I came to see you," he stuttered.

The girl, Libby, stared at him with flat black-fringed eyes. There was no hint of welcome in them.

"I guess so," she said, and stood there, motionless.

Josh couldn't think of what to say. He didn't know if he wanted to flee or just sink into the floor. He had never seen her so thin, her features sharpened, older looking, her eyes huge and unblinking. He felt as if he had stepped into the wrong movie altogether.

"What about your parole?" she hissed, finally.

Students filed by, and several of them turned to stare at Josh when she said this.

"Could we, could we go somewhere else and talk? I haven't had anything to eat… I think I need to sit down." He hated his own weakness in the face of this flinty young woman.

She took him by the elbow and steered him back down the hall. She seemed impatient, irritated.

"Aren't you even a little glad to see me?" Josh hated the whiney sound to his voice.

She stopped, ran her hand through her short hair. "Of course I am, Josh. Just surprised, that's all." She laughed. "Wow. I mean, it's like two realities colliding."

Josh wasn't sure what she meant by that and didn't know if he liked it very much, but more urgent matters were on his mind.

"Look, Libby, I got robbed on the bus. I had money—I wasn't coming up here empty-handed, okay? But I don't have anything now, and I'm starving."

Libby looked at him with concern, and for a moment Josh caught a glimpse of the old Libby.

"Hey, Josh, it's okay." They were outside now, and she put her arm around his waist and leaned her cheek against his for a moment. "I'm afraid we don't have any barbeque up here. But we have Chinese, Italian, deli sandwiches…"

You're acting like I'm up here for a friendly little jaunt, he wanted to say. *Don't you get it? I came up here to be with you, to start over. This is it—what we've always talked about!* But he didn't say anything.

"Whatever, Libby, I don't care." They stopped at a Chinese storefront. He didn't actually like Chinese, but he was too hungry to care. Libby opened the door, herded him in.

Libby ordered for them. Josh still couldn't believe her transformation.

"Why'd you cut your hair? How did you lose so much weight?" he asked in a voice that sounded surly even to him.

"You don't like me like this?" She looked hurt, and he liked that, liked that he could get to her.

Josh shook his head. "No, not much."

"Well, I had to lose weight. I've been trying out for soaps, ya know, to get a start, make a little money. You have to be thin."

Their food came, and Josh dug in to rice and chicken and peas. It tasted good; he could feel his strength returning. He glanced at Libby, who was picking fastidiously at her plate.

"You were really hungry," she said.

"Did you get any jobs? On soaps?"

"No, not yet. But I've gotten some work at conventions, y'know, I pick up gigs like that."

"You didn't tell me much about that." Josh could hear the accusation in his voice.

"I've been really busy, Josh." She put her chopsticks down. "Do you want to tell me why you're really here? How long you're planning to stay? Why didn't you let me know? I mean, you have my number."

Josh felt at a loss. He'd wanted to tell her about the dinner with his mom, how she seemed so willing to let their family fall apart, about how he hadn't planned anything, had just walked to the bus stop as if there were nothing else left to do. About how he'd missed her. Mostly, he wanted to tell her that he felt she was his only lifeline, the only one he had left. But now, with the sunlight shining on her nose ring and her hollowed-out cheeks, he couldn't. He was a little afraid of her, he realized.

"Look, it all happened so fast. I just realized one night there was nothing there for me anymore. I had some stupid notion that if I came up here, I could start over. With you."

Libby looked hard at him. "I'm just surprised, that's all, Josh. And I'm worried, too. I mean, I thought you weren't supposed to leave the state." Here was that professional Libby again, the one that had left him on the curb in Milledge, the one that was "concerned" about him, the one that managed him. He wanted to tell her to come off it.

"Look, Libby, we'll get to that. I can see you're not overjoyed—"

"I'm sorry. I'm so sorry." She bowed her head over her still-full plate. She sounded like she meant it.

"Okay." Josh took a big breath. "Let's back off this for right now. Anyway, how are you, how's your crazy family?"

Libby jerked up as if a string had pulled her upright. Josh saw a momentary glimpse of the old, vulnerable Libby, the one he'd held trembling the night they'd run from Scary Harry.

"Crazy is right, I guess." She tried to summon a little laugh, but it sounded strangled. "My, um, mom is in the hospital. Dad finally lost it, beat her up. I got a restraining order to keep my dad away from the family." Tears glazed her eyes, but she shook them back. "I've got the kids on my own. My plate is full right now—I have to be at home when the kids come back, then I go out at night to work and hope that they'll be okay. So it really wasn't very hard to lose this weight." She laughed again, tossing the absent hair over her shoulder. "It was easy."

Josh stared at her, trying to absorb the information. He

thought she might be lying. He knew what a good actress she was, and she might have just given an award-winning monologue. Or it could have been true.

"Why didn't you tell me any of this? You must have been lying to me for months." He was angry now. Maybe this is what accounted for her short, stilted messages.

"I didn't want to worry you."

"Worry me?" He looked at her, incredulous. Who was she? "What do you want from me, Libby? If you can't talk to me, tell me the truth?"

This time Libby's eyes turned red, and the mascara tears seemed real, making black tracks down her face.

"I didn't want to lose what we had. I wanted to freeze us in time. I didn't know how to talk about it. I didn't want you to come up and rescue me or anything like that." She wiped her face with the back of her hand and blew her nose into her napkin. "That's a laugh, I guess. I'm not going to be like them, like my parents. I've got to make it, no matter what. I'm going to be a success. And I can't let anyone stand in my way. Not even you, Josh." She looked at him kindly, the way you might look at a very sick person. "I don't have any room in me for love right now. I don't have any room for another thing in my life. I'm sorry."

Libby got up. "Look, I've got last night's tips here in my purse…" She dug in her bag, throwing bills and coins on the sticky linoleum table. "Take it. Get back now before they know you're gone." She brought her face very close to his. "What we had was good, Josh. But I was a stupid, naive kid then. I didn't know how hard it all is." And then she kissed him, and her tears seeped into his mouth, and then she was gone, a thin shadow outside the neon-lit window.

***

Josh sat in the Chinese restaurant a very long time. He let the money sit on the table, untouched, while he drank his tea. He was afraid his body would fly apart without the tea, as if it were the one thing keeping him on earth. He seemed to be vibrating internally at a very high speed, even as he turned to stone.

In spite of himself, he began guessing how much money there was—it looked to be about a hundred dollars. He shouldn't take it. He should have done the manly thing and run after her and made her take it back and told her to use it for her brother and sister. Or maybe he should have saved his own last shred of dignity, run after her, throwing the money at her, call her a selfish bitch, a phony who had been leading him on, that her story was right out of a playbook. But was it? He didn't know. He only knew that as she receded from him, something in the pit of his stomach, some connection to her, began to wither, and with it any remaining clarity or resolve he had.

Josh was flooded with a hot shame as he slowly gathered up the money. But in the little time he had been in this city, he had already learned it was a very cruel place unless you paid your way.

He sipped the hot tea and asked for more.

The sun had shifted, so that the light no longer flooded

through the window. He noticed the waiters hovering around him, and the lunch customers began to file in. He slowly counted out the money and carefully put the $114.76 into his pocket. He didn't want to leave the table, his one familiar piece of the city, but it looked like he was going to have to.

She was right, of course. He should just go back. Just retrace his steps, get back on a bus headed home. Maybe he could do it before anyone figured out he was gone. But now that he was here, now that he was away, the thought of going back to Milledge seemed impossible. All of it—waiting for David to live or die, his father's awkward attempts at a relationship, his mother's distance, talk about crazy!—suddenly seemed to have nothing to do with him, with the real him. Who the real him was he wasn't sure. But he wasn't that docile kid being jerked around by everybody else. He'd show them, he'd show them all. He had what it took to succeed, too, not just Libby. She'd be sorry one day, she'd be begging him to let her work for him.

He left a generous tip on the small table. That was the kind of man he was, a generous tipper. He left the small restaurant with what he hoped was a swagger. *New York City, here I come,* he thought, but the thought echoed hollowly in his mind.

TWENTY-SIX

Hal fidgeted with the earphones but didn't put them on. He looked around: most of the people were listening to the news or reading. He hadn't thought to bring anything to read, but the bobbing heads on the screen didn't entice him, either. The man next to him snored lightly, his rather large head lolling dangerously toward Hal. The man was fat, too, which only made Hal feel more uncomfortable in the small seat. He crossed and uncrossed his legs, trying to find a comfortable position.

He looked out the window. He was lucky, he supposed, to have a window seat. He had never really been much of a flyer, for while he understood the physics of flying in the abstract, he disliked putting physics to the test. They were angling up through the clouds and now broke out into a sky so blue and bright that it let Hal forget for a moment how uncomfortable he was in his seat, how uncomfortable he was in the role he was supposed to be playing. If he was honest with himself, he had never really been comfortable anywhere but in his shop and home.

He had very little to go on. Helen had given him the name and address of the school Libby went to, convinced that would be the place to start. Could it only have been yesterday, Sunday, when she had called him to tell him Josh was missing?

He had called Valerie—Meg—to tell her. It had become a habit, telling her about Josh. As angry as he was about her lie, he still felt compelled to tell her. Her interest in Josh seemed genuine enough. She'd been understanding about Josh. With her, he had sensed new possibilities in himself; he'd begun to hope he might be the father he wanted to be to Josh. Not like the failure Helen knew him to be. The failure he evidently was. But now that he knew who she was, well, it made him sick. He hated lies, any deviation from the truth. It had been a double betrayal to learn her true identity. What was her game anyway? She should have hated Josh after what Josh did to her husband. Was she some kind of nut? And she'd been angry with him! As much as he might have been falling for Valerie, he knew he hated Meg.

The seat belt light went on, and the captain announced they were going through some clear-air turbulence, just as the plane bounced and shuddered. Hal tensed, feeling trapped by Fat Man and too far from the exits. Figures Josh would put him through something like this. Hal squeezed the arm of his chair tightly and closed his eyes, willing his stomach to relax. He braced his feet around his carry-on bag in front of him that contained the clock. With every bump, he imagined the possible damage to its delicate workings.

He'd had time to make some an appointment before he got on the plane. He was there to find Josh, but the appointment was his cover. What he hoped was that he'd drag Josh away from his girl, put him on a plane, and get him back before anyone knew he was gone. He was prepared, he'd been rehearsing how he would do it. He would try to listen to Josh, not yell at him. He'd tell him he'd been young and in love once, too, the way Valerie had suggested. He'd promise to support Josh. He'd even promise to support his interest in film, stop trying to make him into an engineer. That grated on his nerves because he thought this artistic phase was a passing fad. Still, he'd swallow that. He'd do it. He didn't want to see Helen's face the way he'd seen it when he'd left—her eyes red rimmed and empty. She'd looked so old and defeated.

He shook off the image of Helen, turned his thoughts to the clock. He'd put Josh on a plane, and then he'd be able to concentrate on business. He'd never met the gentlemen he talked with, but he could sense their excitement when they heard about the clock. He imagined meeting with them, imagined the regard those worldly men would have for him. This was it, at last, his break. Josh and Helen wouldn't be able to think of him as a failure anymore, none of them would.

The plane suddenly leveled out, and Hal's stomach calmed. Guilt flooded Hal for thinking ill of his son. It was just—if he wasn't angry, what would he feel? His fingers drummed his knees. He mentally pushed the door closed on the answer, but still little murmurs of anxiety and hopelessness made their way to him through it. Josh as a boy flashed into his mind, Josh grinning up at him, holding up the small shark he caught at the beach, the fish almost bigger than he was. They'd brought it back to the pine-scented beach campsite, and Hal had made a big deal about it, ceremoniously teaching Josh how to gut and filet it, cook it over an open fire. Josh had finished every charred morsel, his eyes shining. He wanted that Josh back, or some semblance of him. Hal held on to that image—it would give him the courage to do what he came here to do.

He looked out at the clouds below them, which had turned dark and gray. It had all changed so quickly, it seemed to Hal. When Josh started having trouble in school, it had made Hal angry, but also horrified. It was his fault. Josh was like him. Helen was right. She couldn't understand why a parent would repudiate a child that shared his same, as she insisted upon calling it, disability. She didn't understand that it was all too much for him, that he felt everything Josh experienced, every failure, anew, magnified.

It was an old pain, and Hal had seen no way out, just more slogging through tougher and tougher terrain. So he hardened himself to it. What else could he have done?

The seat belt lights went on again, and Fat Man's wife poked him awake. He awoke with a sputter and snort, suddenly taking up even more of the nonexistent room. The plane landed with a thump, and the stewardess near him laughed as if it were just added fun. They taxied and parked, and Hal thought he would strangle Fat Man as the guy unpacked his luggage from overhead, now talking loudly to anyone who would listen. He swung his bag down heedlessly, almost smashing the overnight bag onto the carefully wrapped clock. By the time Hal reached the terminal, he felt almost giddy to be free of Fat Man and the plane.

In the airport, Hal shifted his overnight bag to the other shoulder. He felt competent now and focused. He pushed through the plate glass doors, stepped out into the diesel-filled air, and put his hand up to hail a cab. It amazed him that one actually stopped. He showed him the address of the school, then sat back and closed his eyes.

***

David felt Meg's sorrow flow toward him, like water seeking lower ground. She was crying, going on about New York, about a lost boy. He wanted to pat her back, tell her that boys were lost every day, that sometimes boys wanted to be lost. He wanted to tell her that he had fled to New York, but come back. Her boy would come back when it was time. He was sure of it. He only wished he could tell her.

New York. He was arriving in New York, stepping off the train that first time, his degree and suit equally shiny and new. "Look out, world, here I come," he had whistled.

And it had been all that he'd dreamed, even more, for a while. His firm up-and-coming, his marriage to beautiful Ruth securing his place in Manhattan's Jewish elite. He was drunk on the city, the success, the smartness of it all. Bright lights, big city, indeed. There were great parties, coke lines, liquor flowing freely, and he flashed not once but often, on Anthony, on how he'd like to tell him that their lives were not that far apart, that he, too, had bad habits. Only his were sanctioned and came with a hefty salary, while Anthony's got him sent to jail. And so after a coke high, he'd often wake up depressed, thinking, *Man, I'm a damned hypocrite.*

The feeling of being somehow an imposter would creep up on him unexpectedly. He'd be walking to a meeting and see a black man with dreadlocks dressed in rags, rooting through the trash, and he'd wonder if it was Anthony. He'd be reading briefs on the train and look up to see someone who could be Anthony hanging from a strap, reeking of alcohol and cigarettes, and he'd be snapped out of his complacency, and ashamed, as if he'd been found out. As if the man saw him for the fraud that he was, a man who'd given up on his best friend, a man who, with all his power, had failed the person he cared for the most.

He couldn't tell Ruth about any of it. The first few times he'd brought it up, she'd looked at him blankly and waved her hand dismissively. Finally, once the sheen of their early marriage had dulled, she told him flatly that she found his obsession self-indulgent and unattractive. "Really, David, it's not as if it was your fault. Things happen. You suffer from a messiah complex."

He told her she was right, and tried to forget it, but couldn't. He kept in touch with Anthony's mother, Cornelia, found out that Anthony had been in the hospital, where he'd gone after a brawl, and had submitted to detox. Anthony had been home for a while, but soon drifted back to his old buddies. He'd been in and out of jail. He'd managed to have a sprinkling of children along the way, all of which were added to his mother's household, the young mothers fading away like shadows, and David imagined Cornelia's house overrun with them, the endless diapers and runny noses, the smell of pepper vinegar that always permeated the air.

He'd used some connections to try to trace Anthony and had some luck, but by the time he'd track Anthony down in one place, he'd be gone. It became almost a hobby, and he realized that he'd given up really finding Anthony, but by keeping notes of where he'd been, by tracing his wanderings, he had some record of his friend's existence, some connection to him. He was here. He lives. Like the snail trails they'd follow as boys, shiny threads written on leaves, proof of the invisible snail.

Ruth sensed that David had another life, and she thought he was having an affair. When she found his journal with the notes, she was incensed, called him crazy, said she'd rather he had had an affair—*that* she could understand. It was the beginning of the end of them. When he told her he wanted to go back south, to do community work, she was horrified. She was right; he was more married to his past than to her.

It will be all right, he wanted to say. He felt Meg go then. He could tell by the cool emptiness beside him.

***

Monday afternoon, Helen compulsively checked the ringer on the phone. She sometimes turned it off, but she wanted to make sure it was on now. She had called Hal as soon as she knew the plane had touched the ground. They were polite with each other, cautious, both of them uncertain how to be. She didn't want to nag Hal, had determined to let him handle this his own way. She knew she had nagged him too much in the past about Josh. She'd let him call her next time. But in the meantime, she prowled around the house, nervous as a cat. She had spent most of Sunday afternoon cleaning, doing dishes, vacuuming, changing sheets, doing laundry, as if the order she created could somehow bring Josh home. Today she had nothing to do but wait.

It was as if all Josh's life, she knew something like this would happen, as if she had been waiting for it. So many times, her throat would close and her chest grow tight with panic. It would happen when as a toddler, he'd run into the street, heedless of her cries. It would happen when as a small child, he would run off in stores, and she would frantically look through racks of clothes, peeking under changing room doors, her face hot with humiliation and helplessness. It would happen when he'd try to do his homework in second grade and get so frustrated he broke all his pencils. It would happen in the doctor's office when she tried to help him with a math problem and he threw the book at her. It would happen when he'd cry and hit his head repeatedly, saying, "I'm stupid, stupid, stupid." It would happen when he would lose assignments, shoes, lunchboxes; when he would need to be told things thirty-two times; when he was late for school every morning.

And there was the anger, the guilt over being angry at him for his messy room, at his spaciness, at the constant interruptions when she was on the phone. Because he was the sweetest, most loving child. But he wore her out.

She had thought with treatment he would get better. And he did, for a while. But in high school she suspected that he didn't take his medication. Her brief respite from worry ended, and with its demise began the "coddling" Hal had accused her of, a word she despised. She knew Hal was jealous of the attention she gave Josh. But what was she supposed to do? She had desperately needed to keep a connection, to be there if he fell.

But he had withdrawn from both of them. It was natural

and necessary, she knew, but she wished Hal had not simply dropped out as a parent. If only Hal had reached out to his son! She had seen Josh make overtures that were ignored or simply not noticed, and every time it had killed something in her. She knew Hal suffered in his own particular hell, but knowing that didn't make her any less sad, or angry.

She fixed herself another cup of coffee and went into the sunroom, where she was working on her self-portrait. She had resisted this assignment. She didn't like looking at herself. "Why?" she had asked when Olaffson had said it was absolutely imperative.

"Because you need to learn how to paint faces, and your face is always available!" He had grinned at his own joke. "All artists must do it. Learn something. Just do it."

She looked at the painting now, cold to it. The palette was predominately grayed, with strong black lines so that it was almost a drawing. The face was partly obscured by dark, wild hair falling over her shoulders. There was an odd look in the woman's face, of surprise and attention, but also a look of pain, of wanting to hide. The eyes were wrong, she could see, spaced too far apart and with one larger than the other. The flesh color was wrong, too purple. All in all, she hated it, but heard Olaffson's voice urging her to just go on.

So she picked up her brush. Olaffson had said that anything closely observed was loved. But there had been no softening of her gaze in this rendering. The face that gazed back at her confronted her with all her mistakes, all her losses. She had tried so hard to be a good mother, a good wife. And what had it all come to? No, love was not what she felt.

She squeezed black paint on the dried colors of her palette. Then, very methodically, she painted over every last inch of the painting.

***

Hal tipped the cab driver and got out, anxiously eyeing the school. He'd talked with Helen as soon as he'd landed, and she'd assured him he could do this. But he wasn't so sure.

He went straight to the school's office. Classes were still in session, he realized with relief. It was past four, and he had been afraid the school would be closed. He explained to a woman at a desk that he needed to see Libby Starkweather, that it was urgent, a family matter. The middle-aged woman, who had short, red, spiked hair and multiple piercings, gave him a sardonic look. "Well, that girl is certainly popular today," she said, then leaned into the intercom and called Libby. Hal was afraid the secretary would ask him about the "urgent matter," but thankfully, she didn't.

A girl came in, and he looked surreptitiously down on his lap at the photo Helen had taken from the computer. The girl hardly looked the same at all. She was thin, with short hair and arms covered in inky swirls suggesting dragon scales. He stood up, hesitated. "Libby?" he asked.

She nodded.

"I'm Hal Lovejoy."

She stared at him. He could see the realization of who he was slowly come to her. She nodded.

"It's about Josh. Can we speak out in the hall?" He felt the redheaded woman's eyes on him.

"Sure, whatever."

Hal followed her out into the hall. He looked down at the photo again. "You don't look anything like this."

She glanced at it dismissively. "That's old. So, you're his dad?"

"Yeah, that's me."

She took him in. She seemed as surprised by him as he was by her. "You don't look so bad."

Hal blanched. Of course she would have heard only the worst. He cleared his throat.

"He's disappeared."

"I know."

"Ah, we thought you'd know where he is. It's quite serious, you know. He's violated his parole. Is he with you?"

Libby shook her head no. "He came here earlier today. It really freaked me out. Like two realities or something. Anyway, he'd gotten robbed on the bus, and he didn't have any money. So I fed him and gave him money to go home, get a bus ticket." Her sarcastic tone faded. "I'm really worried about him, y'know, with the parole and all."

Hal looked at this girl his son loved. She looked worn out, too thin. She looked wary. She looked almost old.

"We are worried, too, that's why I'm here." He paused, looking at her again, hesitating.

"What?"

"I was wondering, do you love my son?" He was surprised to hear himself say this.

To Hal's surprise, her eyes filled.

"Look," Hal said, "I'm sorry. It is none of my business. But look, you took care of Josh this morning, so let me take you for tea or dinner. Would that be okay?"

She considered him again. "Well, I've got movement class now, but I guess I can skip it. Yeah, it's a little weird. This whole day has been weird, but okay."

She got her things, and they walked outside. He felt awkward with this girl, but also protective. She was so thin a gust of wind could knock her down. He wasn't very good with people, he knew that. But now he felt as he had sometimes with Valerie, willing to take the risk, because something was there, like a tune faintly heard, that he found himself following.

She suggested Chinese, but he insisted on a Tuscan restaurant.

"I'm vegan," she said petulantly.

"Well"—he held the door open for her—"the Italians fix good vegetables."

They settled into a booth and ordered.

"Libby," Hal said. "Look, you know Josh better than I do these days—"

She made a snorting sound.

"—do you really think he went back on the bus?"

She shrugged, but Hal thought he saw concern on her face.

"What else could he do? I mean, I think he came here for me, but I burst that bubble."

"Well"—and the idea was a new one to Hal—"well, I wondered if he might have decided to stay."

"For what?"

"Well, that's what I'm asking you."

She made an irritated click with her tongue, looked away. "Who knows?"

"Come on, help me out a little here. Help me know my son." Hal was surprised at his urgency. It seemed suddenly as if Libby might be the best one in the world to help him.

The girl bit her lip, looked around nervously. "Well, he did always want to come here, ya know. He thought he would be a great film director. We made plans, we were going to make it here. But it's rough—you have to be tough. And Josh, he's too dreamy for the real world." She looked away. "I guess that's why I liked him. He made me believe in a kinder world."

"But why would he come here now? Did you break up with him, anything like that?"

She looked horrified. "I'd never do that long distance. You have to do that in person."

Hal looked down. "I see. Maybe the relationship was a little one-sided... ?"

Libby sighed. "Not at first. But look. My folks are useless. My mom's mental and my dad disappeared—he's probably on a bender—and I have my sibs to take care of, and you know, sometimes Josh can just be so lost. I can't take care of anyone else now."

Hal took this in. It was unimaginable. A child this age.

"I, uh, that is quite understandable."

Hal saw a tear drop onto her lashes.

"Damn, I hate to cry." She blew loudly into an oversized napkin. "I just want to know," she said in a strangled voice, "why you grown-ups don't—grow up!"

Hal winced. Libby's anguished face brought something back. He saw Josh the night of the accident, heard his own voice screaming at him, saw Josh's face close off in an expression he knew so well. It was his own.

Hal reached across the table and patted Libby's blue-veined, tattooed arm. "You have a point there, Libby," he said. "You have a point."

Hal gave Libby two hundred dollars to reimburse her for the money she had given Josh. "It's too much," she said and tried to give it back, but he firmly closed her hand around the bills. "I wasn't very nice to Josh," she added, biting her lip.

She asked him to let her know as soon as he found anything, and he said he would, taking down her number.

"I wish you well, Libby." He hesitated. "I hope you and Josh can be friends."

She nodded, then turned quickly, striding away with her head up and her shoulders thrown back. He watched her small, brave figure until it disappeared into the rushing crowd.

TWENTY-SEVEN

Hal stood on the busy corner, cold and disoriented. He called Helen and told her what Libby had told him. Helen said she would try to call the bus station and have Josh traced. "Do you think he got on a bus, Hal?" There was a slight lift in her voice. "That would mean he'd be on his way home by now, wouldn't it?"

Hal didn't want to disillusion her, but he didn't want to worry her, either. He tried to be precise. "There is no way of knowing, Helen. I'm hoping that's what he did. There's no way to know for sure. Did you check with the phone company again?"

"They say there is no signal." She sighed, and he winced at the flatness in her voice. "I guess you're right. What will you do now? What about your business—the clock?"

"I've made an appointment to have the clock appraised tomorrow morning. I found a place nearby for the night."

There was a long pause. Hal knew Helen was fighting back fear. He tried to be upbeat. He said, "I'll wait to hear from you, I guess. I don't want to get the police involved any more than they are. He might contact us—he probably will. Just hold on to that."

"Yes, he might. I think he will eventually. It's just this waiting, Hal. It is killing me."

"I know, Helen. I don't know what else to tell you."

He heard a strangled cry. "It's okay, Hal. Good-bye."

"Helen—" he said, and he took a breath, wanting to add something, but she had hung up.

He'd let her down again. He hated that tone in her voice, the tone that didn't let him in. He tried to shake it off. What would he do with himself now? He hated waiting, too, but there was nothing else he could think to do. He started walking.

Hal looked around him at the light glancing off the big plate glass windows. He walked by Starbucks, inhaled the coffee, hurried across a crowded intersection. He'd never been to New York before; he and Helen had always talked about going. But their life had gotten smaller, had turned in ever tighter circles. Now, in the city, he felt as he had with Valerie, as if he were someone else, or a different version of who he was. The constant oppressiveness of being Hal lifted as he took in the sights and sounds and smells—the skyscrapers, the horns honking just like in the movies, the hot dog stands. He had always loved the original *Out-of-Towners*, and now he felt as if he had entered the set.

The shop owners had called him to ask if he could come in at nine instead of ten tomorrow; they'd had a cancellation. He looked at his map and pointed himself in the direction of his hotel. After several blocks, he began to notice that most of the stores gave way to art galleries. He slowed his stride. He gazed in the windows at paintings and prints, at sculptures and installations. He was amazed at what some people considered art. He knew he was a bit of a rube, but he had perused Helen's books when she'd studied art history, and some of the stuff—toilets

with mannequins or rubber duckies in a kid's wading pool—
didn't strike him as art.

He passed a window, though, that made him stop. Here
were paintings that seemed somehow familiar. He looked at
the artist's name, but it didn't ring a bell. There was something
about them, though, some feeling... they were all suburban
landscapes, but here and there was something startlingly out of
place, an elephant or cheetah or a golden python wrapping itself around a street lamp. He thought for a moment, and then it
came to him: the paintings Helen had strewn around the house
when he'd gone by a few days ago. He looked at the window
again. Helen's were much less realistic, much looser and more
dynamic in composition, but there was something similar. Hal
stood, considering. He hadn't thought this way in a long time,
and it was as if the gears were rusty. Maybe it was just that el-
ement in the paintings of unexpectedness, of strangeness, of
mystery, of something wild breaking through the tight surface
that caught his attention.

And then it came to him. Helen was good. She was an artist.
She wasn't crazy. Or at least not just crazy... maybe a little crazy.
But she had this, this other life, and it had nothing to do with
him. All these years he had thought she lived for him, so much
so that her much-needed help had grown to chafe, so much so
that she had become for him, more than anything, a symbol of
his own failures. His failure to be an engineer, his failure as a
father, as a husband.

He had discounted her life. She hadn't seemed to have one.
Maybe she had discounted it, too. All those years, helping him,
tutoring Josh, getting Josh treated, fighting with Hal, all those

years—what were they in the light of this other life that she had secretly harbored?

He couldn't put together the woman shuffling around in her robe, her lips pursed with repressed displeasure at him, with the authority he'd glimpsed in her paintings. He felt a second large dislocation. Unfamiliar feelings and thoughts threatened to flood him, to make him lose his moorings. He steadied himself against the brick facade. A door opened and flashed the fading sunlight in his face, and he found a man on the sidewalk, smiling at him. He took a step back. The man, who had had his hands behind his back, considering Hal, gestured at the window. "Would you like to come in, sir? We have much more inside…"

It took Hal a minute to realize the man saw him as a potential buyer. He looked around and realized that this was not the kind of place one browsed.

"Um, no, thank you," he said and began to move away, feeling more disoriented than ever. He felt exposed in some way. He clearly didn't know how to navigate this place. The old panic started up. He wished he could go to Time Pieces now. He needed to get back to the world he knew, the world he had mastered, where he was safe. He consulted his map again.

***

Josh walked the streets of Manhattan, taking it all in: the Calder mobile, Rockefeller Center with its giant lit tree and skaters, the flags in front of the UN, the taxicabs on Broadway. He should, he knew, be thinking of shelter, but he was too excited. He would live here. Somehow. He walked down residential streets with well-tended brownstones and small gardens, passed women in furs walking little dogs. He sauntered through neighborhood bistros festooned with gilt decorations, glimpsed patrons lifting crystal wine glasses. He could hear Christmas music. Two older men on a street corner gestured with their hands, arguing animatedly, grins on their faces. Everywhere there was ease, prosperity, and life being lived large.

Josh was drunk with it all. He thought of himself in a few years, worldly, successful, like Woody Allen without the nerdiness, walking with a girl like Emma Stone, a girl smitten with him, a girl who got him. He saw himself with a megaphone, arguing good-naturedly with his ensemble cast. He thought of the sheer concentration of talent in the city—who knew, maybe he'd bump into Scorsese or Wes Anderson. Anything was possible—in The City.

It was everything Milledge was not. He thought of the mall in Milledge, the depressing stores, the fat, ugly people who had no idea another, better world existed. He shuddered to think he had ever lived there. He felt embarrassed for the place.

It began to grow darker. The sky between the buildings turned indigo. He saw the Chrysler Building again, festooned with lights, its needle slicing the sky. Broadway now was a river of light bisecting mountains of light. There was a throb to the city that got into him, as if he were inside a giant heart.

He was beginning to get tired, and he was hungry again. He didn't know what time it was; he'd left his watch at home, and he still had his phone turned off. He patted the money in his pocket, told himself it would have to last, that he'd have to find a deli, get a sandwich. But he didn't seem to be in a part of town that had cheap sandwiches, just fancy restaurants. Each eatery he passed had more tempting treats than the last.

Finally, so hungry he could think of nothing else, he stopped inside a touristy German restaurant. He told himself he'd just get a coffee and put lots of milk in it. He could nurse it a long time, get refills, rest up, and decide what to do next.

He ducked in, found a booth in a corner that looked out on the pulsating street, and ordered his coffee. The waiter tried to talk him into ordering more, but he resisted. He'd been broke, he didn't want to go there again anytime soon. He drummed his fingers on the table. He'd get a room at the YMCA—that's what they always did in books. And he'd look for work at a restaurant. Some place like this, with good tips. He'd have to get some other clothes, a jacket maybe, and wash what he had on. Maybe he could find a Salvation Army store or a Goodwill.

The coffee came. He looked into the cup and saw a murky reflection. He framed it as a shot in a movie, the coffee still sloshing slightly, a shot that said something about the protagonist. Something like, his girlfriend screwed him. Something like, he belongs nowhere, man, just lives from shelter to shelter. He remembered the leering panhandler. No way, he wasn't gonna end up like that. He just needed to get his bearings, and he'd be fine. He put three packs of sugar in the coffee and stirred, the rich fragrance dispelling his dark thoughts.

He sat a long time, looking at the map. He had three refills, and still the hunger was there. The place wasn't very busy, and Josh was glad—he didn't want to be shooed out. On the table next to him was a plate of half-eaten Wiener schnitzel and potatoes. He had been smelling it since the waiter had put it on the table. It glowed with a kind of satiny glow, the meat under some sauce and the potatoes barely touched. The patrons had just left, the thin woman protesting that it was too rich, too much for her. Josh looked longingly at it, and then eyed the waiters, relaxed and chatting at the bar. His waiter had been rather terse, displeased by Josh's meager order, and he looked over occasionally to check Josh. He hoped the waiter couldn't see how desperate he was.

Josh had to have that food. He asked his waiter for the check, got up to go to the bathroom, lifting the plate as he went. His heart raced. He didn't feel guilty, as he expected, but smart and daring and excited as he blocked it from their view with his body, walking rapidly toward the men's room. He locked himself in a stall and sat on the toilet, amazed that his hunger could override his disgust at the smell. The meat and potatoes had cooled and had a slightly gelatinous consistency, but at the first bite, all his gastric juices were set in motion. This was food! Not that thin fare at the Chinese restaurant. He ate it all, using his fingers to wipe up the gravy.

Just as he was finishing, someone walked in. He froze, sure that they were coming to get him, that they had discovered the missing plate. He suddenly felt the urge to cough, and he strangled it. He heard unzipping, and a torrential flood emptying into the urinal, the zipper again, and then, miraculously, footsteps and the door opening and closing.

He was trembling now, aware of the sweat cooling uncomfortably under his arms, running down his back. He carefully placed the plate on the floor, went out, and found the bill on his table. He placed the few dollars under the saucer and left, not daring to look over his shoulder. Outside, walking past the restaurant's window, he quickly glanced to see if he had been discovered, but the waiters were arrayed as before at the bar. He walked quickly and then began to run. He didn't know where he was running to, but it felt good and necessary.

He ran a long time, past tony restaurants and boutiques, sometimes in the streets, running around dog walkers and strollers, couples laughing, holding on to each other's arms. He sucked in air, and then more air, feeling the blood flowing into his legs and arms, feeling the hard contact of his feet against the pavement. He thought of Dustin Hoffman in *Marathon Man*, the pounding footfalls as he ran by the Hudson River. He was sweating Libby from his system, pounding every memory, every foolish hope.

He ran, noticing how the neighborhood slowly changed. Here the neon was grungier, the stores covered in colorful graffiti, and the people moved more slowly. No one looked at him as he raced by, just stepped aside to let him pass. Yet he still felt as if all of them could tell that he was out of place.

He belonged nowhere. He thought of his mother's distant face that night, how she had seemed to be letting go of him, of his father. Letting them fall away from her, uncaring. He thought of his father's slow desertion over the years. And he thought of that night, of the sickening thud, of waiting for his father, of the twisted expression of rage that met him, his father's face no more familiar to him than a Kabuki mask. No, he belonged nowhere.

Finally, gasping, the air abrading his exhausted lungs, he slowed to a walk. He had no idea where he was, but he had crossed some invisible border into an entirely different city. Here, men in rags rummaged through smelly garbage, old people shuffled along with carts of food, some of them muttering to themselves, and young toughs hung out on street corners.

Josh leaned against a wall, his head hanging down, sweat streaming off him. He had to think of a plan. Find a YMCA. He had to find a Y. He shut his eyes for a moment, trying to focus. Suddenly, he was aware of something else, a presence near him. Jerking his head up, suddenly alert, afraid of muggers, his eyes met those of a girl about his height. Large brown eyes outlined with kohl stared at him. Silver hoops swung through a waterfall of black hair, and her breasts flowed out of the top of her pink T-shirt. She smelled of cigarettes and tortillas and some heavy, flowery perfume.

"Hey, cutie, you want a good time, honey?" She licked her full red lips suggestively, ran her hand up her leg. "I give you a good time, baby. You come with me." She tried to hook her arm through his.

"Don't touch me," he yelled, pulling away from her.

"Fucking freak," she yelled back, waving her arms. "I call the police on you, man." She joined a group of girls, and they all turned to stare and point at him. He walked away quickly, trying this time to blend in.

He jogged past the barkers at the porn shows, past the all-night groceries, the bars. At one seemingly decent cigarette stand where he went in to ask directions to the Y, the guy didn't speak English and gave him a suspicious look. "Buy cigarette?"

the wizened old Chinese man asked, but it sounded more like he was demanding something of Josh. Josh wanted to just stay there for a moment, alight somewhere. His feet and legs hurt. But the man's hostile expression propelled him onto the street again.

He limped along. The law of the street, he was beginning to realize, was to keep moving. Like a shark in the ocean. Kill or be killed. He felt that he had been asleep all his life, in his safe little world, and now he was waking up. He clutched his arms to his chest, trying to fend off the wind that came funneling down the canyon-like streets. The smells of the street nauseated him—the exhaust, the garbage, the heavy smell of fried food, the overwhelming smell of alcohol as he passed too close to someone. A man sat in a doorway, his elephantine leg stretched out in front of him, moaning and begging. Josh hesitated in front of him, transfixed by the sight. He had never seen such a deformity; he'd never heard such sustained sounds of pain. He dug in his pocket for a dollar and tried to throw it in the man's basket, but it floated to the ground and Josh had to pick it up and actually hand it to the man.

"Thanks, oh, bless you, man," the fellow muttered. Josh awkwardly saluted him, then rushed from the sight.

Josh patted his pocket, found the map he'd gotten at the station. He unfolded it now, trying to figure out where he was. He leaned under a street lamp to read the fine print. He had to figure out how to get to a better neighborhood, at least. He could find an all-night bar, maybe, or maybe a coffee shop to wait out the night. He ducked into a Block Drug Store, asked the black clerk where the Y was. The man didn't look at him as if he might rob him, but just gazed at Josh calmly for a moment. Then he called to someone in the back, his voice soft with Caribbean rhythms, and a similar voice called back, "On West Sixty-Third and Fifth." The clerk circled it on the map. Josh was so grateful that the man didn't treat him like a pariah that he bought a candy bar from him, although he was past hunger now.

He walked outside, got his bearings, turned east and north. He'd been going in the exact wrong direction. He was somewhere in the Lower East Side. His arms and legs felt filled with sand, and the thought of walking all those blocks back seemed impossible. *Just keep walking north,* he told himself. The colored lights around him merged together into a fantastic anemone. Things began to blur. He couldn't tell if sounds were behind him or coming toward him. If he knew which bus to take, he would take it. But he didn't, so he put his waning energy into just moving north, just staying alive.

He walked undisturbed for what seemed like a long time. He seemed to be in a safer neighborhood now, and he relaxed his vigilance a little. Every now and then he pulled out his map, made sure he was going in the right direction. The noises around him melded into one giant white noise. He no longer felt the pain in his legs. He was a walking machine.

SECTION 10:
THE END OF HOPE

TWENTY-EIGHT

A strange sound penetrated Josh's fog. First just a noise that separated itself from the surrounding din, it resolved itself into a human voice, and then into words. "Hey! Hey, fella!" Josh stopped, looked around him. "Hey! Down here!" He looked into the street and saw a silver Lexus with the window rolled down and, inside it, a man looking up at him.

Josh pointed to himself with a questioning shrug. "Me?"

The man laughed. "Yeah, you. I saw you looking at a map. Are you lost?"

Josh squinted at the man. He was fiftyish, with blond hair and a big, shiny watch.

"Why do you want to know?" Josh retorted, panicked.

"You're not, as they say, from around here, are you?" The man's eyes bore into him.

Josh blushed, shook his head.

"Look, where do you want to go? I can give you a lift."

Every red flag inside Josh went up. But he glanced at the street, and then back into the interior of the car. The seats were leather. Oh, to sit down! To not be walking.

"I need to get to the YMCA," he heard himself say, although he had not intended to say it.

"That's no problem. I'll take you there."

The man looked at him with a friendly, casual smile. He could have been one of the dads from the better suburbs at home, Josh rationalized. He looked like the kind of man he'd see at soccer games sometimes, making a token appearance at his kid's game. A banker or lawyer or something like that. Maybe harmless. But what was he doing here in the middle of the night? *No, you can't trust anyone in the city. You can't trust anyone, period.*

Josh shook his head. "Thanks, but I'm fine."

Josh walked briskly, but the car kept pace with him.

"Hey, look, kid. I can tell clearly that you are not fine. You look lost as hell. If you were my kid, I wouldn't want you wandering the streets like this. Just get in and I'll take you to the Y."

The guy sounded so reasonable. So he was a dad. Maybe he was a dad who even cared about his kids. Or maybe he wasn't. Josh glanced down again at the leather seats. His legs suddenly felt as if they might give way beneath him.

Josh ran around the side and got in.

Just as he had imagined, the seat was heaven. He sank down in it with a sigh. The car accelerated smoothly, joining the traffic. Soft jazz played, and the car smelled of olives.

"I'm Ted," the man said. Ted offered his hand, and Josh shook it, noticing that he was the first to let go.

"I'm Josh."

"Would you like a martini, Josh? Or some weed?"

Josh shook his head. He wanted to be alert in case he needed to get out. He was beginning to think he'd made a mistake. But the car was moving slowly—he could always just jump out. The seat molded around his body. Exhaustion washed over him.

"So, you're a long way from home… ?"

"Georgia."

"Hm, that's what I thought. The South."

"Look, do you know where the Y is? That's all I need, just a lift."

"Hey, okay, I'm just trying to be friendly here, just trying to help." There was an edge to his voice.

Josh shifted toward the door. "Hey, look, man, I appreciate it," Josh said. He knew that edge, his father had it. You had to back down sometimes and gentle the guy, handle him.

He watched Ted's jaw loosen, saw his grip on the wheel relax. "Just trying to help," he repeated.

"I appreciate it, too. Hey, this is some car."

"Yes." The man looked around appreciatively. "I enjoy it."

"You must be a banker or something…"

"I'm a broker. Wall Street."

"Cool." Josh said. The trick seemed to be keep the guy talking. "Interesting work?"

"It's all right. I'm good at it."

"Got a family?"

He saw Ted's jaw tighten again. "Oh, yeah, got the whole picture. Beautiful wife. She's a perfect size six. Blond. She works out all the time. Two kids—straight-A students—a boy and a girl, nine and eleven. They haven't hit puberty yet, so the picture is still perfect. A beautiful house. A beach house on the Cape. We ski in the winters at all the best places. A perfect life, that's what I have." He reached down and took a long drink from a glass with two plump olives in it. "What about you, Josh? You come from a perfect family, too?"

"Oh, yeah," Josh matched his tone. "Let's see. I'll give you the pretty version. My mom, Helen, is a painter. She used to be a nurse and a mom. But she had to find herself, so now she paints all the time. Doesn't cook or clean. My dad. He has a clock repair shop. He knows all about every kind of old clock there is. And he is crazy about time, and punctuality and order. And he used to take me camping and fishing and stuff, but then everything changed." Josh left out the part about David, about the accident.

"And you?" Ted said.

"Me." Josh laughed a short, harsh laugh and tried to match Ted's arch tone. "You wouldn't know it to look at me, but I'm a talented though undiscovered film auteur."

"Well," Ted said dryly, "I thought there was something special about you. So you've come to the Big Apple to make your fame and fortune, huh?"

"Something like that." There was a silence, and Josh gazed out the window. He noticed then they seemed to be leaving the city.

"Hey! Where are you taking me? Hey, man, what are you pulling?"

Ted looked over at him then, his face suddenly naked and hungry. "Look, I can turn the car around, okay? Really. But I'd like to talk, just talk. Drive around in my beautiful, comfortable car."

"Look, I don't do that. I'm not some kind of male prostitute, okay?" He was close to tears, the handle of the car digging into his back. "You'd better let me out."

Ted pulled into a gas station. "You can't get out here. This place isn't safe. Look at it!"

Josh looked. The people milling around the station looked rough. A group of white kids with bandanas around their foreheads and tattoos on their arms sat drinking on top of an old car. Next to them, a van boomed out rap music. The sleek Lexus was already drawing attention.

Ted parked. He turned to Josh. "Look." His voice was shaking. "It's true. I trawl, okay? You looked like maybe... but I can see you're just a kid. Okay? I'm not a monster. I'm not going to force myself on you. I'm just lonely, damn lonely. God, I mean, I just want someone to talk to." He struck the steering wheel, and again Josh was aware of lurking anger the man was struggling to control.

"Look, if you want, we could drive down to the coast now, get a big breakfast, talk, and listen to the waves, watch the sun come up. Just talk. Then I'll bring you to wherever you want to go. I promise not to lay a hand on you." He held up both his arms as if under arrest. "Scout's honor. Or I can turn around and take you to the Y."

Josh looked out at the seedy filling station and thought about what waited for him in the city: more walking, maybe finding the Y closed. Did he trust Ted? No, but he thought he could overpower him if he had to. Ted was a small man, and drunk, and Josh wasn't large, but he was strong and young. And tired. Very tired. And for now the car seemed like a perch, a place to rest. If he could just rest, he could figure it all out.

"Okay, but if you touch me, I swear I'll slug you. I'll beat you. I've already put one guy in a coma. Don't think I won't do it." Josh was amazed at the assurance with which he said those words—he who thought he abhorred violence of any kind. Josh gestured roughly with his hand, surprised at the surge of energy he felt. As if he really had it in him.

"Oh," Ted said coyly, "I love tough guys. I swear I won't touch you."

Josh nodded. "I mean it."

"This," Ted muttered, putting the Lexus into gear, "will be interesting."

***

There was nowhere else to go.

Meg took the stairs two at a time, hoping she wouldn't see anyone she knew. Her nose and eyes were raw, and she couldn't stop the tears that came in waves.

She looked at the gray cement blocks, the steel railing of the utility stairs. Sister Antonette had shown her this shortcut, bypassing the flashy atrium, the mahogany reception desk, the smiling volunteers, so she didn't have to go through all the motions of being a "guest visitor." No, the guts of the place, without all the window dressing, suited her fine, especially today.

Her life had been stripped bare as well. It was as if she had been filling herself with Josh and Hal and Valerie, the whole drama, letting it distract her from her loss. When Hal took the clock and left, it all went with him. And now there was this terrible emptiness and nothing to fill it. Now she was headed to David's room, to David, accepting at last that there was no hope for him. For them. And that knowledge made each step she took drag. She felt as if she were forcing her way through mud.

When she opened the familiar door, she saw Sister Antonette's substantial, white-clad body bent forward as if she were listening to something. Meg started, thinking David was speaking, but when the nun straightened, she could see his same, unmoving, sallow profile.

Sister Antonette turned slowly toward Meg, almost as if Meg had startled her out of a reverie.

"My dear," the nun said, holding out her hands to Meg and holding Meg with her dark-brown eyes. There was something sad in those eyes, and tender. Meg knew the nun was taking in her pink nose and red-rimmed eyes. Nothing got by her.

Meg went to her, took her warm, firm hands. "How, how is he today?" Meg stuttered, realizing it was a stupid question she didn't want answered.

Sister Antonette's forehead wrinkled, her gray eyebrows lifting. "There doesn't seem to be much change."

The tears started again, and Antonette pulled a handkerchief out of her pocket. Meg took the hanky, blew her nose noisily. The handkerchief smelled of mints.

"We must always have hope. And faith."

Meg stared at her. She had come to the end of hope. "There isn't much to go on."

"Do you mean, if he'll recover, if he'll live?"

Meg nodded.

"No. I don't think there is too much hope for that."

Meg stepped back as if slapped.

"Then what good is faith, Sister?"

"Faith is knowing that all is held in God's hand, even if we can't see the design."

Meg shook her head. "Not this, surely not. It was just chance, bad luck... I'm sorry, I can't take any comfort there, Sister. I think it is just a way to console ourselves." She felt her anger rise, wanted to tell this kind woman off, tell her how she resented easy pieties, when she saw tears in the nun's eyes.

"I love David, too, my dear. His mother and I were close friends. She died in my arms."

Sister Antonette rose, and Meg could see for the first time how stiffly she moved. Her white nurse's shoes made almost no sound as she passed Meg, but her knobby hand rested briefly on Meg's shoulder.

David was anxious for Peggy to come. He had, suddenly, so much to tell her. He'd been feeling a change coming, the way, even when it is still summer, you could smell a certain sharpness in the air, a quickening, so that you rushed to get all your summer fun in before it was too late. But it was already too late, the languor of summer broken by the very thought of autumn.

Hurry, Peggy, he thought, because it wasn't only the martini he craved, but the rustle of her dress, the way she listened, the way nothing shocked her, the way sorrow flowed through her and was transformed into sweet song.

A door opened, and he heard the falling note of an alto sax, and it filled him with sadness. A door closed, but he could still hear clapping and cheering, then that, too, faded away. He heard a match strike.

"Isn't that bad for your voice?" he asked.

Peggy exhaled languidly. "Believe me, babe, I've cut down. But a girl's gotta, y'know, relax." She stretched, shook out her blond hair. Today she was wearing black leggings and a striped tunic. He'd never seen her hair so long and loose. She looked older, wearier. She, too, was changing.

"Whew, I'm beat. I'm not the girl I used to be. Oh, I'm sorry, David." And she shook a cigarette out of the pack and held it out to him. David took it, and she handed over her own to light his. In his life before, he'd smoked, but he had given up cigs and hard liquor at Meg's urging. Now he'd grown to love these ritualistic vices he shared with Peggy.

They sat there, companionably, in silence. The only sound now was of inhaling.

"'Little boy lost, in search of little boy found,'" Peggy sang softly, at last. "'When will you find, what's on the tip of your mind'?"

"Good question," David said.

"So," Peggy said, stubbing out her cigarette, lying down next to him, her cheek supporting her hand, her hair a platinum waterfall. "So, darling, out with it."

"I don't know how to—"

"Just give it a try."

"I wanted to do good, to be good, but still I caused pain. Not intending to, but there it is—I neglected my parents, and Meg. Meg who'd asked for so little, and I selfishly couldn't give that little."

"'Little boy false,'" Peggy sang on, giving him that enigmatic look of hers. "'In search of little boy true?'"

"And even the communities I served, the people Meg accused me of giving my best to, I hurt them, too, made missteps. I was too cocky sometimes, too uncompromising, too impatient."

"And as for fishing in streams, for pieces of dreams, those pieces will never fit. What is the sense of it?"

David felt his failures, and the crushing knowledge that there was nothing to change the past. The pain of this knowledge radiated out and became all that he was.

"Can't you smell autumn in the air, Peggy? Meg loved fall, but it always makes me sad. A little sad."

"Well, sure, honey, it makes me a little sad, too." She lit another cigarette, inhaled, and looked at him with those smoky eyes. He could smell her perfume, and the sweat underneath. Her silver earring swayed and sparkled. He felt so tenderly toward her earring, her hand, her hair. Tenderness welled up in him, turned to wet tears tracking down his cheeks.

Then he felt a familiar hand take his. Meg. David yearned toward her, the love he felt for her sharp as pain.

"Oh, darling, forgive me!" he cried.

"Oh, she forgave you a long time ago, chum," he heard Peggy say, her voice suddenly far away.

He was back on the hill that night he had stopped to look at his town, and a love for it as sweet as honeysuckle nectar pierced him. Then he got on his bike and followed Anthony through the shadow-dappled street.

TWENTY-NINE

Helen woke Tuesday morning, confused and groggy. She had thought she'd heard Josh cry out as he often did as a little boy, but realized in the thin gray light of dawn that it was just an owl. She listened again, still immersed in the feeling that it was Josh, still primed to respond to him. There it was, the plaintive cry—and then the hoo-hoo-hoo that distinguished it from the sound of a crying child.

She turned over and pulled a pillow into her arms, hugging it close, as if it were Josh's wiry, trembling eight-year-old body cuddling into hers.

"And then the kidnappers got me, but I bit their fingers and got away and ran to Daddy."

"Is that all you remember?"

A shudder, and then, "No, but it's all I'm gonna tell. It is too scary."

"Okay." She had wanted him to tell her other details, had wanted some insight into what was upsetting him, but understood that it was indeed too scary for him to relive it. She wondered where his fears came from—in the daytime, he would engage her in conversations about how tornadoes were better than hurricanes, because you might just land on soft grass, or how you could get away from sharks by poking them in the eyes, or how to escape from quicksand. But at night, he wasn't so sanguine.

Where, where had his fears come from? It wasn't as if they had ever experienced an earthquake or war or any other traumatic event. She wanted to ask other mothers if their children obsessed about those things as much as hers did, but she had never become friends with his friends' mothers, and kept her doubts to herself. When she tried to put herself in his place, to imagine what it would be like to suspect disaster lurking around every corner, she found herself paralyzed. To be Josh, she realized, took great courage.

Sometimes he had told her other dream details—the bad guys were going to push him into a shark tank, but he poked their eyes out and ran to Daddy, or aliens were going to take him in a spaceship, but he zapped them with his laser gun and ran to Daddy. It was always Daddy he ran to in his dreams; it was always her he ran to in the morning.

Helen pressed her fingers to her temples, to her eyes. A few sparse tears squeezed out. She had the vertiginous feeling that Josh was still eight, that she could still hold him and comfort him, all the while knowing, as the light grew stronger, that he was seventeen and wandering somewhere in some city or bus station, god knew where. She clung to the younger boy, but he slowly faded in her arms.

She struggled to get up, to orient herself, to not allow herself to sink back into sleep. There was something urgent to be done, although what it was, she wasn't sure. She'd taken a sleeping pill last night, something she hadn't needed to do since she had started drawing and painting again.

She shuffled into the kitchen, flipping on lights as she went. Buster, ever at the ready, poked his nose in from the laundry room, his tail thumping rhythmically against the wall as he offered himself to her. She'd given up on keeping the wall clean—there was a swath of greasy two-foot-high dog rubbings all along it.

The familiar ritual of grinding the coffee beans, of hearing the drip, drip, drip into the pot, steadied her. *What to do, what to do?* She had called the bus stations all day yesterday but had turned up nothing. His phone still wasn't on. Josh's parole officer had called her again, and she had appreciated what sounded like real, personal concern in his voice.

"It doesn't seem like him, ma'am. I talked with Ms. Jones at the Good Shepherd, and she agrees. What do you think might have been going on?"

And Helen could answer truthfully, "I don't know. We went out to dinner—I know he was a little upset about some things I said—"

"Did you fight, Ms. Lovejoy? Was that it?"

"No, nothing like that. I just said—well, it's personal."

"I know, ma'am, but it could help."

Helen took a deep breath. "Well, I just said I didn't know what was going to happen with his father and me, that was all. It wasn't a particularly dramatic statement."

"But he reacted—how?"

"He just seemed upset, that's all. That's normal, I think. But not angry or anything. We parted amicably. I mean, it is normal for a kid to be upset if his parents are having troubles."

There was a silence on the other end of the phone, then a sigh. "I believe you. It isn't much to go on, that's all."

"I know it isn't."

She had hung up, feeling a mixture of gratitude and dismay. All these people who were involved in Josh's life, yet she didn't know any of them. Mr. Stevens, Ms. Jones, all seemed to care for him. They had always been a family that kept to themselves; only Josh had showed any talent for friendship. Now, these people, these strangers, were involved in her son's life. It felt odd, the way not knowing about Hal felt odd, as if the known universe had shifted, as if all the planets were out of order. It was clear to her now that Josh's life was out of her control. Maybe it had been, maybe for most of his life, but she was just now getting around to realizing it. And maybe that wasn't a bad thing.

Helen sipped her coffee and milk, her stomach too knotted to eat. Her heart raced, she felt an urgency to do something, but couldn't think of what to do. Driving with the brakes on, someone had called it.

Her sketchbook lay on the table, and she pulled it over to her. She found herself making harsh, broad charcoal strokes, covering the paper. She took her cloth, wiped out areas, began sketching people—it was wrong, nothing, just chaos.

Ripping off the paper, she started over, something else forming itself on the paper. Working quickly, before she had a chance to think too much, she drew a man, his attenuated arms outstretched, and a boy, legs blurred with motion, running toward him.

***

Josh struggled to open his eyes. He had been dreaming, a dark frightening dream of trying to run away from something as fast as he could, only to be caught fast. The smell of coffee dispelled the dream, and he opened his eyes cautiously, the memory of last night growing sharper. He struggled to sit upright.

"Ah, the dead awake," Ted said. "Here's some coffee, there's cream and sugar in the dash." He handed the thermos to Josh.

"You think of everything." Josh heard his voice, thick with sleep, and gruff. In the light of day, he wasn't sure he would be able to keep up the pretense of the tough guy. He wondered if Ted had believed him in the first place. He glanced over at Ted, who had his wrists draped languidly over the wheel. He seemed to be in a great mood. All signs of martinis were gone.

"Yes, I do." Ted smiled. If Josh didn't know better, he would have easily taken Ted for a friendly uncle, worldly and fun, with his tan skin and polo shirt. But he knew better.

Josh looked out the car window at the two-lane road. Seedy motels and neglected apartments littered the road. Just beyond them was the beach—a pale strip of gray sand and a sheet of grayer water meeting an even darker sky. The foam on the beach looked dirty. A smell of salt and rotting seaweed crept into the car, along with the startling screech of gulls. It wasn't at all what he had expected: he'd thought the landscape would be beautiful. What he saw was dreary and depressing.

"This is Cape Cod?"

Ted laughed. "Well, no. There's been a change of itinerary. I started toward the Cape house, but then I thought, how boring. So halfway there I turned around, headed south. This is the Jersey Shore."

Josh felt his mouth go dry. Beyond the highway, what little he could see looked desolate.

"So, where are we headed?" Josh tried to sound light, jovial.

"Someplace very special." Ted hummed along with Charlie Parker in a self-satisfied, ostentatious way.

"Okay, can I have a little more to go on?" Josh worked to keep his voice level.

Ted slid his eyes over to Josh and gave him a long, appraising look.

"I don't suppose," he said, "being from the South, you've ever heard of Asbury Park?"

"Doesn't ring a bell."

"An amusement park. In its heyday, one of the greatest rock 'n' roll venues in the world."

"And now?"

"Now, it has aged, fallen into disuse. Seen better days. Like me." Ted glanced quickly at Josh. Josh had to turn away from the need in his face. "At any rate, it is slated to be demolished. I decided I needed to see it one last time. And I think, my young friend, you will thank me for it."

"Well, we'll see. In the meantime, I need to pee," Josh said roughly, trying to dispel Ted's avuncular tone.

"Okay." Ted was all concern. "There's a diner not too far where we can get a decent breakfast, can you wait a few minutes?"

"I guess so," Josh said, embarrassed. He didn't like being treated like a child.

They drove in silence. In the light of day, he knew just how defenseless he was, with almost no minutes left on his phone and with little money. He was a naive kid, and this guy knew all kinds of ropes. Still, Ted hadn't laid a hand on him. Maybe he did just want to talk. The main thing was for Josh to keep his head, to not panic. He looked out the window. There were few cars on the road, and half the businesses seemed closed.

"Well, I thought it was around here," Ted muttered irritably.

"Well, I gotta pee bad, so we better stop soon."

An old sign for a Phillips 66 appeared, but it was deserted. At last they found a BP station, and Ted pulled in there. Josh got out and found the rotten men's room that looked and smelled as if it hadn't been cleaned in twenty years.

Josh locked the door. He fished his phone out of his jeans. His fingers trembled, and he fumbled the phone, almost dropping it. He punched 1, speed dial for his mother's cell. It connected.

"Mom!"

"Josh, is that you?" It was his father's voice, tense and loud.

"Dad?"

"I've got your mom's cell. Son, where are you? I'm in New York, looking for you. We've been so worried…"

"Dad!" Josh glanced nervously at the door, kept his voice low. "I'm almost out of battery. Dad, listen, *I need help*. I got a ride with this guy—"

"Guy? What guy? Josh, why are you whispering?" Josh could hear the old familiar impatience in Hal's voice.

"Dad!" Josh's voice shook. "Dad, listen, you have to listen to me. Okay, he's taking me to a place called Asbury Park. An amusement park. Dad, got that? Asbury Park. You've got to come get me. Dad—"

The phone died. Josh stared at it. Did his dad get it? Did he understand that Josh was in trouble? Hearing his father's voice had given him a flash of hope, but the dead phone in his hand extinguished it. At the best of times, his father didn't really listen. What were the chances he'd listen now?

Josh braced himself against the cold tiles and threw up.

When he came out, Ted was talking to the proprietor, an old, wizened guy with rheumy eyes who reeked of cigarettes. Josh watched Ted closely for any sign that he had heard him call his dad.

But when Ted turned to Josh slightly, to include him in the conversation, he seemed completely unconcerned with Josh. "I'm just in shock. The Blue Plate diner is gone. They had the best breakfasts, the kind you can't get anymore—sausage and bacon and lots of eggs and toast. Now everything is fast food. Well, thanks. I appreciate the tip." He nodded at the old man, who held up a stained hand to him and grinned. Oh, Ted was smooth all right, Josh could see that.

As they left, Josh said, "Guess you haven't been here in a while." A cold wind sheared across him, and he pulled open the car door hurriedly.

"No, not in a long time," Ted muttered.

"I could go for a McDonald's sausage biscuit. I could eat about anything right now." It was true, to his astonishment. Nauseated minutes ago, he was suddenly, truly ravenous.

Ted scowled. "I detest those places."

"Well, they're better than nothing." Josh could already taste the crumbling, hot, oily biscuit in his mouth.

"Actually, they're not." Josh was amazed at the ferocity in Ted's voice, a tone like a warning growl. "The old guy told me of a place still open. It's a little farther along, but worth it." Ted turned to Josh and gave him a winning smile. "You'll see."

They found the place after a few wrong turns, and it was as good as the man had promised. Everyone working and eating there looked to Josh to be about one hundred years old. The waitress was so thin and wrinkled Josh was amazed she wasn't on life support. She herself seemed oblivious and sprightly, though, bringing them hot coffee and more bacon, leaving behind her the ubiquitous smell of stale tobacco.

"Does everyone in these backwaters smoke?" Josh whispered, conspiratorially. He was in a much better mood now that he was full and the caffeine was buzzing around in his head. He was even able to see this as a story. As a short indie film. The sun spilled generously onto their table, confirming him in his optimism.

Ted laughed. "Look at them. What else do they have? Poor slobs, probably living hand to mouth on some retirement pittance. The young ones no better, trapped in a place like this."

"But you said you liked diners like this!"

"No, sonny boy, I mean in a town like this. Cigarettes, alcohol, meth, coke, opiates. TV. Hey, the only difference between them and me is the cost of our drugs. Yep, the good old drugged-up US of A." Ted's lips thinned in a rueful smirk.

Josh was taken aback by his cynicism. "Well, not everyone, I mean, not everyone..."

Ted leaned in closer to Josh, his blue eyes laser-like. "Do you know anyone who isn't addicted? To something? To drugs. To sex. Or work. It's like that's the only way you can survive this f-ing life—get high, don't think about it."

Josh flashed on Libby, on her newfound thinness. What if

she was coked up, just to keep going? There was fun-loving Andy, who was always slightly high on weed. He thought of his mother and the glazed look she had when she painted, the way she seemed to look past, through him. Or his dad, locked in his shop, so fucking uptight about those damn clocks, about everything being just so. But could those be addictions?

"I don't know, I suppose I never thought about it—but why?" he asked Ted.

Ted leaned back in the booth, seeming to enjoy Josh's obvious discomfort with the idea. "Because otherwise, we'd all go mad with the—the strain of reality." He seemed quite serious, Josh thought, as he looked down at his cup, serious and old, the lines around his mouth and eyes more visible in the harsh morning light. And then, as if he'd read Josh's mind, Ted laughed. "God, I sound like such a pompous ass."

What am I doing here with this guy? Josh thought. *How did I get into this mess? Into another mess?* And what were the chances his father would find this Asbury Park, if it even existed, if it wasn't one of Ted's weird stories. Maybe he could go to the men's room, slip out a back way, hitch a ride back to the city. But there were hardly any cars in the parking lot, on the road. He could buy a bus ticket, but where was a station?

"Do you think I'm a pompous ass?" The pleading note in Ted's voice brought Josh back to the table. Ted looked suddenly vulnerable.

"I hardly know you." Josh thought, *Though without a doubt you are*, but then saw that Ted was still waiting for something from him. "No, that's not it." Josh shook his head, tried to sound reassuring. "I just don't understand what you were talking about.

Maybe you're right. Maybe everyone is addicted to something. It's just—sad, that's all."

Now Ted was scrutinizing him again, all traces of vulnerability gone. "Ah, you're an idealist. Well, you're young yet, plenty of time for that to change. But you weren't on the streets for no reason. What's your story, kid?"

Josh could feel himself blush. He didn't want to tell Ted the truth, but he didn't quite know what to tell him.

"It was a misunderstanding."

"And?" Ted's blue eyes riveted him. He squirmed but couldn't look away.

"My girlfriend—I came up here to see her, and well, we broke up is all. So I didn't have a place to stay. She thought I was going home. On the bus."

"And why didn't you?"

Josh looked out the window. "I don't really know." He remembered his mother talking dispassionately about his father, the feeling that night of being untethered. "I guess there really isn't so much to go home to." He didn't mention David or his parole.

"Yeah, well, I know about that."

"You do?" For a moment, Josh was taken off guard.

"Hm, well, it isn't all that unusual, is it? But you still haven't given me much information." Ted clearly intended to get Josh's story out of him, one way or another.

Josh looked down at the table. He felt his heart beat fast and hard. He felt hot, as if he were under an interrogation lamp. "I've, I guess I've always wanted to come to the city—I won some filmmaking competitions, and I thought Libby and I could start over here."

"And? You had a plan? Money?" Ted's voice was clipped, emphatic.

Josh felt confused, angry. "No, okay, I didn't. I mean, I did, but I was robbed on the bus."

"But why not call your folks?"

"They've got their own problems…" Josh picked up his fork and made lines in his napkin. Wasn't it clear he had no plans, hadn't thought anything through? That he was a stupid loser. He wanted away from Ted, who was examining him the way a collector might study an unusual species of butterfly caught in a net. "Hey, it's not really very interesting—it's *banal*." He tried to match Ted's cynical tone. Balancing the fork on his finger, Josh watched the way it reflected the light on the ceiling over Ted's head. He didn't want to tell Ted about his life; he didn't want to have to think about it. He especially didn't want to think about it. He wanted to think about the films he would make, the life he would have.

When he looked back at Ted, the man was smiling with a slightly amused expression.

"Banal?" He seemed to be mocking Josh. "Josh, please." There was that edge to his voice again, Josh thought, and he came to attention.

"Are you done? I'm anxious to move on." Ted hopped up, suddenly all motion. He threw some bills on the table and turned to go. Josh bolted the rest of his food and followed him outside. Ted strode very quickly, his short body ramrod straight, his shoulders back, a little general. Josh had to hurry to catch up with him. When he did, he noticed that Ted had a small secret smile on his face.

"The park would make a great setting for a movie, by the way. As a budding filmmaker, I think you will appreciate that, at least." Ted was smiling pleasantly, an indulgent uncle again.

"What would?"

"Asbury Park. Haven't you been listening? It's just an abandoned amusement park, but it reminds me of something Fellini would use. Amazing architecture, surreal faces painted on structures. But maybe you aren't interested." Ted was frowning now. "Maybe I attribute more imagination to you than you have."

Be careful, Josh thought.

"Sure, whatever." *Come on, Dad,* Josh thought. *Come on.*

They drove on. Josh stared out the window, experiencing the same trapped feeling he had had as a kid on long rides. Dark gray clouds scudded over an empty landscape of marshy flats and derelict strip malls. He noted idly a tattered American flag whipping violently in the wind. He felt his courage falter. How had he gotten into this mess?

Ted asked politely what kind of music Josh liked.

"Hip-hop, rap, stuff you wouldn't know about. Some old-school rock, I guess."

Ted winced, fiddled with the tuner. Loud static filled the car, then the voice of a rabid preacher, salsa music, then a news station. Ted paused for a moment, listening to a report on a terrorist bombing followed a weather report of local storm warnings. Finally, he found a classic rock station.

Josh was glad for the music, for the way it filled up space. Ted seemed relaxed, driving in that languid way he had. He had told Josh to look out for signs for Asbury Park. Josh was looking for more than that; he was looking for some signs of life, a Greyhound station, anything. What he saw were beat-en-down-looking gas stations, cruddy strip malls, seedy motels, their pastel paint faded and peeling. It all looked dispiriting or dangerous, as if there might be gangsters and drug dealers lurking, or at least petty thieves. Nothing looked quite real. It looked, Josh thought, like a movie. A very dark movie.

Josh thought, *This is a movie I'm making. This isn't real. But it is interesting.* Focusing on that, as if everything were a movie, always made it better. It was a trick he'd taught himself years ago. He felt himself relax a little. He wasn't really here, driving down a deserted highway with a crazy, middle-aged, closeted Wall Street banker. No, it wasn't him. It was a character named Josh.

THIRTY

They stood gazing at the clock, that little gem of mechanical perfection. The moment was everything Hal had hoped it would be—the opulent store with its velvet-draped windows, the fine clocks elegantly displayed behind glass cases, the expressions of unconcealed surprise and appreciation on the faces of these two worldly men. He'd thought, when he'd arrived and met them, that he'd picked up a bit of bemusement in their demeanors, as if he himself were a curiosity. He was self-conscious of his accent, of the slowness of his speech, and it seemed they had no reference outside Atlanta for the state of Georgia, or the South at all. But when he described the clock and brought it out, it was his turn to be bemused.

Mr. Kahn spoke first. "Well, I really am amazed. It is in perfect condition." He gently placed the clock on his desk. "What did you say its provenance was again?"

"A woman came into my shop to have it cleaned. Said it was her grandfather's. She is an elementary school teacher, and she thought it would be a good teaching tool."

The other two men gasped. Mr. Elliot, the younger one, looked horrified. "You, I hope, dissuaded her?" The man shot his impeccably starched wrist out of his Brooks Brothers charcoal suit in a kind of shudder. For a moment, Hal regretted his navy polyester sports jacket.

"Uh, um, of course I did. That is why you see it before you."

Mr. Kahn looked at him with narrowed eyes. "And what do *you* think it is?" He took off the dome, touched the delicate machinery with a manicured finger.

"I think in all probability it is a very fine reproduction. I couldn't find an identifying mark. However, I came across this article recently…"

The two men exchanged glances. Mr. Elliot said, "Ah, the *Horology Today* article."

Hal went on, more nervously now. "I realize that in all probability it is not one of the stolen clocks. But I wanted to satisfy my curiosity, at least. And perhaps find a buyer for the clock, as the owner is willing to sell."

Mr. Elliott looked at Mr. Kahn, who nodded slightly.

"We might be able to help you out," he said smoothly. "Of course, that would depend on your finder's fee, things of that nature, our commission… We do have a stable of collectors. Of course, we'd have to determine what we are dealing with first."

Hal nodded. "Of course." His heart beat so hard he was afraid they'd notice. They hadn't laughed him out of the shop. They were looking at his clock, asking him his opinion. As if he knew what he was doing. As if he were a true colleague. Hal allowed himself a moment of satisfaction.

Mr. Kahn said, "How do you feel about leaving it with us? We would of course give you the proper paperwork and surety. I think we would only need it for a day—will you still be in the city?"

Hal was about to respond when the hush of the place was jarred by a loud buzzing. Hal looked around, then realized the sound was coming from inside his jacket. It was Helen's damn cell phone, growing louder and more insistent.

Hal fished in his pocket for it, feeling himself flushing. *Not now,* he thought. *Not now Helen.* "So sorry," he said, turning away. "I'll just be a moment."

He would have liked to throw the damn thing through the window. "Yes," he almost yelled into the phone when he finally found the right button to push.

There was static, and then he heard Josh's voice. "Mom!"

"Josh, is that you?"

There was silence for a moment. "Dad?"

"I've got your mom's cell. Son, where are you? I'm in New York, looking for you. We've been so worried…"

Relief flooded him, followed by the old irritation that accompanied any interaction with his son. *Why now? Here?*

There was another long pause. Hal felt the two gentlemen glancing at him, was embarrassed.

"Dad! I'm almost out of battery. Dad, listen, *I need help.* I got a ride with this guy—" Only then did Hal notice his son's voice tremble.

"Guy? What guy? Josh, why are you whispering?"

Then he realized that Josh was crying and taking big, gulping breaths, his voice hissing over the phone. Something like alarm spread through Hal's chest. "Josh," he said as gently as he could.

Now the alarm had him by the throat, the way it had that time when Josh's canoe capsized at Lake Burton, when he wasn't sure he could swim fast enough to get to him. Alarm, and the sure knowledge that whatever Josh needed from him, he would not be able to give. Just as he had not reached Josh that time, but had watched another father, stronger and faster, pluck his son from the water.

"Dad! Dad, listen, you have to listen to me. Okay, he's taking me to a place called Asbury Park. An amusement park. Dad, got that? Asbury Park. You've got to come get me. Dad—"

The phone went dead even as Hal said, "He? Who—?"

The sudden disconnection, the loss of Josh's voice, stranded Hal between two worlds. He glanced back at the other two men and longed to pick up where he had left off with them. But he had to focus on Josh. *He's with a guy? Taking him someplace?* What had Josh done this time? What stupid, stupid thing? Hitch a ride with a weirdo? Why didn't that kid ever think? Why, why! He had no judgment, drifted along, got caught in crazy scenarios—*Christ, what could it be now?*

Josh had been scared. Really scared. And now Hal was scared, too. "Asbury Park. You've got to come get me," he'd said. Asbury Park. Hal jotted the name down, the talismanic words that would bring him to Josh. Josh seemed to think his father could do it, could find him, save him from "this guy."

What to do? What to do? He'd have to find a car, get directions. How would he ever do it? He'd never driven up here before, didn't know his way around. He felt suddenly hot and unable to get his breath.

He turned around and saw the two men huddled in whispered conversation. In front of them, on a table, was the clock. Its brass gave off a soft light, and Hal almost groaned. His one moment. Everything he had worked for. Why couldn't he have had at least this one small unalloyed triumph?

"I have to go. There's been an emergency with my son. I'll have to rent a car. If you could direct me someplace to do that?" His voice was stiff. He felt again like a country bumpkin, unsure how to navigate these urban waters.

To Hal's surprise, Mr. Kahn looked concerned. "My heavens. I hope he is all right?"

"Yes, I think so—I'm not sure. I need to go." He patted his breast pocket with the scrap of paper, feeling like an engine forced to idle.

"What about the clock?" Mr. Elliot asked, somewhat petulantly, it seemed to Hal.

"Just keep it here as we discussed. Here is my card. Sorry to cut this short—"

Mr. Kahn came round the desk, holding out a set of keys. "Here, Mr. Lovejoy, take these. I'll walk you up to the garage. I hardly ever use the thing anyway, to tell you the truth. Here's my number—when you come back, just take it back to the garage and give the attendant the keys."

"I couldn't possibly—"

"You must. Absolutely." He clapped Hal on the back. "I have a son myself. Besides, we may be doing business together."

They walked to the garage, a short few minutes away, and Hal was grateful for Mr. Kahn's silence. At the garage, Mr. Kahn explained the arrangement to the attendants, and then showed Hal the GPS system. "Just key in your destination here." Tactfully, Mr. Kahn didn't ask what it was. Hal wished the car was old and beat up: he was intimidated by its leather interior, its gleaming surfaces. But when he began to protest, Mr. Kahn wouldn't hear of any objections.

"It would take an hour or more to get you on the road at the car rental. Don't be ridiculous. I'm not worried. Just leave it here with Eduardo, he has full instructions."

Hal was nodding, pretending to take it all in. He wished Mr. Kahn would go now, so he could get on with it.

Mr. Kahn startled him by taking Hal's hand in both of his and looking at him with damp eyes. "I wish you and your son the best. In the end, what else is there?" He hesitated a moment. Hal felt acute embarrassment. "My son... ," Mr. Kahn started, then hesitated. "Well, I wish you the best." And then he turned and left, and Hal watched for a moment as he walked away, noticing the hunch in his shoulders, the tired way he walked. What had he been about to say? Something about his son.

SECTION 11:

IT COMES TO THIS

THIRTY-ONE

Josh saw the sign first. "There!" he said, pointing, and Ted, as if startled as if out of a reverie, swung off the highway, toward the beach.

They drove slowly down an empty street with no people, no cars. Instead, they passed lots full of weeds, abandoned buildings with boarded windows, and rusted street signs. Graffiti covered half the buildings. A once-elegant building stood tall and alone, the door gone, but a sign above it read proudly, Ambassador Hotel. A ghost town, Josh thought.

They drove next to the weathered, dilapidated boardwalk that ran parallel to the beach. Looking around, Josh strained for any sign of life. A plastic bag lifted in the offshore breeze, did a lazy somersault, then drifted around the corner of a building. A few sparrows pecked listlessly in the dirty snow of the car park. Josh thought he saw a cat slink around one of the buildings, but he wasn't sure. Gray water churned beyond the desolate boardwalk, the only moving thing in sight, except for the gulls that wheeled and dove. Even they, Josh thought, looked dispirited.

A large, ornately decorated brick building rose up before them, incongruously gracious with the surrounding seediness. "That's the Convention Hall," Ted said. "Let's take a look at it. It has—or had—fantastic sculptures inside." Josh noticed the excitement in Ted's voice, the lack of his usual smoothness. For a moment, Josh glimpsed an almost adolescent enthusiasm in the middle-aged man. There was yellow tape across the road and a no-trespassing sign, but Ted disregarded the sign and parked the Lexus almost nosing the tape. Although there wasn't a soul around, Ted locked his car. Josh almost pointed out the absurdity of it.

"Hey, how do you know about this place, anyway? It's kind of creepy." The wind whipped around them, sliced through Josh's thin hoodie.

Ted, looked up at him, surprised. "What, the park?" Ted surveyed the boardwalk. "Well, I guess it is now, but it wasn't always. It was happening in the seventies. There was a real music scene. Everyone came to the Stone Pony, the Fast Lane. Bruce Springsteen played here—many times." Ted paused, and then added, "You do know who he is, don't you?"

"Oh, *yeah*." Josh faked nonchalance, but the truth was, he only vaguely knew who Bruce Springsteen was. His parents had not been particularly cool. As a matter of fact, the further he was from them, the nerdier they seemed. But then, Ted hardly looked like a rocker, either.

Ted stood looking up at the building almost reverently, it seemed to Josh. He pointed out the terra-cotta relief sea creatures, a winged Pegasus, and a serpent, all cracked and painted in faded greens and golds. "Look at that ornamentation. Look at the architecture. Can't you just imagine coming here when it was first opened, in the late twenties, the thirties? It must have been the place to be. Swank." Ted looked at him, waiting for enthusiastic agreement.

Josh shrugged. "How do you know all this stuff?" he asked, petulant. "And why do you care? What's past is past." *Let's just move along,* Josh thought. *I want to get out of here.*

Ted leveled his dismissive look at Josh. "I suppose I *have* attributed more imagination to you than you indeed possess. What's past is never past." The acid put-down stung Josh. Ted was always doing that, putting him in his place, making him feel like an idiot.

Ted turned abruptly and headed toward the black hole where doors should have been. Josh followed reluctantly. He heard Ted ahead of him, but couldn't see him in the murky interior. Every muscle of his body tensed. He didn't want to be in the dark with Ted. He imagined what he would do to Ted if the man touched him. The thought of Ted's small manicured hands on him made him sick. He would deck him; he might kill him. He closed his eyes and felt his hands around Ted's neck, imagined the surprise and panic on the man's face. The satisfaction of that image, though, was quickly followed by another wave of nausea. Maybe he was a killer; maybe it was his fate. Not one he sought out, but one that kept coming toward him. He felt grimly bitter at the thought. He saw it, the police questioning him, Josh trying to explain how he'd come to be there with Ted, his mother's eyes red and anguished. Again.

He opened his eyes. Ted was somewhere ahead of him, blathering on excitedly. As his eyes adjusted to the dim light, Josh slowly became aware of figures along the walls. They were more large mythical creatures, seahorses maybe, green like the watery light inside. Josh felt as if he were underwater, submerged in a fantastical watery kingdom, a place both frightening and mesmerizing. He had to admit Ted was right; the place was amazing.

Ted was talking at him, his voice growing more insistent. Josh looked for him in the dark, then saw Ted's small erect figure gesturing excitedly right in front of him. Josh had already learned how to tune Ted out, just like he'd tuned out Hal. Now he tuned back in. Ted's mockingly professorial voice was going on about the arcade, the theater, the beaux arts style, blah, blah, blah. Ted, Josh had figured out, wasn't interested in conversation. He was interested in an audience. Josh obliged him by emitting sounds of amazed awe. What he really was thinking was whether his father would be able to find him in there. How to get Ted out of there, get them outside, so there was a ghost of a chance Hal would find them.

Ted now led him into the deserted theater. Josh flipped up seats as they went, watching the dust rise, glad to make some noise. There was always something compelling about an empty theater, that sense of expectancy, and yet here there would never be any expectancy, it was over, all in the past. Except, evidently, not for Ted. The past again. Josh shuddered. Ted walked up onto the stage and drew back the heavy red curtain. Puffs of dust hit Ted in the face and he sputtered. "I saw the Boss on this stage." Ted turned on his heel, as if trying to take it all in, sighing. "But the real fun was at Mrs. Jay's, drinking beer and watching the Harleys roll in."

Ted's dramatic monologue was growing very old. Josh said loudly, "You still haven't told me about you and this place. Why it's so damned important to you."

Ted, with surprising agility, tripped down the stage stairs.

"Ho-ho. Now who wants to know? I think we should trade secrets, sort of like strip poker—oh, sorry, I mean metaphorically."

"Very funny." Josh felt himself sullen, a dangerous anger moving in him again. He sat down in one of the seats, trying to hold on to himself.

Ted came over, put his two hands on the seat's armrests, and lowered his face level with Josh's. Josh reared away from his coffee breath, from his cynical eyes, from the smell of expensive cologne and damp wool.

"You think this place is interesting, wait till you see the Palace Amusements." He paused a moment, then went on. "Don't you think," he said, as if they were in the middle of a pleasant conversation, "that this would make a good movie setting? Hmm? What kind of movie would you make, Josh?" Ted's face hung in the dark air like a challenging, leering mask.

Josh pushed out of the chair, shoved past Ted, and looked around. He didn't want to play Ted's games but didn't have the energy to fight him. "It would suit a noir movie." He was thinking of the movie he always wanted to make with Susie, his chubby Greta Garbo. "Sort of postmodern noir, I mean." Ted just stood, arms crossed, looking at him expectantly. "But," Josh went on, quickened by the thought of his movie, "there is a sadness here, too. Something melancholy. Sort of the feeling you get in Welles's *Journey into Fear* or Hitchcock's *The Wrong Man*. You could go all kinds of ways with it."

Ted nodded thoughtfully, as if he was really listening. "Well, you have abysmal taste in music, but you certainly know your film."

It took Josh off guard. Few adults had ever actually paid attention to what he thought. Ted confused him. Sometimes he was weird as hell, sometimes he was almost human. Maybe he, Josh, had overreacted, making that call. Maybe Ted was just a harmless rich fuckup, maybe he really did just need someone to tell his story to. Maybe that was all there was to it. Josh was an idiot, calling for help like that. They'd do this tour of Ted's past, then get in Ted's car and get right back to Central Station where he'd take the bus home and no one would ever have to know about this little detour of his. Or. Or they'd get into Ted's car and drive to some deserted beach where Ted would hurt him, maybe kill him. Maybe Ted had a gun. A knife. Josh flashed on the scene—his body behind a dune, blood in the sand, innocent beachgoers finding him. He shook himself. No, he had to stay focused. If he stayed alert, it would be all right.

They left the building, walking down the boardwalk, past shuttered windows, the faded lettering advertising snow cones and ice creams and hotdogs. They walked by a vacant lot, filled with old tires and car parts. Josh kept looking behind him, looking for some sign of his dad. Nothing. Josh thought of Hansel and Gretel, of leaving a trail of something to lead Hal to him. *Yeah, right,* Josh thought. His dad. His stomach lurched, and he thought he might heave again. He didn't know which was more disturbing—his father finding him in this situation and knowing finally what a screw-up he was or being left to fend for himself.

Ted marched on, didn't seem to notice Josh's agitation. The older man leaned into the wind, and despite his suit, hugged his arms across his chest. In the shadowless gray light, Josh could see the pink of Ted's scalp beneath the artificially blond hair.

He could see the lines in his face, the gray stubble on his chin, the sagging jowls. Looked at from this angle, he seemed repulsive, pitiful, nothing to be afraid of.

Ted seemed to be in some sort of discussion with himself, looking around and every so often shaking his head. Suddenly he stopped and gasped. "Oh, my god, Mrs. Jay's." He took hold of the cyclone fence and shook it. "It's… gone. Look at that." He swept his hand in the direction of an empty lot. "Gone."

Josh turned away from Ted, embarrassed by his raw emotion. Instead, he looked out at the deserted beach, at the relentlessly pounding waves, the threatening clouds. He noticed piles of seaweed near a pier, slimy and dark, bits of white shells and shiny debris caught in them. Gulls shrieked and circled, some of them landing near the seaweed. He picked up a stone and threw it at the birds. He thought again about overpowering Ted, about taking the keys and leaving—but where would he go? And even he knew he'd land in jail, so what was the point? He remembered his night spent in the police station holding cell, the noise and the light and the way it seemed it would never end.

The gulls screeched overhead. Suddenly, the beach was covered with wings and beaks, with raucous calls, as if all gulls in the area had been summoned by some mysterious force. It was like the scene in Hitchcock's *The Birds*…

"Josh! Hey, kid, you coming or what?" Ted snapped his fingers in front of Josh's face.

Josh jerked back. "Yeah, okay. So where are we going now, dad?"

"Very funny."

"I want to ride on the merry-go-round!" Josh whined.

Ted laughed, turned around. "Oh, you will, son, you will. Now be a good boy and don't dawdle or you'll get a spanking."

"Righto, dad."

They headed toward the Casino, a ruined copper-and-brick building at the end of the boardwalk. Ted continued his discourse on the way it used to be—the hippies, the bikers, the music scene—with great nostalgia. Josh could almost smell the salt and beer and pot, hear the laughter, the sexual banter. He could hear the bass thumping out a rhythm; he could see the stars shining overhead, the phosphorescence in the waves. It filled Josh with longing for bygone youth, for a youth he would never have, for a time that would never come again.

He was wondering how Ted fit into it all, was curious again, when Ted stopped abruptly and said, "Whoa!" He pointed. There on the beach, marring the view, was an abandoned, half-built concrete-and-steel monstrosity. "Damn developers!" Ted cursed. Then, "That's how money is made. Or not, in this case." He frowned, seemed to Josh to take the structure personally. "Of course, I help finance risks like this."

"Ted, I have to tell you, I just can't see you in this place. Not the way you describe it."

Ted stopped, pivoted around to him, a sardonic look on his face. "It's a long way from there to here, boyo."

Josh frowned, felt again the butt of a joke.

"Here it is!" Ted said excitedly. Josh looked up into a huge, leering grin painted on the side of a large building.

"Ah, dear old Tillie. Here we go!" Ted said with exaggerated enthusiasm. "Little Joshy can go on the twister, the scooter, the fun house, the merry-go-round, and maybe the tunnel of love, if he is a good boy." Ted stepped over the yellow police tape, scooted by the orange barrels and the sign that said "Danger, Do Not Enter! Condemned!"

Josh stood outside the yellow tape. Ted waited for him inside it, the painted face grinning over his shoulder.

"Well?" he said.

"Can't you read?"

"So?" He shrugged.

"It says 'Do Not Enter. Condemned.'"

"Please don't turn into a literalist on me, Josh."

"Yeah, I don't want that building on top of me. I'm going back to the car. I'll see you there after you have your little walk down memory lane."

Ted looked down, scuffed the toe of his shoe in the dirt. "Well, if that's what you want. Fine. I was going to tell you more about my story—I thought this would be the appropriate setting. But if you don't want to, fine. I don't blame you." He shrugged ruefully, his face suddenly slack. He turned, his shoulders slumped, and walked into the building.

***

Hal got into the car, keyed in Asbury Park with trembling hands. Miraculously, the map showed a spot on the Jersey Shore only sixty miles south of Manhattan. Hal put the car in gear, backed it out gingerly, sweat trickling down his armpits and back, and eased into the river of cars. Unsure of what he was doing, he knew he was driving too slowly for the traffic. All around him cars wove in and out, honking angrily at him. He'd never seen such drivers, not even in Atlanta. Here it seemed like a game: who could be the rudest, stopping on a dime, the loud brakes, the skidding tires.

With relief he saw the signs for the George Washington Bridge. He carefully maneuvered the car into the right lane, all the while hating the whole predicament he was in—borrowing a car (he hated borrowing, never did it) from a stranger (didn't like any show of emotion from anyone, but it was almost obscene to have another man so openly emotional), driving in this city (he didn't like cities, didn't like to be away from home), going to find his son (who baffled and irritated him) who had managed to get himself into yet more trouble, trouble of some undefined sort.

He braked suddenly, barely avoiding the car in front of him. Red taillights snaked up onto the bridge. He followed, anxious to get in the right lane, hating the thought of being cooped up in that enclosed dark space. Hot now, he took off his jacket, tried to steady himself with his breath.

He should call Helen. And tell her what? About Josh's phone call? That would do nothing but terrify her. No, better to see it through, get to a resolution, get Josh, then call her. He'd be there in an hour or so.

Over the bridge now, the cars burst out of their confinement, spewing onto the New Jersey Turnpike. Hal saw the toll-booth ahead and reached for his wallet, as the smooth British female voice of the GPS told him to get ready to pay the toll. Annoyed, he muted the thing.

Oil refineries and smokestacks stood like sentinels on either side of the flat highway. Manhattan receded behind him. He felt strangely exposed here, missed suddenly the comforting hills of North Georgia. Cars whizzed by him, many of them weaving and dodging, many of them late-model, sleek cars that seemed to belong to a different breed of person than he was. He felt weary and slow and unequal to whatever it was that awaited him in New Jersey.

He tried not to think of Josh, to speculate about what had happened this time. But it was hard, with all this empty time on his hands, not to. He tried to focus instead on the clock, on the possible sale. He tried to imagine his name under the clock in *Horology Today* or *Clocks*, and maybe a picture of him, Hal, smiling modestly behind the clock. But he couldn't sustain the fantasy. He found himself remembering things he didn't want to remember, things he'd put behind him.

He saw Helen's face the day he came home and had to tell her that he'd failed his mechanical engineering exit exam for the third and final time. Her disbelief. Her disappointment. "We are never to talk about it again," he'd thundered at her, ashamed that he had been so weak, that even though she had corrected and typed his papers, he couldn't pull off the exam. He'd hated her for feeling his own shame.

It was all jumbled up. All these invading memories like flies buzzing around his head. But here, in the gray monotony of the highway, he had no way to distract himself from his own thoughts.

Josh. Josh as a little boy, so bright and open it hurt Hal to think of it. To Hal, Josh's mere existence had seemed to make up for all Hal's screw-ups. He remembered the texture of the carpet they used to sit on, the way it would impress itself on their arms as they lay there building Lego forts. Later, the games involved knights and Star Wars figures, sword fighting, battles. Helen would stand in the kitchen doorway, watching them, a little smile on her face, and Hal remembers looking up, their eyes meeting, each acknowledging the other's contentment. There had been such a sense of wholeness then, the three of them. What had happened, what had happened?

He couldn't bear it, couldn't bear what Helen tried to tell him. That Josh was imperfect, that he too might be blighted by whatever it was that had made life so hard for Hal. And he'd fought her. It was her fault, trying to find trouble where there wasn't any. But he knew it wasn't.

And then they hadn't been three, but two and one. He was the outcast. Or he felt like outcast. But who had cast out whom? And didn't they care? And he told himself it didn't matter at all, that he had his clocks, and it took up his time. But then Josh started in with his crazy filmmaking and failing his classes, and Hal had felt that old strangled feeling again, that something had to be done to keep Josh from sliding into the pit. And he'd tried to take control, to discipline Josh, but now he wondered, was it discipline? Wasn't it punishment?

And he punished Helen, too, because if he was in hell, then it was only fair that she should be there with him. And then he knew he had succeeded pretty fairly in taking her with him. Even before. Even before the accident.

Josh's face at the accident. The nakedness, the fear, the way his eyes bulged out of his head, his slack mouth. Hal shook,

thinking of it. Josh had finally, publicly, exposed Hal's inade-
quacies. As a parent, as a human being. The final failure of Hal's
failed life. But Josh had run up to him, his arms outstretched—

What had Mr. Kahn said? "In the end, that's all there is."
What had he meant? And what had happened to his own son?
Hal wanted suddenly to call Mr. Kahn. It seemed he would
know what to do. But then, Hal didn't talk to strangers about
things like this. He didn't talk to anyone. He didn't even talk
to himself.

And now something else would be required of him. The old
defeat crept in with the cold. He had failed Josh. He would
probably fail him again. He feared for Josh, for himself. What
lifeline could he throw his son on this harrowing sea? Hal was
no one's captain. He wasn't even sure he could find his son.

But he did find the exit. And with dread, turned onto it.

SECTION 12:
THE WAY
THE WORLD WORKS

THIRTY-TWO

Josh turned away and started walking resolutely up the boardwalk toward the car, the wind pushing against him. Damn Ted! Who the hell was he, anyway? Josh didn't give a damn about his stupid stories, his stupid life. He just wanted to go home, wanted this to be over. Ted could find someone else to tell his stories to. Josh was done playing games with him, done with Ted treating him like a baby one minute, like the most fascinating adult the next. The guy was sick.

Josh looked over his shoulder at the Casino. The building seemed to have swallowed Ted. *Fine,* Josh thought. He didn't think Ted would last long without an audience. He'd have to outwait him. He strained his eyes, looking for any place that he could run to. There was nothing but the sea on one side, the highway on the other. No, he'd have to leave the way he came. It had gotten colder, and Josh hugged himself, rubbing his arms for warmth. The clouds that had been gathering all morning hung darkly over the water now. Josh smelled rain and the sharp scent of the ocean. Well, he'd duck back into the Convention Hall if he needed to take shelter.

The salt air thick around him, Josh gazed at the empty stores and concession stands with their faded pastel murals and aluminum shutters. As a kid, he had always wanted to go to a place like this, with fun rides, ice cream, the smell of suntan lotion. His parents had said it was too far, they didn't have the time or money for such things. Now he supposed he was past wanting those things, just like this place was past providing them.

The rain started. Stinging sheets of water slashed him. He looked north to the Hall, then back at the Casino with its gaping windows, its tangle of green weeds on the roof, tossing in the brisk wind.

Where was Ted? He peered at the wide, empty parking lot in front of the Casino, at the meters standing at attention, at Tilly's ludicrous face grinning down at him. For a moment he wondered if he'd made Ted up, if he existed at all. If anyone existed besides Josh, or if he had landed in some twilight zone, the last person on earth. A loose piece of board banged in syncopation behind him. He turned and ran back down the boardwalk, feeling a frantic urgency. Even Ted was better than no one. This time he didn't hesitate; he jumped over the police tape and walked into the cavernous building.

He couldn't see anything at first. Dust went up his nose, and he was overwhelmed by a rotting, mildewed smell. The place was cavernous. He called out, "Ted?" but his voice sounded puny in all the space. He took a few steps, his eyes slowly adjusting to the murky light. The shapes of the merry-go-round, the abandoned rides, the fading fun house all began to emerge. There was the same underwater light, that same greenish cast, that same muffled silence of the Convention Hall, only more so—a surreal underwater world, a world where all the rules of life were suspended.

He didn't see Ted at first. All he could make out were chunks of shadows, gradations of gray. He squinted, then saw Ted sitting in a seat on the twister, his knees up to his chin as if he were a small child, gazing down at Josh. Josh realized he must have been watching him.

"Josh! How nice to see you. You didn't disappoint me."

Josh was in no mood for his sarcasm.

"You have a story to tell, Ted." Josh's voice was too loud, too harsh. "Then I want to get the hell out of here."

"Yes, I do. And we will." He sounded like an indulgent uncle again. "What do you think of it, Josh?" From his perch, he gestured expansively, as if it were his.

Josh looked around. His photographer's eye took in every detail, the way the gray light made the spiderlike mechanism of the rides looked surreal, the negative space creating mystery, the contrast between the laughing faces, and the dead stillness of the place.

Ted materialized at his elbow, startling Josh. "Let's go upstairs, the view is even better," he whispered conspiratorially. Josh followed Ted up the iron steps, carefully testing his weight on each one. Ted seemed oblivious to any danger, taking the stairs two at a time. Josh held his breath, sure the stairs would give way at any moment. And yet, he was excited, too—the sense he hadn't had since he was a child, of exploring an abandoned building, the thrill of transgressing.

On the mezzanine, Josh let out his breath. It was a better view, but it also felt precarious. Looking up, he saw holes in the roof, saw the weeds that had taken hold there. He turned to tell Ted, but the man stared into the dark space below, his body rigid. Ted seemed reckless to Josh, perhaps more unaware of danger than Josh knew himself to be.

Ted turned to Josh, dusted off two rickety chairs. He was fastidious, even in this place.

Josh wanted to get on with it, get it over with, and get back to New York. He would take the first bus home, he thought. But what would be different when he got home? Wouldn't everything be the same, everyone preoccupied with their own lives? Oblivious to each other. Everyone with *their own addictions.*

Ted leaned toward him, his hands clasped around his knees, as relaxed as a doctor interviewing a patient. "Are you going to make a movie of this, Josh? Do you collect stories of people?"

"Hey, you started this. You wanted to know *my* story."

Ted smiled. "I still do. I want to know if your story is any different from all the rest."

"The rest?" Josh resented the man's constant condescension.

"We'll get to that later... Okay, go on."

"Why does this place mean so much to you?"

Ted's eyebrows shot up, surprised. Josh thought he was about to protest that it didn't really, but instead, he cocked his head, nodding. "Good question." He looked around. "It was the first place I could be myself. It was the place I found out who I was, what I was. And it was okay. It was better than okay. I don't know if you can understand... it was before the gay movement. I knew I was different, but until I came here, I didn't know that others were, too. It was a kind of nirvana. All the pretending, all the strain of trying to be who my parents wanted me to be—I left it behind. I didn't have to do that here."

Josh nodded. He was imagining himself with Libby, back then. The two of them hippies, her free of her parents, him free of his dad bearing down on him, free of his unexpected rages, of his mother's depression. Free. He'd like to find a place like that.

"Can you understand? A little?" Ted looked vulnerable again, but it was only for a fleeting moment. Then his face resumed its smooth, sardonic expression.

Josh could see himself and Libby on a bed covered with a cheap, colorful Indian spread, smoking a hookah, sitar music playing in the background. He saw Ted, thirty years younger, entwined with his lover. Yes, he could understand.

Josh nodded. "But why the wife, the kids? What's the point of that? I mean, that's pretending, isn't it?"

"Ah, the young. So idealistic. So simplistic." He reached into his pocket and took out a vial and sniffed it. He offered it to Josh.

"I don't want it. Whatever it is."

"Ah, too bad." Ted sniffed a few times, stuck the vial back in his pocket. His eyes were brighter, his face flushed. "Life betrays the sweet promises of youth. Hate to clue you in."

"You know, I'm not here to be insulted, okay? I mean it— why the whole thing?"

"Well, I have to make money. To make money on Wall Street, you have to fit in. To fit in, you have to be married. Besides, I am good at living a double life. It suits me. It makes everything a story, so to speak. It allows for 'narrative invention,' shall we say?"

Josh felt a jolt of recognition. He knew what that was like. Yet he felt an intense dislike for Ted at that moment.

"And do they know? I mean, do they all accept this arrangement—your family, your—"

"Boyfriends?"

"Yeah."

Ted shook his head. "Hey, I give them all a good time. I make so much money they can have anything they want. They all go along."

Josh tried to see Ted's face but couldn't read his smile. Josh's stomach clenched. Acid licked the back of his throat. He looked over the railing into the murky darkness below. It looked, suddenly, abysmal. A void, bottomless. The stilled rides menacing, torturous.

"But—what happened? To make you—go from, uh, nirvana to… ?" Josh gestured helplessly. "I mean, the story."

"Specifics?"

Josh nodded. "That's what makes a good story."

Ted's eyebrows shot up again. "All right, then. Let's see, I had been coming here every summer since I was sixteen. My first lover—the love of my life—was older than me. Actually, only six years, but at the time, he seemed so much older, so worldly-wise. He was actually a bartender here, at the Stone Pony." Ted paused, looked away from Josh. "Anyway, he was gorgeous—tall, muscular, dark eyed. I was surprised he picked me, although I have to say, I was a good-looking enough kid— blond, blue eyed. Jerry had come from the same kind of background as me—the Connecticut suburbs, all about martinis and money and connections. He understood all that. I had, as a boy, a yen for, an eye for, pretty things. By that time my interests had refined themselves to collecting ancient Chinese porcelain. At first my folks had encouraged this, but as I got older, they had become wary and then alarmed. Why didn't I go out for sports? Why didn't I date their best friends' daughters?

"But Jerry, he got excited about my collecting, encouraged it. It was before the Internet—it's probably hard for you to imagine how difficult it was to get information then. But Jerry would go to libraries and photocopy articles, would look out for pieces at flea markets for me. Could he barter! He had that charming manner, made it seem like a game, that the seller was lucky to be in his presence.

"Once, we went to an estate sale in the Hamptons. Some old folks—Jerry had read the ad in an antiques newspaper. Anyway, the guy had been an ambassador to China, and the place was a virtual museum. His widow—an acerbic, wizened old bitch, dressed in black and nobody's fool with her thin New England lips—looked askance at us when we first walked in. We were the earliest customers. But by noon, by god, Jerry had her charmed and we were invited for lunch, wine and all. We left there with porcelain that now is priceless, with an agreement to pay over time—twenty-five dollars, I think, a month. Poor thing died shortly afterward."

Ted's face was alive with pleasure at the memory. Finally, Josh said, "What happened to Jerry?"

Ted frowned. "Ah, yes, the turn in the story."

"We were together for three and a half years. But that last summer, I guess things here really were dying." He sighed, his hands falling to his sides. "I drove down here as soon as the park opened, just in time to see Jerry walking out of his apartment with an older man—I mean, really older. I ran up to them, reckless, and demanded to know what was going on. Didn't do that with much aplomb, I'm afraid."

Ted gestured helplessly with his hands, smiling ruefully.

"Well, anyway, Jerry looked at me sadly and told the other guy to go on, he'd catch up with him in a minute. Then he took me by the arm as if I were a child. I shook off his hand angrily. In a patient voice, he tried to explain to me that the scene here was dying and he needed security and Rick had been interested in him for some time and could I try to understand. By then I was snotty nosed, crying. I just wanted him to put his arms around me, say he would never leave me. I felt as if I were being split in two, cleaved down the middle. He had been my world."

Ted hung his head, his voice was thick with emotion. But when he raised it again, there was the old hard look in his eyes.

"So, what happened then?"

"Well, in short order my parents found my porcelain collection, what was left after Jer had taken his 'share.' They figured out the road I was headed down and got me to a shrink who convinced me I wasn't the way I was. But part of me knew. I guess I wanted my parents' approval, at any cost. It was a relief in a way, to have them accept me again. But I would watch myself acting, it was as if I really were two people. The more I tried to ignore the things I knew, the more compelling the other life seemed. But I dated their best friend's daughter and married her, and all the while grew to despise them all for not knowing me, not seeing me. Not that I gave them much of an opportunity."

"But was it better, the other life?"

Ted looked searchingly at Josh. "What is better? I certainly felt more alive, more excited, more real. But you get older, it takes more and more to get the thrill. I've had a few long-term relationships. They didn't last. I guess I was always looking for him."

"Did you ever see him again?"

Ted didn't seem to hear him. He didn't answer for a long time. "Funny thing you should ask. I actually did find him again—the Internet is a wonderful tool. He had been in France, and recently moved back to the city and opened an antique shop. I had actually gone over there yesterday and waited in my car to catch a glimpse of him."

"And did you?"

Ted closed his eyes and spoke in careful, measured sentences.

"It had closed, and I was afraid he might go out another door. I was about to leave when this older, ravished-looking man wearily locked the door. He walked with a limp, and he had a belly on him. I thought it must be an employee, but as he passed me, I could see that the eyes were the same."

"Didn't you go after him? Ask him for a drink? Catch up?"

Ted shook his head. "You don't get it, do you?" He had opened his eyes now, and there were tears them. "I wished I had never seen him like that." Ted took a deep breath. "Of course he would change. I had anticipated that. But—" Ted took a deep breath. "But the thing is—it wasn't Jerry. The old verve, the confidence. It wasn't there... I slowly drove alongside the curb for a few minutes, wondering if he'd glance down, if my feelings would change. Until I couldn't stand it. The stoop in his shoulders."

Josh spoke carefully. "What did you want from him?"

Ted startled, as if he had forgotten Josh was there. He didn't speak for several long seconds, but when he did, there was no hardness in his voice. "I wanted to be real again, to feel whole. The way I had when we were together." He looked away, as if embarrassed.

"Maybe you could just—talk to him. Maybe it would help—"

Ted laughed, a harsh, abrupt laugh. "You don't get it, kid. It is just one more betrayal. I was stupid to even hope. An object lesson, kid. So you don't waste time looking for perfect love and understanding. You can only pretend for a while, and then the game is over. It's all a lose–lose proposition. Or a use–use proposition."

Josh shivered. This world of Ted's. Was it the real world, stripped of illusions? "What kind of world is that?" Josh gasped out finally.

Ted smiled thinly. "It is *the* world, Josh. Expect to be betrayed, as I suspect you already have been. Isn't that right?"

Josh felt himself blush. "I never really thought about it that way."

Pieces of Ted's story felt familiar to him, as if he'd heard the rhythms of the song before but in a different key. He saw Libby's thin, beaten face, felt again the unreality of her turning away from him, buying him off with a few dollars. He saw his mother's closed, resigned expression, the way she had just stopped being a mom, given up. And he thought, although he didn't want to, of standing alone in the road over David's body, of waiting for his father, and of his father's unbreachable rage.

A feeling of something hot and piercing in his gut made him almost cry out in pain. And now he felt he was falling down a deep black pit, a pit he would never get out of. He didn't care. It was so sweet to fall, to let go. He had been betrayed. It wasn't just him being a loser. It was them. They had played him for a fool.

He was shaking with rage. Ted was right.

Ted watched him carefully. "You see?"

Josh was about to say, *Yes, yes, you're right. That's the way the world works,* when he heard a sharp crack overhead. He looked up through a hole in the roof. The wind had torn a piece of roof off—Josh could see the rusted corrugated metal edge slapping now against the rafters. As he peered at it, the clouds shifted, and the sun alighted briefly on the white wing of a gull passing overhead.

Midfall, he was arrested. The brief image of the bird recalled something to Josh, something important. He groped like a dreamer awakened, the last few images of the dream dissolving. What was it? And then he had it: reading *The Snowy Day* to Marius. The page with the snow angel on it. Explaining to Marius about snow, getting down on the dirty carpet and scissoring his arms and legs, Marius staring at him as if he were nuts. Then, slowly, Marius bringing his arms out and flapping them jerkily. "That's it, Marius!" Josh had said, sitting up. "Air angels," Marius had said, giggling.

That had felt like the way the world worked.

Stunned, Josh clung to that memory, struggling hard against the pull of resentment. The world had betrayed Marius. It had crippled him and killed his mother.

But that day, that day, with Marius flapping his wings, Josh had felt *right.* He'd felt good, whole.

The rage began to seep out of him. Maybe Ted was wrong.

There was a creaking sound, louder this time, and both of them looked up. Another piece of the roof sheared off, slowly and sickeningly.

"We've got to get out of here!" Josh yelled, pulling on Ted's sleeve. "Come on." But Ted stood there, an unnatural calm on his face, and slowly shook his head. Josh hesitated. "Are you insane? You've got to get out of here!" A crash came then, shaking the mezzanine.

Josh ran for the stairs, taking them two at a time. Wood splintered around him, cracking loudly like thunder. Dust rose in great clouds, clogging his throat and eyes, so that he was forced to stop and get his bearings. The stair under his feet twisted sickeningly. He wiped at his eyes, craning back to look for Ted, hoping he was behind him. Ted stood motionless just where Josh had left him. Covered in white plaster, he stared straight ahead, as if transformed into a funhouse statue, while pieces of roof and wall crashed around him. "Ted," Josh shouted, but his voice was lost in the din.

The building gave another shudder, and the stairs rippled again, throwing Josh forward. He covered his mouth with his shirt to keep the dust out and kept his arm over his head to protect him. At the bottom of the stairs, he stopped again, disoriented. Where was the door? Josh's breath came in harsh gasps, his heart beat frantically. What if he died in here? What would it do to his mother? Oh, god, he can't think about that, not now. He saw her face, anguished, old. If he made it, he would be better, he would be.

He made out the spidery arms of the twister, looming like an alien monster in the dust. He went toward it, then backed away, remembering that it was placed deeper in the hall. He spun around and saw the merry-go-round and groped his way toward it. It had been the first thing he'd seen when he'd entered the building, so it would be closer to the exit. That seemed so long ago now, ages ago, as if in another lifetime. And the call to his dad—that seemed to belong to someone else's life altogether, someone still in the normal world, someone entirely more innocent than he felt now.

Just as he made it to the merry-go-round, his hand resting on a plastic horse, he glimpsed a vague lightness in the gray. He squinted and thought he saw a dim slice of light. The door. Was that it? The door he'd left ajar when he'd come in? That must be it. The building heaved and torqued again like a thing alive. Josh pushed off the merry-go-round, keeping his eyes on that slice of light. He ran as fast as he could, his legs pumping, his lungs filling with dust, yet nightmarishly, he didn't seem to gain ground. All around him, things fell—a red seat from the twister flew past him, a banister from the stairway landed by his feet, the leg of a plaster starfish blocked his way ahead. Something hit his shoulder hard and almost knocked the breath out of him. He stumbled but regained his footing, keeping his eyes fixed on the slice of light, and slowly it grew and became an open door, and then, miraculously, he was through it.

He kept running up the boardwalk until he was out of breath, then collapsed and turned back to the building. Sobbing and coughing up dust, he watched the roof collapse inward in a slow, awful way, Tilly grinning even as she swayed. "No, no, no," he heard himself screaming. He looked around, crying, calling for help, but only the gulls answered him.

"Oh, god, oh, god," he cried, then found himself on his knees on the asphalt, throwing up again.

THIRTY-THREE

Josh's eyes burned. He pulled his shirt over his mouth and nose. He wanted to run away, but he stayed there, unable to move, choking in the billows of dust, watching as the building collapsed in slow motion. It seemed to go on forever. Then, slowly, the dust began to clear, and the awful creaking and moaning of the old metal structure faded to a hum. And there, in the clearing debris, stood Hal. His back was turned to Josh, and he was walking toward the disintegrating building.

"Dad!" Josh screamed. "Dad, I'm over here!"

Hal turned, and Josh almost flinched, reflexively afraid and ashamed. But his father's face wasn't angry. Hal looked terrified, his face streaked with dust and tears.

"Josh," his father yelled, coming toward him. "Josh, thank god!" Hal pulled Josh awkwardly into his arms. "Thank god you are okay. You're okay!"

Josh allowed himself to rest against his father. He inhaled the familiar smell of him, the always-lingering clock oil smell, the too-sweet odor of spearmint gum. Beneath the unfamiliar suit, Josh could hear the steady beat of Hal's heart, as steady as the clocks he surrounded himself with.

"What on earth happened, son? Are you all right?" Hal said finally, pulling away to look at Josh's face.

Josh kept seeing Ted standing on the mezzanine, pieces of roof falling around him, that eerie, crazy calm he had. If he couldn't explain to himself what had happened to him there, how could he explain it to Hal?

"I'm okay, Dad. Really. I can't explain it all right now. Just give me a little time, okay?"

He saw Hal struggle with himself, his brow creased, his lips pursed. His dad liked everything accounted for. He liked things in working order. He didn't like mysteries. He didn't understand the way Josh approached things, how Josh was always drawn to the enigmas, the gray areas.

What was it Ted said about despising his parents for not knowing him? Is that how he felt about Hal? Because he remembered it; it had felt familiar.

Hal helped Josh to his feet, brushed the dirt off him. "Okay, Josh. Okay."

Josh was colder and hungrier and more tired than he had ever been in his life. He didn't think he had the energy to despise Hal. He was tired. Tired of trying to make Hal love him, or understand him. He knew what Ted had meant, a secret pride develops like a callus, and you think, *He can never know me.* It is a lonely, hard place, but it was the place he knew himself best. Could he give that up?

"We've got to call the police, Dad. There's a man in that building. He might still be alive."

Hal blanched. "My god! Josh, what have you gotten yourself into!"

"I'll explain it, but I need a phone."

Hal drew the phone from his jacket pocket and gave it to Josh. Then he sank to the curb and put his head in his hands.

***

Hal looked up at the cop.

"So, this guy—is he going to be okay?"

Behind the cop, Josh watched as they loaded a dust-covered Ted into the ambulance. Ted must have seen him, because he raised his arm in a weak salute.

"Yeah, he's in serious condition, but he'll recover. Evidently, he had so much alcohol in his blood it saved him. We actually got a statement from him—he said Josh tried to get him out, but he, uh, didn't want to, uh, go on living. A real nut."

"So Josh is free to go?"

"Yeah, we got his statement. He'll have to deal with the authorities in Georgia. Get a girlfriend closer to home next time, kid."

Josh managed a weak smile.

Josh followed Hal out into the parking lot, everything around him surreal, the fuzzy streetlights, the beat-up pavement, the fancy car his dad was unlocking. His dad was saying something about a Mr. Kahn, an antique clock collector or something or other.

"So you weren't really looking for me? You had an appointment with Mr. Kahn?" Josh felt the old resentment begin to rise in him again.

Hal turned to Josh, his face ghostly in the streetlight glare. "It was a pretext. I thought I could find you and get you home before the authorities found out. So you wouldn't get charged with skipping parole. No chance of that now, I guess."

Josh didn't miss the disappointment in his voice.

Hal put the car into gear. "You might as well put your chair back and get some sleep."

For the second time that day, Josh felt like a little kid again. But this time, he relaxed. His dad was there, taking care of things. The steady shh-shh of the tires, the soft undertone of the radio. Hal had come to get him. That was big. That was huge. *I have to remember this,* Josh thought as he was tugged deeper and deeper into sleep. And just before sleep claimed him completely, something inside him knew Hal would never really understand him. But he also knew that Hal loved him. In his way. And that would have to be enough.

***

Meg sat with David's body for a long time after the nurses unhooked him from the machines. Without the monitor's green glow, without its whirrs and hums, without the merciless florescent light, the room had the deflated hush of a broken-down stage set. Now there was only David, and not even him, but what was left of him, what was quickly becoming not him.

Sister Antonette had told her to take as much time as she needed with him. Time? Meg thought of all the times she had waited, wanting more of his time, more of his attention. How what she had wanted was only just out of reach—they would go away together after the next project, after the next campaign. And now, suddenly, there was no next time. There was only now, this quiet room, with only the sound of her own breathing.

The two women had taken turns watching through the night. Meg had never seen anyone die before. She was heartsick and afraid, and ashamed of being afraid. She sat on his bed as his unseeing eyes flew open, as he convulsed suddenly, gasped for breath, and then quieted. His living will clearly stated DNR, and yet Meg could almost not bear to see him struggle.

"Is it always like this?" she had cried, almost angry at Antonette for being party to such cruelty, angry that she didn't know this would happen, angry that despite everything, he was being taken from her and there was nothing she could do to stop it.

Sister Antonette stood by the bed, her white habit glowing in the dimness. Her broad face sagged, and her blue eyes, embedded in their folds of wrinkles, looked out at Meg sorrowfully. "He's not in pain, dear," she told her, and yet Meg thought such a struggle could only be painful.

"Does he even know I'm here?" Meg had asked later, after a long period of quiet, when nothing seemed to be happening.

"I don't know. He very well may. Hearing is the last thing to go. Keep on talking to him, Meg. Tell him how much you love him. Tell him that he can go. That you will be all right."

"Will I be?" Meg whispered.

The old nun patted her hand. "Yes, I think you will be," she said.

And so she did talk with him, as she had been doing all along, although now it felt more urgent, and the urgency made her awkward. She realized then that she had been waiting all those months for some sign from him, some last word—that all her conversations in this room had held out just that hope, that fantasy. She knew now there would be no last word. She had held his hand in hers, and wept onto it, feeling the faint pulse still coursing through.

She must have fallen asleep, because she was being gently shaken. She saw Sister Antonette's gnarled, burnished hand on her arm and remembered where she was. A faint reddish light came in through the window. She was still on his bed, still holding his hand. She looked at his beloved face, his eyes closed, his features thinned and sharpened. It was over. A strange calm came over Meg. It was over. Even as his hand grew cool in hers, she knew, finally, how alone she was, how alone everyone was. And yet it didn't dismay her as it once might have. It was simply the truth.

Ever since they'd met in the kitchen of Common Cause, he had been the sun around which she revolved. Despite the hurt they'd inflicted on each other—or because of it?—she could never fully imagine her life without him.

And now he'd given her this final gift.

He'd set her free.

***

Helen kept checking her watch. Eleven thirty. They should be home any minute. She tried to distract herself but couldn't settle down to anything—not drawing, not knitting, not TV. She kept jumping up and pacing. She pulled out the sideboard drawer and attempted to organize years of junk that had accumulated. But sorting through the old Uno cards, pens, photos, rubber bands, and Legos only made her weepy. Everything reminded her of Josh. Finally, she gave up. She put on some music and rocked in the rocking chair, trying to breathe.

She'd had a day to try to take it all in, a day that seemed like a year. There had been overwhelming relief that Josh was safe, confusion about what had happened, why he hadn't been on the bus home as they had thought. She still didn't understand who Ted was or how Josh had somehow helped save his life. It had almost seemed as if she had dreamed the whole sequence of events, or as if it were a film she'd seen and confused with her real life, and when the lights in the theater came on, she would walk back outside into the sunshine of the solid world.

Only it was real. When she held that thought, she plunged again into icy despair. It was as real as the news this morning from a friend at the hospital that David Masters had been taken off life support. Cruel, cruel timing. What would happen to Josh now? He had skipped parole, gotten into some other scrape, and now David Masters was dead. A dullness settled over her, a heaviness. She felt as if they were in the bottom of a pit and there was no way out, no handholds or lights to guide them. It was the old feeling of wanting to protect Josh, to help him, but not being able to. Not being able to make the world safe for him. Of failing him.

And so she careened through the day, relief giving way to

despair, despair wearing itself out, faint glimmers of hope surfacing, then disappearing.

She needed to talk to someone. Her neighbor Alice had moved, and her mother would blame her somehow. Still, she picked up the phone and listened to the dial tone, as if she could by that action summon a listening ear. Then she began to dial Olaffson's number, but her courage failed her and she hung up. He, she realized with a start, was her only friend. He was the only one who knew her, who saw her. For the first time in her life, she wasn't afraid to be seen—all of her, her raggedy parts, all the parts of her she was ashamed of—in his eyes they seemed less shameful. He *knew* her. He had taught her to see, but he'd also taught her to be seen.

She picked up the phone again and dialed the full number.

"Hullo." His voice sounded half asleep. That was how he sounded when he was deep into his painting, and she felt an urge to hang up, to not interrupt him, not impose herself on him.

"It's me. Helen. I'm so sorry, it sounds like you are right in the middle of painting."

"Naw, that's okay. Just finishing up here. What's going on?" He had a welcome in his voice, a way of easing the other person.

"Josh ran away to New York to see his girlfriend, broke his parole, and got into some kind of trouble there—it's all confused, he was robbed, got picked up by some freak, and was almost killed in an accident. I don't know how much more I can take, O. I'm so worried about him."

"Where is he now?"

"Hal's coming home with him. They'll be home soon." She blew her nose, not caring how she sounded. "Hal. He went up there and was supposed to find Josh and just took the girl-friend's word that he'd taken a bus home and then went on his merry way to some clock dealer. Oblivious as always to what is really going on. Meanwhile, Josh gets picked up by some alcoholic—he could have been hurt. He could have been killed!"

Molten, her rage against Hal poured out of her. "It's a nightmare. Nothing ever changes with him. He lives in his own world. He doesn't care about us, he's abandoned us. He's abandoned me."

Olaffson let her cry on until, until the hiccupping, snorting gasps subsided.

"Feel better?" he said, as if this sort of thing happened every day, people calling and spilling their grief and rage to him.

She took a deep breath. "Yes."

"Hal is with him now, Helen. He hasn't abandoned him. Maybe he didn't do things the way you would have liked, but he went. Can you entertain the possibility that things are not the same? Can you be open to that?"

"What, what do you mean?" Helen stuttered, feeling herself getting defensive. Olaffson was supposed to be on her side.

"You know how when you are painting, you have an idea of how things are supposed to be? The ideal painting in your mind? But then you set out to execute it and you just can't get it to work. So you get frustrated, you turn your back on it and feel angry and ashamed that you even had such an ambitious notion. But then you stumble on what you started one day, and you see some possibility there that you hadn't seen before. And you pick it up and start working with it, maybe this time just seeing what is there, discarding your ideal notion. And something new happens, something you didn't expect. Do you think a relationship could be like that?"

Helen felt stunned. She knew what he was talking about, but she had never thought of it before. "Yes," she said slowly, "I guess I see that. I have to think about it some more."

"Helen, take care of yourself today. Don't try to solve all the problems. Take care of yourself so you can be there when they come home. They are coming home to you."

Helen started to protest that Hal wasn't, Hal had moved out. But she stopped herself.

"I love you, O," she said, and she meant it, but not in the way she'd meant it before.

"I love you, Helen. You can always call me." And then she felt him begin to fade, his attention shift, saw him in his studio, looking at a painting, becoming absorbed back into it.

"Good-bye, O."

"Good-bye, Helen."

When she had hung up, she knew she would not call him again. He had already given her all that she had needed from him. She felt complete. She felt strangely content and orderly, like a well-swept room.

She heard the car and held her breath. They were home.

***

Josh saw his mother silhouetted in the window as they pulled into the driveway. She must have heard them because the door flew open and she came running out in her nightgown and slippers and had a hold of him before his foot touched the ground.

"Josh, Josh," she cried, holding him tight and rocking him.

He felt her tears wet against his cheek, and his arms encircled her. "Mom! I'm okay, really!" She stood back, holding him at arm's length, scrutinizing him, looking for signs of damage. "Mom, I'm tired, but I'm okay. I'm intact." He glanced at his father, standing diffidently on the other side of the car, saw a shadow cross his face. "Mom," he said more softly, and cocked his head toward Hal.

His mother reluctantly took her eyes from him and looked over at Hal. He saw her face, so open to him, begin to close down. He braced for their clash, felt himself grow small and cold inside, his stomach churning. And then Josh witnessed what would remain for him one of the most astonishing and singular moments of his life. Helen released him and went over to Hal, and she offered her uplifted, naked face to him, and she put her arms around him and kissed him. Josh watched his father's ramrod figure bend to hers, saw the weary sag of his shoulders as he put his arms around her. They stood there, his parents, their faces hidden from him, in a long, silent, and, what seemed to Josh, somber embrace. Josh felt a long way away from them, and yet it felt all right. He remembered when he was little and they hugged, he would always try to get into the middle, to make a family sandwich. But he wasn't little anymore, and he didn't need to be in the middle.

Helen whispered something to Hal and took him by the hand and led him around the car to Josh. She took Josh's other free hand and led them onto the porch. "Come on, my boys," she said. "It's been a long day. Come and sleep. We'll sort it all out in the morning."

And then they went in the house and closed the door and turned off the lights, as if it were the most natural thing in the world.

EPILOGUE

The funeral procession wound slowly through the old cemetery. It was a gray day, proper for a funeral. Strong gusts of cold wind blasted through bare branches, and caused the screen of silvery bamboo to violently toss its leaves. The gleaming black hearse and beads of cars snaked along the narrow, winding road. On either side, soft hills rose up, covered with silvery, gnarled oaks and monuments in various stages of decay—marble angels without noses or fingers or wingtips, inscriptions and dates worn away, moss effacing names, families, dates. Despite such degradations, or perhaps because of them, the old gravestones could inspire in the susceptible a feeling of the brutal swiftness of time, but also of timelessness, of a strange peace. *All Who Lie Here,* as one tombstone read, *Have Run Their Race.*

If those in the procession had time or inclination to stop and explore, they might see on the largest monuments and crypts and family plots the venerable names that still dominated street signs and adorned buildings, names seen frequently in the written proceedings of the city government—the Mosses, the Hardigrees, the McWhorters, the Finleys. They might note the tenacity and stability of these families, but also the shortness of individual lives. The careful observer might imagine the encroachments of the outside world, the toll of wars and flu and infant deaths. Yet still, this steadiness, a sense of a settled place, of community, abided here.

The procession passed the old Jewish section of the cemetery and headed toward the newer, more egalitarian plots. There was no black cemetery here—those were in other parts of town, some of them overgrown with smilax and honeysuckle, some forgotten, some well-tended. In those cemeteries, there were more nameless ones, more stones fallen over, the inscriptions erased by age and neglect. But there were also honors and names that persisted—the Wootens, the Sheats, the Greshams, although these names would not be found on grand buildings, but painted on signs above barber shops, in front of car washes or nightclubs. But in these times, there was only one cemetery. It was an inclusive cemetery now. Race alone would not keep one out, although as in the world at large, the price for such real estate prohibited many from adding their names to the stone record of the city's illustrious past.

The observer might consider, perusing stone after stone, the persistence of families. Whatever adventures the individual may have had, in death there was no escaping history. Whatever the disagreements, you were claimed by your kin. Freer spirits might reinvent themselves, disgruntled ones leave, but in the end, there you were, a Smith or Burton, still. The stones did not give up their inhabitants' secrets; whatever the flesh had suffered, whatever momentary joys or epiphanies, none were revealed here.

The town was used to absorbing its deaths—the hapless infants who, even now, didn't survive; the ordinary attrition of accidents and the usual diseases; the hardy old finally dropping to the ground like overripe fruit; the green fruit of the young shipped back in standard-issue coffins from places only vaguely imagined, from wars many in the town thought had nothing to do with them. But this death felt to some to be an untimely betrayal—of what? Of hope? Of vision? Of some yearning to be the place they purported to be?

Was it a betrayal or a fulfillment, or was it both, the way all deaths are? It was a cold gray day, and those prone to melancholy shivered in their jackets, perhaps unaware of the cardinals flashing vermillion in the branches overhead.

The casket was lowered into the hole that had been prepared for it, and Meg threw a handful of dirt on it. When she straightened, she saw at the edge of the crowd, standing by themselves, Hal, Helen, and Josh. Hal was in the center, his arms around Helen and Josh. His head was bent, as if he was listening to Helen, who was turned toward him. But Josh looked straight ahead and caught Meg's eye. She raised her hand to him, and he raised his to hers.

ACKNOWLEDGEMENT

I would like to express my gratitude to the many people who saw me through this book. For their unflagging support and belief in me through many years, David Foss, Jean Cantu, Susan Gill, and Madeline VanDyck. To my generous beta readers, David Foss, Jean Cantu, Rebecca McCarthy, Janet Geddis, Carol Myers. To Laura Petrella, for her superb editing, insight and encouragement. To my poetry group: Sarah Gordon, Betty Littleton, Rebecca Baggett, Mary Anne O'Neal Ingle, Lee Ann Pingle, Lisa Reeves, Emily Hipchen, and Clela Reed, for not letting me get away with lazy writing. To all the staff at Deeds Publishing, for their professionalism, integrity and talent: Bob Babcock, Jan Babcock, David Ingle, Matt King, Mark Babcock, and Ashley Clarke. To my mother, Claire, who shared her love of books and stories with me from day one, and for my brothers, Mike, Jon, Joe, and my sisters, Elizabeth and Megan, for always being there. For my children, Geoff, Andy, Hannah and Adam, who continue to delight and inspire me, and finally, for Todd, my rock.

ABOUT THE AUTHOR

Sara Baker's fiction has been published in *Cleaver, Confrontation, H.O.W. Journal, The China Grove Journal, The New Quarterly,* and other venues, and has been shortlisted for the Bridport and Fish contests. Her poetry has been published in *Stone, River, Sky: the Negative Capability Press Anthology of Georgia Poetry,* The 2011 Hippocrates Prize for Poetry and Medicine, *The Apalachee Review, The Healing Muse, Ars Medica,* and elsewhere. Her work has been shortlisted for the Eludia award, and she has been a finalist for the Gertrude Stein award, and the Hemingway Days First Novel Contest, among other awards. Sara lives in Athens, Georgia, with her husband, physicist and writer Todd Baker, and they have four wonderful grown children. They are grateful to live in such a vibrant community. When not writing or teaching, Sara is an avid gardener, dancer and dog lover. Her work in the field of expressive writing led her to blog about writing and healing at Word Medicine, www.saratbaker.wordpress.com.

CPSIA information can be obtained
at www.ICGtesting.com
Printed in the USA
FSOW01n1743200217
30954FS

9 781944 193560